SACRAMENTO
WITH KIDS

SACRAMENTO WITH KIDS

*A Family Guide
to the
Greater Sacramento Region*

By Dierdre Wolownick Honnold

Manufactured in the United States of America

Design and typography by Tempel Typographics
Illustrations by Katy Hardeay

Library of Congress Catalog Card Number: 94-60204

ISBN 0-9640370-0-9

First Edition

I dedicate this book to Charlie,
my travelling partner in life,
without whose help, patience, understanding
and love it would never have come to be,
and to my two favorite assistants,
Stasia and Alexander,
whose travels are just beginning.

I would like to express my heartfelt thanks to:

Jo Chandler,
without whom there would be no book;

all the wonderfully helpful, friendly people at the
Chambers of Commerce and the San Juan School District;

and all those family members, friends and colleagues
without whose assistance and encouragement this book
would not have become a reality: Forrest Honnold, Alice
Honnold, Michael Honnold, Carol Honnold, Winnie
Bachmann, Brian Bates, Niki Bates, Henry Burnett, Len
Cramer, Ellen Cunha, Tom Dayton, Judy Ege, Lauao Ellis,
Bud Gardner, Hal Harrington, Brenda Hartley, Bill Irwin,
Linda Jackson, Nancy Kramer, Kathy Lefforge, Jim Levy,
Bob Lyman, Bill Morris, Toni Morris, Charlene Parsons,
Kathie Read, Kathleen Reimer, Shelley Rink, Sandy Van
Horn, Shipley Walters, and my parents, Joseph and Stasia
Wolownick, who always knew this would happen someday.

Special thanks to my three partners in research, travel and
fun: Charlie, Stasia and Alexander.

CONTENTS

INTRODUCTION

When I moved to Sacramento with my young family, I assumed (having lived in several big cities) that I'd be able to find countless resources that would help me find places to go with my children. After all, I knew that Sacramento's the heart of northern California (San Francisco being a world of its own), the state Capital, gateway to the Sierra Nevada, only an hour from the Bay, the snow and Gold Country. How could a place so ideally located not be overrun with guide-books?

So I began combing the bookstores, the libraries. Networking. To my surprise, in this gold-mine of exciting places to visit and things to do, information was scattered and hard to track down. But the kids were ready, Mom was willing — and so this book began. As I began to compile information, I realized that other parents would also benefit from what I had amassed. We had such fun being detectives! And what we discovered surprised even my husband, a native Sacramentan.

One of the first things you'll discover about Sacramento is how friendly the people are here. The second thing you'll discover is that they're even friendlier than you thought in the first place. Kids are welcome in restaurants, museums, or just about any place you can imagine — and many you couldn't possibly imagine! This attitude probably stems partly from the fact that Sacramento is itself in its childhood, as cities go. The Gold Rush, in 1849, was the beginning of Captain Sutter's sleepy little settlement at the confluence of the Sacramento and the American Rivers.

But there's nothing sleepy about it now. Sacramento is an international port, the capital of a state that, if it were a country, would have the seventh largest economy in the world! Here, you can learn how genetic engineering happens or how a bustling newspaper newsroom functions. You and your kids can delve into ancient history at the State Indian Museum, or wander through Old Sacramento and imagine yourselves in the Old West. If you're into outdoor sports, there's no place quite like Sacramento. Its two rivers afford an unending variety of water sports and appropriate settings, including miles of parkways, and there's a wide variety of other sports to choose from. If your interests lie in more cultural endeavors, Sacramento has the Symphony, the Ballet, the annual International Jazz Festival, many college and local orchestras, theaters, dinner theaters — my list is still not exhaustive. And for children, special programs abound in all areas — music, theater, dance, nature programs, literary programs, science and art museum workshops, sports.... Why this book wasn't written years ago is a mystery my kids and I have yet to solve.

But now it's here, and whatever your family's preferences for having fun, you'll find something here to please everyone. A warning, though: some of the entries are not what you'd expect to find in a guide-book. That's only natural, since kids aren't standard issue.

And as the children have grown, so has the scope of our discoveries. Thanks to that wonderful variety of experiences inherent in each age of growing up, this book contains listings of places appropriate for all age groups. The focus here is on the family, but, of course, these listings can also be a resource for day-care providers, teachers planning field-trips, individuals, anyone in the Sacramento area looking for a place to spend a few pleasant, fun-filled hours or a whole day.

So whatever your family focus is for fun, welcome to Sacramento, a city born of adventure. In these pages you're sure to find some exciting ideas to tease your little tourists' sense of adventure and keep them asking for more. I hope you have as much fun exploring the places listed here as we had finding them!

As you expand on this book and make your own discoveries, please contact us at P.O. Box 1941, Carmichael, CA 95609-1941. We'll be happy to send an autographed copy of the new edition to the first person to suggest a new entry, or a way we can make Sacramento with Kids even more helpful for families and teachers. With your help, the next edition will be even better!

Unless otherwise indicated, all telephone numbers listed here use the 916 area code. For numbers inside the 916 calling area but outside the city of Sacramento, dial 1 before the number.

Please note: information contained in these listings is effective as of this printing; always telephone first for up-to-date prices and hours.

❧ 1 ❧
Places To Go

Real Sacramentans recognize each other by the way they pronounce the city's name — something akin to "Sakamenna." Another way to fit in is to become familiar with the attractions in this chapter. Not all of them, maybe; but at least a nodding acquaintance with most of the places listed here is de rigueur for anyone claiming to really know Sacramento.

Sutter's Fort is where it all began. Once you've laid the historical groundwork of visiting the Fort (see Sutter's Fort, this chapter) and the Indian Museum (see California State Indian Museum, this chapter), right next door, you're ready to explore and understand the rest.

Since Sacramento "grew up" during the Gold Rush, a good place to get the feel for the place and to begin to understand what Sacramento is all about is in Old Sacramento, which was the financial center of this jumping-off point to the beckoning gold fields in them thar hills. I'll begin this chapter with a walking tour of Old Sacramento. All of its attractions will be listed alphabetically under the section called Old Sacramento; attractions in the rest of the chapter are also alphabetized. And for your convenience, attractions found in Old Sacramento will be cross-referenced from other parts in this chapter or from other chapters.

If there's an attraction you expect to find here but don't, it's probably listed in Chapter 2, which contains equally popular but usually smaller attractions.

OLD SACRAMENTO

The Old Sacramento Historic Area is a State Historic Park and a National Historic Landmark. Located on 28 acres of waterfront on the Sacramento River, it's been a place of business since 1849, when James Marshall discovered gold at John Sutter's mill and Sam Brannan made his fortune here selling to the rush of gold-seekers. It's home to the greatest concentration of historic buildings in California.

In 1839, John Augustus Sutter chose the Sacramento Valley to establish his permanent settlement in California. By 1849, there were several permanent buildings on the waterfront, and when the news of the discovery of gold started to spread, the streets of Sacramento swelled with visitors from all over the world. But natural disasters, in the form of fires and floods, destroyed the town several times, until finally, in 1862, the city was actually raised above flood levels by adding land dredged from the Sacramento River. On the southwest corner of 2nd and I Streets, a courtyard shows the original level of city streets.

Now, let's go see Old Sac. Get ready for a trip back in time, and a plain old good time! As you wander the covered boardwalks and cobbled streets — in solid, comfortable shoes — imagine yourself part of the excitement of that incredible time of unbridled imagination. Gold was the magnet, the hope, the dream of those who came through Sacramento en route to the foothills. It colored every aspect of life here. This was a place of limitless dreams, a frontier of human expectations that quickly grew into a thriving city. It's a mix of civilization and wilderness, gentility and abandon; the wildness and passion of the gold-seekers has left its permanent mark on this frontier town, and you can experience some of that feeling as you wander through Old Sacramento.

There are many ways to plan your tour of Old Sac. You can begin at the Old Schoolhouse, next to the parking structure, and simply walk all the streets in any order that strikes your fancy. That's my family's style. Kids enjoy visiting the Old Schoolhouse and seeing what it was like "back then." The docents there are very helpful and friendly, and love kids. Or you can park at the other end, under the freeway, and begin with the Railroad Museum, History Museum and Central Pacific Passenger Station, <u>then</u> wind your way through the streets.

However you do it, though, leave lots of time for shopping, which is unparalleled here, with over 125 shops to choose from and no two alike. No matter how much time we spend in Old Sac, my kids always have to visit the kite shop, the candy shops, the rock shop and the puzzle shop, and always have to stop at the Pony Express monument to sit and re-group. Whatever your family's preference, you'll find it here.

Kid tips:

- For running off some energy, picnicking or just taking a break, there's a large grassy area in front of the History Museum and Railroad Museum, across from the Passenger Station. While kids romp here, they can climb on the large blue buckboard wagon and let their imaginations play too.
- For a water-side romp between stops, riverside picnic, etc., there's a park below the railroad tracks, accessible in front of the History Museum. Paths wind along the river, shade trees, lots to explore. A great place to be if one of the bridges happens to go up or around! (If you go in the winter, though, be prepared: the park is sometimes under water in wet months.)
- Dashing up and down the many ramps or stairways leading down to the waterfront where the boats are moored is my family's favorite Old Sac riverside activity. Especially exciting is the walkway that moves, leading out to the private craft moored here. Waterbirds are plentiful here at times, and it's a photogenic place to capture your explorers with the paddlewheel Delta King.
- From K Street in Old Sac, you can walk under the freeway to K Street and the new Downtown Plaza. Here, you can shop, browse and find lots of eateries to please any kind of taste or budget.

Location: Bordered by I-5, Capitol Mall, and the Sacramento River. Directions: Take the J Street exit from I-5 and follow signs for Old Sacramento. Parking: Long-term parking at reasonable rates is available under the freeway, on I and J Streets, and at the end of Front Street (south end of Old Sacramento). Limited parking is available on the streets. And if you enjoy walking and panoramic views, you can park FREE on South River Road in West Sacramento (across the river) and walk across the Tower Bridge. This 5 to 10-minute walk (depending on the age of your walkers) affords you a spectacular view of the whole Old Sacramento waterfront area, as well as the river itself. It's especially memorable if the bells clang and the elevator bridge goes up!

- *Old Sacramento Visitor Information - 264-7777 (weekends and holidays) - 442-7644*
- *Old Sacramento Events Hotline - 558-3912*
- *Old Sacramento Merchants Association - 558-3912*

Note: However you decide to visit Old Sac, you'll want to make the <u>Visitors Information Center</u> one of your first stops, to pick up the necessary maps and brochures.

∾ B F Hastings Building

2nd and J Streets, Sacramento CA 95814 ∾ 445-7373. Hours: B.F. Hastings Building and Supreme Court: call first; Wells Fargo Museum: 10am-5pm daily. All three attractions FREE.

In April, 1853, B.F. Hastings opened a bank on the corner of 2nd and J Streets in Sacramento, to help bring capital and supplies to the '49ers swarming the city. Soon after, Wells Fargo & Company moved into the building, and when Sacramento was chosen as the state capital, the State Supreme Court moved into the second floor here. For a while in 1860, the Alta Telegraph Company operated out of the building, but was soon bought out and turned over to Western Union. And the Hastings building served as the western terminus for the famed Pony Express, which carried mail across the frontier for a short time during 1860. (In 1861, the completion of the first transcontinental telegraph line put the Pony Express out of business.)

The Building now is a museum dedicated to Communication and Transportation. Explore the beginning mail routes to California; meet Showshoe Thompson, the man legend credits with introducing skis to the western United States; see how newspapers were printed then; try writing with a quill pen, and send a real message in Morse Code from one telegraph booth to another.

Next door, where Hastings' bank was, you can now wander through the small Wells Fargo Museum. Small gift shop available, and a modern ATM machine.

Upstairs, you can sit in the actual State Supreme Court, visit the Justice Chambers, hear an actual court case from 1851. But there's one drawback to all this: despite its considerable historical significance, both the Hastings Building and the Supreme Court are seldom open, due to recent state budgetary restrictions. Call the above number first to verify hours, or call Ranger Joanne Ellison, the Living History Ranger, in advance to arrange your visit (322-8034).

❧ Bike and Surrey Rentals

916 2nd Street, Sacramento, CA 95814 ❧ 441-3836. Open Thur-Mon, 10-dark. Sat, 9-dark. Closed Tuesday and Wednesday. After May 15, open 7 days a week. Begins at $6/hour for bikes, up to $50 for a surrey for 8 hours. Bikes and Tandems can be rented for 24-hour periods. Deposit required for all rentals.

Rent mountain bikes, surreys (shaded 4-wheelers for Mom, Dad and 2 kids) or tandems for pedaling throughout Old Sac and/or on the bike trail along the river. They also offer child seats or trailers for bikes, wheelchairs, strollers, and some bike accessories and repairs. A pleasant way to tour Old Sac and more.

❧ California Citizen-Soldier Museum

1119 Second Street, Sacramento, CA 95814 ❧ 442-2883. Between K and L Streets, on east side of 2nd street. Tues-Sun 10-5. Adults $2.25; Service members in uniform, $1.00; Seniors (55+), $1.50; Children (5-17), $1.00; under 5, free. Children under 12 must be accompanied by an adult.

The goal of this museum is not to glorify war, according to the founder, Brigadier General Donald E. Mattson, but rather "to honor the dedication, sacrifice and contributions of Californians throughout history who have assisted in the growth, development and defense of their State and their Nation." This unimposing structure houses some impressive displays, dating from Mexico's expeditions into California in 1770 to Operation Desert Storm. Uniforms, swords, photos, musical instruments, memorabilia — even a cannon which is still fired annually, and one of the most complete collections of military firearms you'll find anywhere.

This museum is unique. Usually, military museums are located on a base or other military installation, and pertain only to that particular branch of the service. Here, though, you'll find it all! And downstairs your young historians are in for a real treat — a vast, extensive library of military history. Come browse, read, research or talk to the docents, who are happy to help. Call ahead to reserve a guided docent tour of the museum, no extra charge.

∿ California State Railroad Museum

2nd and I Streets, Old Sacramento, CA 95814 ∿ 552-5252, Category #7245. At the northern end of Old Sac, overlooking the large green area, near the I-street parking area. Open daily, 10-5, except Thanksgiving, Christmas and New Year's Day. Adult, $5; 6-12, $2; under 6 free. Admission also gets you into the Central Pacific Passenger Station.

The railroad is intimately linked to the history of Sacramento. Four of the most influential men in the Old West — Collis P. Huntington, Charles Crocker, Leland Stanford and Mark Hopkins, the "Big Four" — met in a hardware store in Sacramento with Theodore Judah to design and plan the first transcontinental railroad.

This museum celebrates that history, with many self-explanatory exhibits and collections of memorabilia. Many of the locomotives displayed here are unique. The massive Southern Pacific No. 4294 was the last of the giant cab-forwards to cross the snowy Sierra Nevada ("cab-forward," because it put the passengers in front of the engine, so they weren't asphyxiated by fumes in the long Sierra tunnels).

Walk <u>under</u> a huge locomotive. See the train that used to haul the silver ore out of the Nevada mines. And as you step into the St. Hyacinthe, a restored 1929 sleeping car, you'll feel the slight rocking motion, see the lights "whizzing by," and experience the feeling of actually being in one of these Pullman sleepers. A thrill for the kids, and a nostalgia trip for those old enough to remember.

- An orientation slide show and movie is shown at scheduled times throughout the day, with the last showing at 4pm.
- Although the museum is self-guiding, docents offer tours at 1pm every day.
- Kids — and model train buffs of all ages — will enjoy the impressive model train display upstairs.
- Gift and souvenir shop at the entrance, with lots of things for kids to do.
- Turntable outside the museum where you can occasionally see some of their "rolling stock" turned.
- Very wheelchair-accessible.

↝ Central Pacific Passenger Station

J and Front Streets, at the north end of Old Sacramento, opposite the History Museum and the Old Eagle Theatre ↝ 322-3676. Open 10-5 daily, except Thanksgiving, Christmas and New Year's Day. Included in admission to Railroad Museum only.

Part of the Railroad Museum, this restored railroad station was the first California terminus of the Transcontinental Railroad. Everything is as it used to be — the waiting rooms (with men's and women's separate, of course), the train cars, the platform. Even if your little travellers wander all through the cars and linger on the old-fashioned platform or waiting rooms, this will only take about 15 minutes.

🍃 EATING OUT IN OLD SAC

There are lots of places to eat as you wander through Old Sac, but few really fit the category of "family restaurants." Perhaps the closest to it is the **Whistle Stop** (1115

Front St.), a good place for breakfast or lunch, and **Annabelle's** (200 J St.), a spacious, reasonable family place for pizzas and salads. The **Garden Court Cafe** (106 L Street, across from the Excursion Boats) is also a nice family place to eat a wholesome, quick meal without spending a lot of cash.

Barnum's Ice Cream and Cafe (916 2 St.) offers lunch and desserts, the **Croissant Connection** (1026 2 St.) has yummy croissant sandwiches and specialty coffees, and **Subway** (1125 2 St.) serves long or short submarine sandwiches. For grabbing a quick picker-upper on the go, stop at the **Pony Express Bakery** on the waterfront side of Front St. and munch away at their outdoor tables/benches/barrels or simply on the lawn.

As you wander, you'll see lots of restaurants, like **Los Padres, California Fats** and others; these are for "fine dining." Prices are higher, food is slower in arriving, and kids have to behave like adults.

For the fast-food experience, there's **Carl's Jr.'s** (hamburgers) and **Straw Hat Pizza**. And for desserts, you'll see fudge shops, ice cream, all sorts of sweets and goodies; but for a candy stop that can't be beat, stop at **the Candy Barrel**. This deceptively large shop is filled with barrels of all kinds of candies — a sweet-tooth wonderland!

❧ Excursion Boats

Waterfront at L Street Landing, Sacramento, CA 95814 (if the ticket booth here is closed, the office of Riverboat Cruises is as 110 L Street, across from the Old Schoolhouse) ❧ 552-2933 or (800) 433-0263. April to October, with special tours (charters, etc.) the rest of the year. Lunch: 11am departure, 1pm return. Sat and Sun brunch: 10am boarding, 12:30 return. Sightseeing: Wed-Sun (June-Aug), F-Sun (Apr-Oct): departures 1:30pm and 3pm. Sightseeing: Adults, $10; under 12, $5. Various combinations of snacks, meals and cruises: call for information.

Old Sac has two excursion boats currently available, the Matthew McKinley and the Spirit of Sacramento, with another one, the City of Sacramento, coming into service in 1994. You can take a 2-hour luncheon cruise, a 1-1/2 hour narrated sightseeing cruise, dinner cruise, happy hour cruise... even a murder mystery cruise.

The Spirit of Sacramento, an 80-foot paddlewheeler, was the star of John Wayne's 1954 movie "Blood Alley," and looks like it's straight off the 19th-century Mississippi. It's a trip back in time as well as up the river, as you leave Old Sacramento behind and glide under the I-Street Bridge, one of the very few remaining pedestal (swing) bridges in the nation; it turns 180 degrees to allow big ships to pass. As you float past old cottonwoods and water birds, the captain will fill you in on some of the local lore and history.

If your little adventurers are old enough to sit still for a while (you can walk around the boat, of course, but space is limited), this is a delightfully relaxing, pleasant way to spend a few hours and to experience a view of Sacramento that went out with the last century. Re-capture the excitement of the riverboats that plied the Delta, the Sacramento and the American Rivers during the gold rush; arrive at Old Sac's waterfront like our forefathers did.

- Excellent cuisine on the lunch and dinner cruises; definitely one of Sacramento's better "restaurants."
- Both open and enclosed decks, for the fresh-air experience as well as a warm meal and relaxing ride protected from the Delta breezes. Dining "al fresco" in warm weather.
- Can be chartered for any occasion. (Lots of weddings take place on board.)
- Group rates (10 or more adults).

Note: as of 1994, the third boat, the City of Sacramento, will be moored permanently just south of the Tower Bridge, where a new parking facility and park will be constructed. This will be an immobile restaurant boat. Call for current information.

❧ Excursion Steam Train

Freight Depot, Front Street, Sacramento, CA 95814 ❧

552-5252 Ext. 7245. Every weekday from May through Labor Day, 1st weekend of month October through March. 10-5. Adults $4; kids 6-12, $2; Under 6 free.

You can share the excitement of the era of the steam engine and of the expansion of the Old West by riding this old steam train along the Sacramento River. Thrill to the whistle as you chug south out of Old Sacramento, rolling past the Passenger Station, the Steamboats, the Old School-house and the Tower Bridge. Soon you're out on the levee as it winds through the rural landscape along the River, passing signs that indicate long-disappeared stops. Close your eyes and just listen and <u>feel</u> — it's easy to imagine you've gone back in time!

✒ Huntingtion, Hopkins & Co. Hardware Store

101 I Street ("Big Four" Building), Sacramento, CA 95814 ✒ 323-7234. 10-5 intermittently (due to budget restraints); call first. FREE.

Between the History Museum and the Railroad Museum, this store is part museum and part authentic hardware store. You'll find a fascinating collection of old tools, hardware, and artifacts from the mid 1800s, some of which are sure to puzzle your modern little builders. But maybe better than the hardware is the selection of old-fashioned wooden toys they offer. Kids love them. Between the old-time housewares, hardware and the wood toys, this is your chance to take home a practical little chunk of history.

✒ Horse-Drawn Carriages

You can usually board in front of the Railroad Museum, and sometimes at other locations throughout Old Sac. $10 per tour. Wagon rides also available, $2 for adults, $1 for children.

Roll through Old Sac at a clip-clop pace, with ample time to absorb the sights. Delightful architecture, great people-watching. Perfect for when the troops are tiring!

❧ Old Eagle Theater

925 Front Street, Sacramento, CA 95814 ❧ 323-7234 (information about slide shows and the theater); 446-6761 (information about plays). Across Front Street from the Passenger Station, across the green area from the History Museum. Performances Friday and Saturday at 8pm. Call for other hours. Tickets to weekend performances: $12 general admission; $10 students. Call for other fees.

This unimposing little building facing the Passenger Station on the waterfront was the first building constructed as a theater in California (in 1849). When the '49ers began streaming through the tiny fledgling town of Sacramento, there was no entertainment at all. So they took lumber from their boats and canvas from their sails and built themselves a theater.

The present building is a historically accurate reproduction. The Eagle became quite acclaimed in its time, and today you can still see live theater there. Chattauqua, a theater production company, performs in the Eagle Theatre on weekends; occasionally they do children's theater. And a free slide show about Old Sacramento is available for viewing; call for current information.

❧ Old Sacramento Schoolhouse

Front and L Streets, Sacramento, CA 95814 ❧ 483-8818. M-F, 9:30am-4pm. Weekends 12-4pm. FREE.

Built in the style of one-room schools found in the area in the 1800s, this little yellow school is a favorite with kids. They love to examine the handwriting lessons on the blackboards, sit at the old wooden desks, compare lessons with their own, and play in the schoolyard outside.

- Docents usually on hand to explain, describe, demonstrate and generally enhance your visit.
- Memorabilia for sale, like individual slate boards or old teacher's rules.

ᕈ Pony Express Monument
2nd and J Streets, Sacramento, CA 95814

This action-like monument depicts a typical young rider of the Pony Express. Sacramento was the western terminus of the Pony Express in 1860, until the completion of the Transcontinental Telegraph Line (see B.F.Hastings Building, this section). Mail made its way from St. Joseph, Missouri across the vast western frontier, over the Sierra Nevada and into Sacramento, from where it made the trip to San Francisco and other points by boat, down the Sacramento River. The young men who rode the Express line had to be rough, adventurous riders, and their exploits in that very brief period of history inspired many a young cowboy. That admiration is still alive and well; watch the faces of your youngsters as they gaze at this statue!
- Benches nearby make it a perfect picnic spot.
- A very photogenic place for pictures (better sun in the afternoon).

ᕈ Riverboat Delta King
1000 Front Street, Sacramento, CA 95814 ᕈ *444-5464.*

This magnificent paddlewheeler was the last of its kind to operate between Sacramento and San Francisco. Meticulously restored to its previous grandeur, it now serves as a permanently-moored hotel, restaurant and theater.

Unless you stay in the hotel, they don't appreciate having children running on board just to see it — which is fine, since it's best seen from above (street level), or from the dock. Walk along the dock down-river, towards the Tower Bridge. Kids enjoy walking out on the moving pier to see whatever private boats are moored there, and to see the ducks and assorted other birds that play in the water.

If you're lucky, the Tower Bridge will go up while you're down there, or the I Street Bridge (to the right) will turn. Small children enjoy the clanging bells and the odd sight of a bridge that moves; big people marvel at the engineering.

❧ Sacramento Museum of History, Science and Technology

(formerly the **Sacramento History Museum**)
(see also **Sacramento Science Center**)

> *101 I Street, Sacramento, CA 95814 (Old Sacramento)* ❧
> *264-7057. At the north end of Old Sac, near the Passenger Station, overlooking the large grassy area and the river. Wed-Sun, 10-5. Tours offered at 10 and 11:30 and at 1:30 and 3. If you call ahead and if the docents aren't busy with a school tour, they'll be happy to schedule a tour for your family. Adults 17 and up, $3.50; children, $2.00.*

Beginning in 1994, this museum will be the consolidation of the former **Sacramento History Museum** (this location) and the **Sacramento Science Center** (3615 Auburn Bd.). As of this publication they are still two separate museums, so they are described here separately. Call for updated information.

Sacramento History Museum

About 150 years ago, the founding pioneers of the new city of Sacramento formed the city's first library, called Pioneer Hall, which eventually became the city's first history museum. The artifacts brought together by that Pioneer Society became the nucleus of the Sacramento History Center's extensive collection, which is Sacramento's only history museum dedicated to preserving, exhibiting and interpreting the unique and exciting heritage of California's Capitol City.

It's a walkable museum, not overwhelming, just big enough for a visit of 1 or 2 hours with the kids. Well-organized walkways guide you through an innovative adventure, from Indians to pre-Gold Rush to the present, offering interaction through video stations. Kids will enjoy the Indian Community exhibit, the moving assembly-line of canned almonds, the big machines, the old carriages, the 1940s TV set.... Lots to see and do!

An extra bonus: as you tour the second floor, be sure to

stop near the almond assembly-line (overhead) and look out the big picture-window. Below, near the riverfront, you'll see the big turntable used for turning the Central Pacific Railroad cars at the end of the line. Still used today to turn the Railroad Museum's "rolling stock," this is an unusual part of train memorabilia.

And as you approach the museum from across the square, be sure to point out the flagpole to your little trivia fans: it's the tallest, free-standing, fiberglass flagpole in the country, standing proud at 113 feet.

Sacramento Science Center (3615 Auburn Bd.)

All kids love learning about the world they live in, and this is a great place for exploration. The Science Center is dedicated to fostering curiosity about the world by revealing the link between science and our everyday world. They pursue this goal through a combination of exhibits and hands-on activities, with exhibits changing twice a year, and partnerships with schools, businesses, government and industry. Many of their exhibits go on the road after the Center, and have travelled as far as Memphis and Dallas.

At the gift shop next to the main entrance, you can get a tape and player (free with entrance to museum) to guide you through the Discovery Trail, a quarter-mile self-guiding nature trail. This pleasant, meandering walk has labeled exhibits that explore the interdependency of various natural communities. Feed the ducks, surprise a quail or a snake, meander through redwoods and coastal shrubs. Picnic tables available. Nature trail is free, and you don't have to enter the museum to enjoy it. Even if the Science Center isn't on your itinerary, the nature trail is a nice place to just walk with your young naturalists, or enjoy a meal out among nature.

Besides the bi-annual exhibits and planetarium, they also offer: holiday classes for kids; live animal exhibits; educator's workshops; an adopt-a-classroom program; travelling exhibits; tours; interpretation for the hearing-impaired (call first); a gift shop.

～ Theodore Judah Monument

L Street and 2 Street (on east side of street).

This monument is dedicated to the memory of Theodore
Judah, the man with a vision who, with the "Big Four"
(Crocker, Huntington, Stanford and Hopkins), dreamed,
designed and created the Transcontinental Railroad, which
shaped the West and the nation.

～ Underground Railroad

*128 J Street (2nd and J Streets), Sacramento, CA 95814
～ 443-7777. Located one block south of the Railroad
Museum, on the south side of J Street. Since it's in the
basement, all you see is a door, no windows, no
"storefront"; easy to walk past without realizing you've
passed it. 11-5 daily; weekends sometimes open till 5:30
or 6, depending on demand. 12-adult, $2.50; 3-11, $1.50;
under 3 free.*

If your miniature people love seeing the world in miniature, or if any of your group are model railroad enthusiasts,
this place is a must. In this little basement shop, you can
enjoy one of the largest miniature railroads in the country.
The owner, Ray Oakley, has assembled trains and towns
from all over California. The scenery is faithful to the real
thing, and with a little imagination you can identify the
locales without reading the labels.

Travel with the HO model trains through Sacramento,
Stockton, Roseville, the Sierra, the desert, up into the
Tehachapis, over the Tejon Pass. You can operate the miniature passenger shuttle train, the Sierra snow-plow locomotive, the ski run, the log-loader, and lots of other moving
parts, by pushing buttons.

After your "trip," you can browse through their little gift
shop, where you'll find all kinds of things related to model
trains. If they don't have it, they can get it.

～ Visitor Information Center

Front Street, at the end of K Street, Sacramento, CA

95814 ~ 264-7777 (M-F); 442-7644 (Weekends and Holidays). 10-5 daily.

This is a logical place to begin your tour. Stock up on brochures, maps, etc., to be sure you don't miss anything. Don't forget to pick up the brochure called "Old Sacramento - State Historic Park and Natural History Landmark," which outlines a self-guided walking tour, highlighting and explaining all the important historical landmarks.

- Brochures and maps available, for all major attractions in Old Sac.
- Self-guiding brochure for walking tour.
- Personnel available to answer all your questions.

SACRAMENTO TODAY

Now that you've absorbed some of the local lore and gotten a feel for what Sacramento was like <u>then</u>, you're ready for Sacramento <u>now</u>. The following attractions are listed alphabetically.

~ Cal-Expo

1600 Exposition Boulevard, Sacramento, CA 95852 ~ (263-3000). Business 80 to Exposition Boulevard / Cal-Expo exit. 10-10 daily. Adults, $6; 5-12, $4; 4 and under, free. As the Fair approaches, there are specials to look for, like Seniors' Day, Kids' Day, with reduced prices. Also special prices for large groups.

Once a year, at the end of August, something magical happens at Cal-Expo: the California State Fair. Several midways and more rides than a family can possibly handle in a day sprout from this flat expanse of land that's visible from Business 80 as you near what's called the Arden Curve (where Business 80 and Arden Way meet). Rides, of course, are the first thing you see as the free tram carries you from the vast parking area to the many entrances. But if you can drag your kids away from the excitement of the midway, you can explore the animal shows, petting zoo, plant shows, craft shows, shops, food stops, and all the rest that helps make this one of the biggest state fairs in the nation.

A whole section of the Fair, called Exxon Park, is devoted to kids, with puppets shows, games, children's dance troops, professional jump-ropers (sic) and more. And located near the Main Gate is the Kiddie Carnaval, with rides and attractions for children and parents, such as a baby coaster, a carousel and a miniature Rio Grand train that even parents can ride.

But there's lots more to Cal-Expo, which offers attractions year-round. Some of the regulars are a huge Christmas-tree farm, a Halloween pumpkin patch, yearly shows (guns, coins, gems, boats, etc.), simulcast racing, and lots, lots more. There's always something happening; call for current information.

Also located on the grounds is Waterworld, a fantasy of water-based attractions open all summer long, when Sacramento bakes in temperatures that frequently go over 100. Slides, pools, fountains, wading pools, everything needed to help beat the heat and have a splashing good time (see Waterworld listing).

- ample parking in several extensive parking areas, accessible from Exposition Boulevard.
- wheelchair accessible.
- drinking fountains — essential in Sacramento's blistering summer — scattered throughout the park.
- snack bars, restaurants and restrooms conveniently located.

～ California State Capitol and Museum

10th and L Streets (in Capitol Park), Sacramento, CA 95818 ～ 324-0333. From I-5, take J Street exit east. From Business 80, take 16th Street north to L Street. Public parking garage on 11th and L Streets, limited parking on the street. Tours hourly, from 9-4, 7 days a week, except Thanksgiving, December 25 and January 1.

FREE. Tickets are given out in the basement, in Room B27, a half hour before tour times.

The Capital of California is perhaps the most well-travelled Capital in history! California became the 31st state in 1850. Its first capital city, San Jose, was too uncomfortable, since visiting statesmen had to stay in huts and tents. In 1851 General Vallejo offered his land for the purpose, but visitors had to stay on a steamer moored at the wharf, which didn't set well on many of the political stomachs. Then the Capital hopped to Sacramento, after which it moved back to Vallejo and then on to Benicia. In 1854, it moved permanently back to Sacramento, where it has remained ever since.

The current Capitol building, between 9th and 15th Streets and L and N Streets, is located in a 40-acre park, surrounded by trees and plants representative of all the continents and climates of the world. The Capitol is an impressive, gleaming white granite classical building that dominates the Park, topped with a golden dome. Before you go inside, be sure to look at the Great Seal of California set in the ground outside the west entrance. Within the circle you'll see 31 stars, for the 31 states at the time, and the word "Eureka" (the state motto, which means "I have found it"), a Grizzly bear (the state animal, now extinct in California), and other state symbols.

Inside the Rotunda, a popular first stop is the Carrara marble statue of Columbus and Isabella. Then you can wander through the building on your own, or you can get tickets in the basement for the complete tour, which lasts about an hour. Here you can see where California history-in-the-making takes place. You can visit the Senate and Assembly rooms (even available for viewing from the Gallery while in session), and view the portraits of past Governors.

- Restrooms, drinking fountains, cafeteria and bookshop in the basement. Also in the basement you can examine a cut-away view of the construction of the inside of the cupola (the dome), which fascinates kids who like to know "how".

- Lower gallery corridors contain exhibits of all 58 counties of California, which offer an overview of the state and all it has to offer.
- Recreation of Governor George Pardee's (21st Governor) ante-room and main office, located on the 1st floor. These offices were last used by Earl Warren in the 1950s.
- Elevators for general public and handicapped access.

Combine your tour here with a visit to the State Library, located right across the street from the Capitol (to the west). The building's twin, State Office Building #1, faces it across a fountain. The two were conceived and constructed as a pair, and are referred to collectively as the Capitol Extension Group. The Library is on the National Register of Historic Places, with most of the original fixtures still in place.

The State Library contains a major law library, a large California history collection and a general research collection for use by state officials. The general public has access to its books only through loans from local public libraries.

❧ California State Indian Museum

2618 K Street, Sacramento, CA 95818 ❧ 324-0971. Business 80 to J Street west. Left on 28th Street; park with Indian Museum and Sutter's Fort is on the right. Daily 10-5; closed Thanksgiving, Dec. 25 and Jan. 1. Guided tours Thursday morning, at 10 and 11. Reservations required: call 445-4209. Ages 6-12, $1.00; 13 and up, $2.00; under 5, free.

For many centuries before the arrival of white men in the Sacramento Valley, this region was inhabited by several tribes of peaceful Indians. The Miwoks, the Maidu and the Nissenan (or Nishinam) all shared the abundance of this fruitful area with each other and the wildlife that thrived here.

In the Indian Museum, you can learn what life was like back then. A marvelous permanent exhibit offers displays of clothing, weapons, musical instruments, religious artifacts, animals and their uses and significance — every aspect of local Indian culture. The display of baskets is remarkable, especially the ones that are so tiny you need a magnifying glass to see them. One wall contains authentic family photos from many of the local Indian families that still live here.

There's a video program at the beginning, to help orient you through your visit, and all the displays are clearly marked and explained. Docents are also available to help. If there's no school group scheduled, they're happy to guide you through the exhibits. They're very knowledgeable, and add a personal dimension to what you're seeing.

- Changing exhibits
- "Living history" days, with activities like acorn-grinding
- Located in a pleasant park which also includes Sutter's Fort

❧ Cathedral of the Blessed Sacrament

11th and K Streets. Take I-5 to J Street exit; Business 80 to J Street or 16th Street exit. Light Rail to Cathedral Square.

Built in 1889, the 217-foot tower is visible for miles. Its architectural design came from Paris, its stained glass from Austria. On the K Street mall, it's accessible by Light Rail, a cool stop on a hot summer day of shopping. Concerts throughout the year.

❧ Crocker Art Museum

216 O Street, Sacramento, CA 95814 ❧ 264-5423. Take I-5 to J Street. Right on 3rd Street, then right on O Street. City parking lots on west side of 2nd Street; bring quarters. Limited parking on street. Wed-Sun 10-5, Thurs 10-9, Sat 1-3 (special time for kids' activities). Adults, $3; 7-17, $1.50; 6 and under, free.

Located in a restored Victorian house, the Crocker is the oldest art museum in the West. It has grown continuously since 1873, and now includes European paintings and master drawings, California paintings, sculptures, Asian art, contemporary art and photography.

- Special temporary exhibits.

- Musical performances throughout the year.
- Special workshops, classes, etc., for adults and children.
- Every Saturday is Kids' Hands-on day, with crafts, classes and lots of things to do.
- Large gift shop.

∽ Effie Yeaw Nature Center

6700 Tarshes Drive (in Ancil Hoffman Regional Park), Carmichael, CA 95608 ∽ 489-4918. Tarshes Drive starts on California Avenue, which runs parallel to the north-south section of Fair Oaks Drive in Carmichael (slightly north of El Camino/Van Alstine Avenue). Follow Tarshes Drive into the Park, past the golf course. Follow signs; turn left into the Center. M-F 10-5, every day except Thanksgiving, Dec. 25 and Jan. 1. FREE. In "park season" you may have to pay to enter the Park before you reach the Center. The cost as of this printing is $4 per car.

This small but nicely-laid-out facility interprets the riparian natural habitat (river-dwelling animals and birds) of the Sacramento area. As you enter the Visitors' Center building, there's an exhibit of live local animals that were either wounded or caught and raised by humans, and as such, cannot be returned to the wild. Their cases are placed very low for easy child-sized viewing.

The Center is home to a permanent exhibit of local natural history that children love to explore. It's an ingenious combination of hands-on activities that instruct in a fun way.

- A favorite I have to drag my kids away from is the bird-stamping (get the pages there), and the computer game that lets you pretend you're a fish.
- Bird calls controlled by little fingers make imitation and memorizing fun.
- Child-manipulated animals and birds that move around a relief tree help them learn which animals live where.
- Puppet shows and animal shows, story-telling, all sorts

of free activities available; call or stop by for a calendar.

- Kids' Corner, to keep the really tiny tots busy coloring and such, while the older ones explore.
- Bookstore — stocked with lots of books and guides to nature-viewing and understanding the natural world — and souvenir shop.
- Picnic tables in front of the Center.

After you've explored the Center and whatever outdoor exhibits are available beside it (they often offer interpretive exhibits about the Nisenan, the Indians who lived here), you're ready to get a trail guide and wander through some of the 77 acres of nature trails. These take you along the river and allow you to experience the peace and abundance of this riparian environment, affording glimpses of the wild turkeys, deer, muskrats, squirrels, hawks, woodpeckers, egrets, or countless other birds and animals who make their home here. The best time for viewing the wildlife is in the early morning or at dusk. My little scouts love counting all the deer tracks and "critter" burrows along the way.

ᴥ Fairytale Town

1501 Sutterville Road, Sacramento, CA 95822 ᴥ 264-5233 (recording) or 264-7061. I-5 to Sutterville Road (only goes one direction), then left on West Land Park Drive. Park is on your right, across from the Zoo. 10-5 daily, except Christmas and rainy days. Front gate closes at 4:30. Weekends: 13 and up, $2.50; 3-12, $2; Weekdays: adult, $2.25; 3-12, $1.75. Under 3, free.

This is the place where your small children can really live out their fantasies. Mother Goose is here (to climb on), the Three Pigs (live), the Old Woman and her Shoe (to slide on)...Fairytale Town has them all; every fairy tale you can think of is here, plus some you may not have heard of. Kids'll recognize some of the props before Mom or Dad do. They can slide down from the second story of Old MacDonald's farmhouse, be pirates on Captain Hook's ship, pet the three Billy Goats Gruff, ride in Cinderella's coach — their imagination is the only limit.

- Snack stand and tables available. You can picnic in Sherwood Forest and sit in Robin or Maid Marion's chair.
- Theme restrooms available, and lots of drinking fountains scattered throughout, disguised as animals or toy soldiers.
- Puppet shows in the afternoons; call for hours.
- Two-for-one tickets available; entrance into Fairytale Town gets you into the Sacramento Zoo, across the street. Same day only. The two together, with a picnic in William Land Park, are just the right size for a whole day's outing.
- Special events year-round; call 264-5233.

❧ Funderland

Sutterville Road and 17th Avenue, Sacramento, CA 95822 ❧ 456-0115. Located at south-eastern end of William Land Park, at Sutterville Road. Entrance off South Land Park Drive. Open daily, except Thanksgiving and Christmas, from mid-January till early December; 11am-6pm (after October, 11am-5pm). Free entry to park. Weekdays: 60¢ per ticket (most rides take one ticket); Book of 10 tickets, $5.00; All-day pass, $5.00. Weekends: 75¢ per ticket; book of 10, $6.00.

Funderland is a small amusement park perfect for kids from 2 to 12. It was completely renovated this year, so all 8 of the rides are new and up-to-date. Spin, climb, whirl, roll, and enjoy the pleasant atmosphere of William Land Park.

And when it's time for a change from the frenetic pace of amusement park rides, next door they can ride the ponies (not affiliated with the amusement park). You guide them around a circular track, under large sycamores. A good place to wind down after the rides. Call City Parks and Recreation (see Chapter 8) for information.

- Across the street from Land Park picnic areas.
- Birthday party packages available: 2 hours of unlimited rides (see Chapter 8, Birthday Party Ideas).

∾ Governor's Mansion

16th and H Streets, Sacramento, CA ∾ 323-3047. Take Business 80 to J Street west, right on 16th. Limited parking on street. Open 7 days a week, 10-5 (last tour begins at 4). Adults, $2; 6-12, $1; under 6 free.

California's Executive Mansion, popularly called the Governor's Mansion, was built in 1877-78 on land that was part of the Mexican land grant to John Augustus Sutter, the founder of Sacramento. It served as home to many governors, and has seen four weddings, an assassination attempt, a dynamite explosion and many refurbishments. Earl Warren lived in it the longest, from 1943 until he was appointed to the U.S. Supreme Court in 1953, and Ronald Reagan lived there during the first part of 1967.

Allow about an hour to see the Mansion, which will be of special interest to history buffs or architecture students.

↬ PARKS AND PLAYGROUNDS

Sacramento is an outdoor kind of place. Nine or ten months out of the year, the weather is perfect for outdoor activities, and the topography of the area makes it ideally suited to almost all outdoor pursuits. A trip to the playground is the biggest adventure for small children; and everyone in the family can enjoy an outing at the park, a picnic, a game of badminton, some tennis or roller skating or simply wandering in the shade of the old trees and stopping to listen to a creek.... Sacramento has lots to choose from. The following list is far from complete; but these will get you started. And although playgrounds are most often found in parks, the two are not always synonymous, so I've listed them separately to facilitate your search. First...

∾ PARKS...

A glance at the map will show you how important parks are to Sacramentans. Starting at the western edge of the city, an unbroken swatch of green stretches for 23 miles across the middle of the metropolitan area, from the Sacramento River all the way to Nimbus Dam, just west of the Folsom Lake State Recreation Area. This enormous length of greenery, called the American River Parkway, encompasses a number of smaller parks and recreation areas. Cyclists, walkers or skaters can enjoy the Jedediah Smith trail that runs its entire length, through sylvan, unspoiled riverfront. Come swim, hike, bike, climb, fish, raft, picnic, stroll, enjoy the abundant wildlife, refresh, renew, be restored by nature's beauty and peace.

A word of caution, though: each year, many people drown in the American and Sacramento Rivers. This tragedy is easily avoidable, if proper precautions are taken. Don't let your kids swim out of sight; don't let them swim alone. Stay out of the middle of the river, where the current is swift. When boating, be sure everyone has a snug-fitting flotation device (last year, a toddler floated out of a life-vest that was too big for her and became one of the sad statistics; <u>be sure yours fit</u>). If you rent a boat, be sure life-vests come with it. Don't become one of the statistics; have a safe, happy time.

Most entries to the Parkway have a kiosk; during peak season, or on weekends, you must pay an entry fee. These kiosks seem to be somewhat sporadically manned, due to budget cuts, but during the warmer weather and on week-ends you can usually count on paying. The current fee is $4 per vehicle (free to cyclists and pedestrians).

For the future, there are plans under consideration for another parkway along the Sacramento River. Keep in touch with County Parks and Recreation for more on that.

AMERICAN RIVER PARKWAY
Ancil Hoffman Park

Main entrance at 6700 Tarshes Drive, Carmichael. Golf Course, walking trails, bike trail, Effie Yeaw Nature Center (see same, this chapter), picnic facilities, rest rooms, lots of wide-open green spaces, river access. Our toddlers' favorite place for throwing rocks in the river. Lots of riverine birds and wildlife — deer, wild turkeys, hawks, aquatic birds, foxes, raccoons, possums, squirrels and more. Lots of shade trees.

Annual Kite-flying Day.

Bannister Park

From Fair Oaks Boulevard, take Bannister Road south (east of San Juan Avenue). Located on the Sacramento Bar, where the American River makes a gooseneck turn. Par-course for exercising; walking or bike trail winds its way through natural riverine scenery to the San Juan Rapids, the only rapids on the American River.

Discovery Park

Entrance from Natomas Park Drive, north side, or across the bridge from Tiscornia Park, south side (see below). Lots of picnic facilities, rest rooms, trails, wide open space. Access to river, but in places it's only accessible down a steep embankment my adventurers call "the cliff"; hold onto your exploring toddlers!

Goethe Park

The locals pronounce it "Gatey". Off Rod Beaudry Drive, Rancho Cordova. Picnic tables, rest rooms, lots of space for walking, running, exploring, throwing rocks in the river or swimming, wading, etc. Also accessible by foot over the Harold Richey Memorial Bridge from the William B. Pond Recreation Area, at the end of Arden Way.

Tiscornia Park

Take Richards Boulevard off I-5. This is where my family loves to go "to the beach." A lovely sand beach extends around the bend where the American and Sacramento Rivers meet, with ample room for swimming, wading, playing at the water's edge, picnicking (rest rooms available). Be careful of the strong current out in the middle. Watch the swimmers on the cliffs opposite swing out on ropes into the water. From here you can drive or walk over the bridge to Discovery Park.

OTHER PARKS...

Capitol Park

Boundaries: L, 15th, N and 10th Streets. Sacramento, also known as the City of Trees, is liberally sprinkled with tree-studded parks. Capitol Park is the heart of them all, having sprung literally from the hearts of the people. In the 1860s, the citizens of Sacramento levied a property tax on themselves to raise money to buy land between 10th and 12th Streets. The state eventually acquired the rest, to create the beautiful park you see today.

For a whole-day excursion, pack a picnic lunch and plan on walking the whole park. Park in the garage at 10th and L Streets, then walk clockwise around the perimeter of the park. Along the north side, as you walk under the long arcade of giant, old native California fan palms, you'll pass the elegant, semi-modern Hyatt Regency Hotel. (See Hotel Hopping, Chapter 2.) Wander inside and stop at the shops, watch the continual flow of people, have a cup of coffee at the cafe, watch TV or listen to whatever entertainment's going on in the lobby.

Continue east and pass the Community Center, home of the Sacramento Symphony (at 14th Street), then turn south along the east edge of the park. At 15th and N Streets, as you turn the corner to continue along the park, you'll pass the spot that was discussed as a possible location for the new Governor's Mansion (it was eventually built in Carmichael, a suburb east of Sacramento, but no governor ever lived in it).

Now's the time to wander back into the park, which contains 100 species of trees and plants from every climate and continent in the world, and see if your little explorers can find some of the following:

- a giant Sequoia and coastal Redwood, the official state tree (on the corner of 12th and N Streets);
- a Bunya-Bunya tree from Australia, whose cones weigh up to 30 lbs. (at N Street between 10th and 11th);
- a sugar maple, a gift from Canada's prime minister, Pierre Trudeau;
- Pioneer Camellia Grove (L Street), planted in 1953 to honor the early builders of California. Come here in February and March for a spectacular display of beauty and color. Sacramento is the Camellia Capitol of the world; see "Camellia Show" in Chapter 5,

Festivals and Special Events;

• Deodar Cedars (west side of the park), grown high in the Himalayas, dug up and shipped 'round the Horn to the Park in 1870;

• a statue of Father Junipero Serra and a relief map showing the missions he established in California;

• Memorial Grove, next to Fr. Serra's statue, planted in 1897 as saplings from southern battlefields of the Civil War, in honor of those who died there;

...and much, much more. Stroll through the park, stopping at the occasional drinking fountains, benches, statues, and read the signs that identify the flora. The kids will spy lots of ground squirrels (they arrived in Sacramento in 1921, natives of Missouri); they can bang on the Liberty bells, watch the fish play in the Trout Pond (12th Street), picnic, and just plain have fun. All the trees make it a nice, shady place to play on a blistering summer day.

Curtis Park

Bordered by W. Curtis Drive, Sutterville Road, E. Curtis Drive and Curtis Way. A long, tree-shaded park with tennis, a small Tot-lot, a softball diamond. About 1/2 mile from the Sierra II Community Center, which offers community classes, theater, exhibits, a restaurant and other cultural activities.

Elk Grove Regional Park

Just off Highway 99 in Elk Grove (follow the signs). Elk Grove has all the facilities for family fun — walks, picnic and barbecue facilities, ponds to play by, Tot-lots, tennis, shade trees, lots of space, even an island where concerts are held in the summer (Strauss Island). Bring a picnic and spend the day.

Gibson Ranch County Park

8552 Gibson Ranch Road, Elverta. 991-7592.

Gibson offers lots of space, and amenities for picnicking, barbecuing, walking, playing. Equestrian center for horse lovers. Many cultural events take place here each year, like the Hmong New Year's celebration where young men and women get to choose their courtship partners for marriage; check local newspapers.

Charles C. Jensen Botanical Gardens

8250 Fair Oaks Bd., Fair Oaks. 944-2025; 485-5322 for group tours. On the south side of Fair Oaks Boulevard, about 2 minutes east of the Manzanita Avenue separation. Open daily from 8am-sunset, this small garden is only for enjoying nature. No sports allowed, no picnic facilities, just a lovely, peaceful place to wander and admire the flora. FREE.

Miller Park

Follow Broadway west till it ends at the Sacramento Marina and Miller Park. This is a nice place to forget you're just blocks away from the city. The Park extends along the Sacramento River; one side is lagoon with a Marina full of boats, the other is the River. Lots of picnic tables, a brick barbecue pit, shade trees, rest rooms, a small snack bar (in season). Open from sun-up to sun-down; 5 minutes from the Towe Ford Museum and Old Sacramento.

William Land Park

Bordered by: 11 Ave., 13 Ave., Freeport Bd., Sutterville Rd. and West Land Park Drive. This lovely patch of greenery defines a neighborhood (the "Land Park area") as well as a way of life. On land that was obtained during Sacramento's early years, this inviting, shaded park offers hundred-year-old trees, shaded groves of camellias and azaleas, and sits in one of the oldest neighborhoods of Sacramento. A drive around the area in springtime offers breathtaking azalea-viewing, and in the winter, camellias fill the neighborhood with color. Located within the Park you'll find:

- many picnic areas, some with barbecue facilities.
- several softball diamonds.
- a state-of-the-art playground, near the 13th Avenue corner.
- a golf course.
- Tiny Tot Time, a pre-school run by the City of Sacramento (near the 13th Avenue corner).
- a fenced wading pool, perfect for waders from infant to about 5 or 6.
- the Zoo (see Sacramento Zoo, this chapter).

- Funderland, a child-sized amusement park (see Funderland, this chapter).
- Fairytale Town, where your children can live out their nursery-rhyme fantasies (see Fairytale Town, this chapter).
- a small botanical garden to wander through.
- an outdoor amphitheater which hosts Shakespeare in the Park, concerts and other activities throughout the year; call the Department of Parks and Recreation (264-5200).

❧ ...AND PLAYGROUNDS

Sacramento's playgrounds say a lot about the city's attitude toward its children. The playgrounds listed here offer well-tended, beautiful places to climb, swing, dig, play, feed the ducks, congregate and eat, enjoy nature and just be together in natural surroundings. These are our family favorites; don't stop with this list. With a little creative exploring, you'll find other spots in and around the Sacramento area that are tailor-made to fit your little gymnasts' physical and esthetic needs.

Bryte Park (West Sacramento)

Bordered by: Todhunter Ave., Carrie St. and Riverbank Rd. Four lighted softball diamonds, picnic and barbecue facilities, Tot-lot (sand-filled play area with equipment), basketball courts, soccer fields. Less than a mile from the California State Highway Patrol Academy (see Chapter 2, Tours of the Working World).

Carmichael Park (Carmichael)

Bordered by: Fair Oaks Bd. and Grant Ave. Tennis, swimming pool, Tot-lot, picnic facilities, shade trees. Near many fast-food restaurants and shopping.

Del Paso Park

Bordered by: Auburn Bd., Business 80 and Park Dr. Some play equipment, picnic facilities, shade trees, a creek to explore. But <u>be careful here</u> if you have very small children. There is no barrier to speak of to keep them from toddling onto Auburn Bd., a large, busy, major thoroughfare, and the noise from I-80 and Business 80, right behind the park, can make it hard for them to hear you. Right near the Sacramento Science Center (see Chapter 1).

Garcia Bend Park

Bordered by: Pocket Road and the Sacramento River. Tot-lot, picnic facilities, a nice view of the river. Located in the Pocket area of Sacramento.

Gibbons Park

Bordered by: Gibbons Dr. and Cypress Ave., west of Walnut Ave.

Two well-equipped Tot-lots, picnic and barbecue facilities, tennis.

Howe Community Park

Bordered by: Howe Ave., La Paloma Way and Cottage Way. Several well-equipped Tot-lots, duck pond, pool, tennis, picnic and barbecue facilities, community center; site of Sacramento Symphony summer concerts.

Linden Park/Touchstone Park (West Sacramento)

Bordered by: Linden Rd., Summerfield Dr. and Constitution Ave. Tot-lot, picnic and barbecue facilities, large duck pond filled with ducks, geese, occasional egrets and other wetland birds (West Sacramento lies at the edge of the Delta). Portable toilets only.

McClatchy Park

Corner of 33 St. and 5 Ave. Picnic facilities, Tot-lot. Across from Rainbo Bread (see chapter 2, Tours of the Working World).

McKinley Park

Bordered by: H St., Alhambra Bd., McKinley Bl. and 33rd St. Two large Tot-lots, picnic areas, Shephard Rose Garden and Arts Center, pre-school and community center, duck pond.

Memorial Park (West Sacramento)

Bordered by: Regent, Alabama, Delaware and Euclid Sts. Baseball/softball diamonds, picnic tables, basketball courts, volleyball and Tot-lot.

Mission-North Park

Bordered by: North Ave. and Mission Ave. Tot-lot, picnic facilities, large, winding creek for exploring.

Southside Park

Bordered by: 6 St., T St., 8 St. and Business 80. Pond, picnic tables, running or jogging track; noisy from the freeway overhead. Close to downtown Sacramento.

William Land Park (Land Park)

Bordered by: Freeport Bd., Sutterville Rd., West Land Park Dr. and 13th Ave. Sacramento Zoo, Fairytale Town, Funderland Amusement Park, pony rides (see Funderland, this Chapter), 2 large, well-equipped Tot-lots (tree-shaded), picnic and barbecue facilities, wading pool, flower displays/ botanical gardens, outdoor stage/amphitheater (summer Shakespeare in the Park), duck pond, golf course, baseball diamonds, pre-school.

Note: For information on Parks & Recreation District offerings, community programs, summer classes, camps, etc., see Chapter 8, Resources, Special Assistance Telephone Numbers under Park & Recreation Districts.

❧ Sacramento Children's Museum

1322 O Street, Sacramento, CA 95814 ❧ 447-8017. Business 80 to 16 Street exit north. Left (west) on P Street to 13 Street. On weekdays, only on-street parking (can be tricky). On weekends, parking in the State lots right next to the museum. Tues-Thurs 10-2 by appointment. Sat-Sun 10:30-4:30 open to the public. Closed Monday and Friday. $2; under 2 years free; members free. In 1994, the museum is considering moving to a new location, so call first before planning to visit.

Unlike a "real" museum, here kids are <u>supposed</u> to touch — everything! Walk into the 1880s-era General Store and handle all the authentic merchandise — material, food (not real), things to weigh on the scales. Walk through the Post Office, read the old letters, drop stuff in the mail bags. Assemble your own wheelbarrow and see how it works in the Wheelbarrow Shop. Try on costumes related to all the "shops" and have fun role-playing! They have a real Chevron gas-station, a replica of the American River with boats, piers and other related realia. Kids can even produce their own plays in their theater exhibit.

- Saturday workshops for school-age children — arts, crafts, all sorts of projects with learning as a focus.
- Friday morning Tiny Tot program — movement-based activities and art/craft projects.
- Once a month Kids Night Out — parents drop off children and leave, then hear all about the excitement later!
- Birthday parties (see Chapter 8, Birthday Party Ideas).
- Wheelchair-accessible.
- Museum store — books, games, and toys.
- Just a block from Capitol Park, for picnics. Two blocks from Light Rail. Six blocks from the Stanford House.

❧ Sacramento Science Center
(see also **Sacramento Museum of History, Science and Technology,** in Old Sacramento)

3615 Auburn Boulevard, Sacramento, CA 95821 ❧ till June 1994: 277-6181; after June, 264-7057 (the Sacramento Museum of History, Science and Technology). From Business 80 or I-80 east, take the Watt Avenue South exit. Left on Auburn Boulevard. Center is on the left, about a quarter-mile past Watt Avenue. From 80 west, take the Auburn Bd. exit, turn right on Auburn. Center is on the right, about a half-mile from the freeway exit. Open Wed-Fri 12-5; Sat-Sun 10-5. <u>Planetarium hours:</u> 15-minute free shows: Wed-Fri 3pm; Sat-Sun 1pm. 45-minute paid shows (age 6 and older only): Sat-Sun 3pm. Science Feature: Sat-Sun 2pm. Adult, $2.50; youth (age 3-15), $1.50; Adult planetarium, $2.00; youth, planetarium, $1.00.

As of June 1994, this museum will be merged with the Sacramento History Museum to form the new Sacramento Museum of History, Science and Technology. For a description of the Science Center, see **Sacramento Museum of History, Science and Technology** in the section on Old Sacramento, this chapter.

After June 1994, most of the Science Center's Educational Outreach programs (classes, workshops, etc.) will still take place at the Auburn Bd. location. The Discovery Trail nature walk will remain open to the public.

❧ Sacramento Zoo

3930 West Land Park Drive, Sacramento, CA 95818 ❧ 264-5885; Education Dept., 264-5889; to reserve a Docent tour, 264-7058. In William Land Park. From Business 80, take the 16th Street exit, go south on West Land Park Drive. Zoo is on the right, about 2/3 of the way through the park. From I-5, take Sutterville Road east. Turn left on West Land Park Drive, zoo is on the left. Bus #5 or #6. Open daily 10-4, except Christmas Day. Age 13 and up, $3.50; age 3-12, $2; under 2 free.

There's something about wild things that appeals to kids — and the Zoo's got 'em. Big cats in abundance, bears, giraffes, lots of African mammals in settings as close to natural as possible. The Australian exhibit offers lots of emus, wallabies and kangaroos for a taste of down under. There's an indoor reptile and amphibian exhibit that my kids love to wind their way through — sometimes several times in rapid succession! Birds of every hue and cry lend a jungle atmosphere, filling the air with their strange sounds. Acrobatic monkeys are always a crowd-pleaser as they leap from bar to bar in their two-story cage, and the chimpanzee exhibit is state-of-the-art.

This is a people-scale zoo, just right for a whole afternoon or for just a few hours. There are snack bars and lots of picnic tables available with umbrellas.
- Classes offered throughout the year.
- Gift and souvenir shop.
- Educational trailer for kids to wander through and learn.
- Lots of special events throughout the year, for kids,

amateur photographers, community involvement; call ahead.
- Combination ticket available, for same-day entry to Fairytale Town, across the street (see Fairytale Town, this chapter).
- Family membership available for reduced-price entry. Family pass also gets you entry to many outstanding zoos around the country.
- Snack stands, rest rooms and picnic tables throughout.
- Located in a wonderful park (see William Land Park, this chapter), just across the street from Fairytale Town.

∾ Stanford Mansion State Historic Park

802 N Street (8th and N Streets), Sacramento, CA 95814 ∾ 324-0575. Business 80 to N Street exit or 10th Street exit, or I-5 to Q Street exit. Tours 12:15 Tues and Thurs, 12:15 and 1:30 Sat. Call to confirm. FREE.

Leland Stanford, for whom Stanford University is named, was born here, and this is an unusual opportunity to see "above-ground archaeology", since the Mansion is currently in the process of being restored. You can learn about the process involved in readying a landmark for restoration — the kind of seismic work required (for earthquake protection), how they evaluate the pieces of furniture, what they've discovered beneath the floor boards and other tidbits that you'd never see elsewhere. Probably not very interesting for very small children, but older ones will be fascinated by the "detective work" being done, the mystery involved in reconstructing history.

At Christmastime they offer a special program with lots of old-fashioned games, toys, ornaments to make. That happens the second Saturday in December, from 10am-4pm, and it's free. And on May 14, or the closest weekday, they celebrate Leland Stanford's birthday with an old-fashioned ice-cream social, complete with band concert, from 11:30am-1pm. Also free.

❧ Sutter's Fort State Historic Park

27th and L Streets, Sacramento, CA ❧ *445-4422.*
Business 80 to J Street exit west. South on 28 Street, and
west on L Street. The Fort in on the right, just past the
hospital. From Downtown, take L Street east to the Fort.
Open 10-5 daily, except Thanksgiving, Christmas and
New Year's Day. Age 13 and up, $2; 6-12, $1; 5 and
under free.

In 1834, John Augustus Sutter, a young officer in the
Swiss Army (or so he claimed) and a failed businessman,
fled Switzerland, leaving behind his wife and family, to
come to America. After a tumultuous beginning, he found
his way first to Kansas, then to Fort Vancouver. From there,
he sailed to the Sandwich Islands (Hawaii), where he be-
friended King Kamehameha. But his goal was California,
the El Dorado he'd heard so much about; so after about
four months in paradise he persuaded the King to grant
him several of his strongest, biggest men, and sailed with
them first to Sitka, Alaska, and then to California.

He became a Mexican citizen (California still belonged
to Mexico at that time), and was granted 11 leagues of land
(48,839 acres). With the help of his Hawaiians, the local
Indians and several other friends, he built Fort Sutter, which
he called New Helvetia (New Switzerland).

This first settlement in the Sacramento Valley became
noted for its hospitality. When the Donner Party (see Donner
State Park, Chapter 6, Day Trips) became trapped in the
snowbound Sierra Nevada during the winter of 1846-47,
rescuers left from Sutter's Fort to find them. Sutter developed a reputation as a "bon vivant," enjoying his guests
and even treating them to his ultimate display of friendship
— firing his cannon (he loved to fire it, but whenever he did
the noise broke the brittle glass of the Fort's windows!). But
eventually his friendliness to the Americans who passed
through began to worry the Mexican government who'd
granted him the land. During the political turmoil of the
1840s, his allegiance was suspect by both sides, Mexican
and American. Eventually, the American flag was raised

over Sutter's Fort in 1846, and Sutter was given back his command the next year.

In 1847, he contracted with James Marshall to build a sawmill on the south fork of the American River; but Marshall discovered a "yellow rock" in the tailrace of the mill, and the rest, as they say, is history. The Gold Rush was Sutter's undoing. He lost all his men to the lure of the Mother Lode; people stole his materials and his animals as they passed through on their way to the hills. Neither he nor Marshall succeeded in obtaining mineral rights to the land where the gold was discovered.

Of course, you can see Sutter's Fort without knowing all this history. But history is, after all, people — and Sutter was undoubtedly one of the most colorful folks to leave his imprint on this valley. He was by no means a great success, having lived (and died) in constant debt and having been rescued from the debtors by his son, who eventually came from Switzerland to bail him out. But his name lives on at the Fort, in many place names around town, and in the hearts of all true "Sackamennans." He represents the combination of independence, recklessness, adventure and the fun-loving spirit that shaped the city of Sacramento.

As you enter the Fort, you can get an earphone self-guiding tour, or you can just wander around the Fort on your own. The Fort has been restored to look the way it looked when Captain Sutter lived here, and gives youngsters a good idea of what life was like then. They can see people making candles, baking bread and weaving cloth. The fort has its own blacksmith, carpenter, and cooper, or barrel-maker.

Plan on visiting the Fort the same day as the Indian Museum, which is right next door in the same park. Allow about an hour or two (depending on the age of your children) at the Fort, and the same at the Indian Museum (also depending on the availability of any special exhibits).

- Special Living History days, where docents wear authentic clothing and demonstrate how people lived and worked there.
- Self-guiding audio tour; inquire at entrance.

- Environmental Living Program allows students to spend all day and night at the Fort; inquire at your child's school, or at the Fort.
- Special information/tour for the hearing-impaired.

❧ Visionarium Children's Museum

Sutter Square Galleria, 29th and K Streets, Sacramento, CA 95816 ❧ 443-7476. Located in Sutter Square Galleria, J and 29 Streets. Enter the parking structure off J Street as it goes under the freeway (Business 80). Just a few blocks from Sutter's Fort and the Indian Museum. Open Mon-Sat 10-4:30; Sun 12:00-4:30. Special activities at special hours; call for information. Children 2-14, $4.00; adults, $2.50. Prices vary for special programs; call. Family memberships also available.

In this hands-on museum, kids can make bubbles, learn about light and the principles of motion, create their own movies, experience physical challenges, pretend, and otherwise learn while having a great time. Imagination is the medium. Besides their regular exhibits, they offer: art classes, Family Fun nights (first Friday of every month), special guests, Kreative Kids gift shop, birthday party packages (see Chapter 8) and workshops on music and art, reading, literacy and more. On Grandparents' Day, Grandma and Grandpa are admitted free (first Saturday of every month).

❧ Waterworld

1600 Exposition Boulevard, Sacramento, CA 95815 ❧ 924-0555. Business 80 to Exposition Boulevard exit. Open daily, 10:30-6, from Memorial Day to Labor Day. Adults and children over 4 feet tall, $13.95; under 4 feet tall, $9.95; 3 feet tall and under, free.

This is where Sacramentans cool off during those blistering summer days. There's something here for everyone, regardless of size or age, and you can have a great time even if you don't swim.

- Features Breaker Beach, the largest wave pool in Northern California, plus 25 other water attractions, including the highest water slides in the west, 2 speed slides, paddle boats, a kids' play area and fountains to run through, splash in, play under or just watch.

- Snack bars, changing rooms, water fountains throughout.
- Appropriate swimming attire required.
- Lots of picnic facilities.
- Handicap accessible.

❧ 2 ❧
More Good Things To Do

The attractions in this chapter may be somewhat lesser known than those in Chapter 1, and in some cases they may be smaller; but those are about the only differences. Some of these rate high on my kids' list of favorites. What I like most about the items in this chapter is that in many cases the attractions are unclassifiable. Surprises lurk in the most unusual places! Just like with kids, you never know what to expect. But Sacramento is like that.

Have fun; explore!

OFF THE BEATEN PATH

These may not be the first places that come to mind when musing about what to do in Sacramento; but that's exactly what makes them a valuable resource for family fun. Chances are you might even find a family favorite among them...

∾ American River Fish Hatchery

2101 Nimbus Road, Rancho Cordova, CA 95670 ∾ 355-0896. Highway 50 east out of Sacramento, Hazel Avenue exit north. The Hatchery is between the highway and the river, on the left. Open 7 days a week, about 7:30-4. FREE.

Located adjoining the NIMBUS FISH HATCHERY (see below) on the American River, this somewhat smaller installation has tanks filled with all kinds of trout. Kids love to watch them dart and dive. The California Department of Fish and Game stocks streams and lakes all over the state with babies from here. This year, for the first time since its opening in 1968, it was closed for two months because of the drought conditions, and there can be other seasonal variations in hours; call first.

⌇ Cosumnes River Wildlife Preserve

6500 Desmond Road, Galt, CA ⌇ 684-2816. I-5 south to Twin Cities Road west (about 20 miles south of Sacramento). Take Franklin Road south, turn left on Desmond Road (1 mile south of Twin Cities). The trailhead is on Franklin, before you reach Desmond, outside the gates of the Preserve. Open daylight hours. FREE.

4,500 acres of riparian (river-dwelling) wildlife preserve await visitors here, but the goal is to keep it in its wild state; be sure your children understand the rules. No trampling or picking of flora, don't disturb the wildlife, and if you carry it in, carry it out. In short, respect for nature.

Run largely by the Nature Conservancy at present, this wetlands Preserve abounds with watchable wildlife. It's in the process of change, and may soon be part of a Parks system. In late 1993, there will be a Visitors' Center on Franklin Boulevard. At present, there are some interpretive signs at the entrance to the Preserve.

The trail that winds along the Cosumnes River, through the wetlands, is always open, and affords views of migrating cranes, ducks, geese and other waterfowl. Deer are regularly sighted, as well as beaver and river otters. There are no facilities at present, but you're welcome to picnic here if you remove all traces afterwards.

⌇ Discovery Zone

6351 Mack Rd., Sacramento ⌇ 688-7529. Near Valley Hi Dr. Open F-Sat, 10am-9pm; other days 10am-8pm. $5.99 per child for unlimited play; adults accompany children free (they can play too). Special rates for birthdays; call.

Parents can join their kids in this safe, indoor play area, or they can sit in the full-service diner and sip and watch. The diner serves food kids eat, like pizza and hot dogs, so kids can stay and play all day. Coaches oversee the play areas for parents' peace of mind, and they also help with birthday party packages, which include various combinations of play time, food, drinks, utensils, cake, and tokens for the arcade games.

∿ Fun For All

6412 Tupelo Drive, Unit G, Citrus Heights, CA 95621 ∿ 762-2111. Adjacent to the west side of I-80, just off Antelope Road. Open Mon-Sat 10-9, and Sun 11-7. $5.95 per child for unlimited play time; adults accompany children free (they can play too). Special rates for birthday parties, group play; call.

An indoor play area for children from 18 months to 12 years, this clean, attractive facility offers completely safe play on familiar, challenging "soft" play equipment. Parents can join in the fun, or sit at the many tables and chairs and read while the kids play. Parents and children are matched with computerized IDs before leaving, for complete peace of mind. Several birthday party rooms, token-operated games and a snack bar that offers pizza, hot dogs and other things kids eat, like Cheerios. Future plans include a single-parents' night, cappucino mornings, and other family-friendly activities. Call for more information.

∿ Green Acres Mini-Golf and Arcade

7411 Fair Oaks Boulevard, Carmichael, CA 95608 ∿ 483-2368. On Fair Oaks Boulevard just south of Manzanita Avenue, near the curve where Fair Oaks turns east. Open Wed and Thurs, 1-10; Fri, Sat and Sun, 10am-11pm. Kids 5 and under, free with a paid admission; age 6-59, $5; adults 60 and up, $3. One admission entitles you to play all three mini-golf courses. Group rates available for 10 or more people, if reserved in advance.

A nice place to spend a few hours of fun. Green Acres has three 18-hole championship mini-golf courses, an arcade and a bumper-boat pool. My kids' favorites are the dinosaurs in the miniature golf course that borders Fair Oaks Boulevard, and the fact that it's within comfortable walking distance of several fast-food places. Whether your little gourmets favor tacos, burgers, pizza or sandwiches, you can have lunch and an afternoon of outdoor fun without spending a fortune.

❧ Mine Shaft

*2300 Mine Shaft Lane, Rancho Cordova, CA 95670 ❧
985-4840. Highway 50 to Sunrise Boulevard south. Left
on Folsom Boulevard. Open M-Th, 11-10; Fri, 11am-
midnight; Sat, 10am-midnight; Sun, 10-10. Mini-Golf:
adult, $5; age 7-12, $4; 6 and under, $2.75. Batting
cages: $1.25 for 26 pitches. Maze: adult, $4.50; 4-12,
$3.50.*

This is the place that looks like a castle, off the south
side of Highway 50. They have miniature golf, batting cages,
a maze to get lost in (outdoors), a snack bar, over 100 video
games in the arcade, and Kiddie Rides for children under
70 lbs.

❧ Nimbus Fish Hatchery

*201 Nimbus Road, Rancho Cordova, CA 95670 ❧ 355-
0666. Highway 50 east out of Sacramento, Hazel Avenue
exit north. Nimbus Road left, just before the river. Open
7 days a week, about 7:30am-4pm. Occasional seasonal
changes in hours; call first. FREE.*

There's something about the perpetual motion of fish
that appeals to kids of all ages. Come see the King or Chi-
nook Salmon flash through the froth as they climb the fish
"ladders" on their way upstream to spawn (November and
December). Sleek Steelhead trout perform the same incredible migration in January and February. You can watch the
Fish and Game people take the eggs from the females or
sperm from the males — a process that proves fascinating
to budding scientists. Your little naturalists can feed the fish
(bring lots of nickels) or themselves, picnic-style. The Hatchery is located on a bend of the American River, overlooking
cliffs and a river of rugged beauty just a few miles from
Sacramento. If you're patient, you can sometimes see wild
turkeys, egrets, or a snake or two.

❧ Sacramento Old City Cemetery

*10th Street and Broadway, Sacramento, CA 95865 ❧
449-5621. Business 80, exit at 10th or 16th Street.*

*Broadway to Riverside Boulevard and turn south. The
entrance to the cemetery is on the right. Tours assemble
at the main entrance, 10th Street and Broadway. Open 7
days a week, 7:00-4:30. Gift Shop and Archives open
10-3, Mon, Tues & Fri. FREE.*

The purpose of the tour of the Old City Cemetery,
according to John Bettencourt, Tour Coordinator, is to "introduce kids to a little of Sacramento's history through stories about our pioneers, and at the same time to introduce
them to death and dying in an un-personal way."

More than 20,000 pioneers from every part of the globe
are buried here, including John Augustus Sutter (founder of
Sacramento), three governors, the first mayor of Sacramento,
and the son of Alexander Hamilton. If you've never toured
a cemetery, you're in for a historic surprise. You can use the
self-guided tour map, or take advantage of their tour, which
includes:

- a guided walking tour, full of historical background
  tidbits;
- work sheets for the kids, which give them the
  opportunity to be detectives as they search for specific
  tombstones;
- tombstone rubbings to release their creativity and
  imagination.
- Gift shop and Archives.

It's a different way to absorb some history and have lots
of fun. As you exit the cemetery on Riverside Boulevard,
turn right and drive south down into the Land Park Area
for a short, scenic tour of some of the older homes that date
back to Sacramento's beginnings. Turn left, east, on
Sutterville Road, then left and north on West Land Park
Drive (see also William Land Park, Chapter 1). This is especially beautiful in the spring, when the azaleas are in bloom.
All the streets are lined with big, old trees (Sacramento is
called the City of Trees), and in their shade azaleas and
camellias thrive and create incredible masses of color in
springtime. This street will take you north, back to the freeway (Business 80).

～ Safetyville, USA

3909 Bradshaw Road, Sacramento, CA 95827 ～ 368-4250. Highway 50 east from Sacramento to Bradshaw exit. Hours arranged in advance; call ahead with three possible dates (this is a popular school trip). FREE (donations accepted).

Injuries are the leading cause of death among children 5 through 14. Safetyville USA, the only facility of its kind in the U.S., was created to reduce deaths and injuries through safety training. It's been proven that early education is an effective method of injury prevention, and Safetyville USA has made a commitment to that education.

Located on 3 acres in Sacramento, its one-third scale buildings and streets teach children to recognize hazards in a realistic but controlled environment. They have fun in this "pretend city" complete with sidewalks, streets, traffic signals, gas station, school, police and fire station, etc. After the tour, they discuss what they learn in a classroom setting. The activity books they receive are fun to do, and the injury prevention lessons learned here can last a lifetime.

At Safetyville, kids learn about: Pedestrian safety, Bicycle and skateboard safety, Home and recreational safety, Fire education, Safe vs. dangerous strangers, Construction safety, Electrical safety, Water safety and Alcohol/drug education and prevention.

This program is offered primarily for field-trips and school groups. However, any group of 8 or more children is welcome, from pre-school through sixth grade.

～ Scandia Family Fun Center

5070 Hillsdale Boulevard, Sacramento, CA 95842 ～ 331-5757 (or 331-0115 for general information). I-80 at Madison Avenue exit. Open 10-8 daily. Mini-golf, $5; Racers and Bumper Cars, $4 per 5 minutes; Batting cages, $1.25 per 20 pitches. Cash only.

Whether you have a few hours to spend or a whole day, everyone will find something to do here. Two 18-hole miniature golf courses, Little Indy racing cars, bumper boats, an arcade, batting cages (for softball and hardball), and a snack bar to retreat to in between.

- Monday evening is Family Night: $1 off the price of miniature golf, the Indy Racers and the bumper boats after 5pm.
- Special Birthday Party plan; see Chapter 8, Birthday Party Ideas.
- Multi-attraction ticket for reduced rates, and group rates available.

～ Silver Bend-Kirtland Farms

34600 South River Road, Clarksburg, CA 95612 ～ 665-1410. Highway 160 south to the Freeport Bridge. Cross the bridge, then take South River Road south to Silver Bend. Open June-Dec., about 10am till sundown. Closed November to get ready for the Christmas season, which begins immediately after Thanksgiving. FREE weekdays and off-season weekends. Weekends in October and December, $4.50; under 4 FREE. When there's no admission fee, there's a charge for the train ride (which is otherwise included in the admission fee).

This is a delightful seasonal afternoon's entertainment for small children. Located on a bend in the Sacramento River, Silver Bend has acres of inviting things to do. In October, they feature a Pumpkin Patch; the tour includes a ride on the locomotive-driven train, a talk about history and Pilgrims and harvests, fun activities, like a walk through a hay-bale maze, and a shop for sampling the apple cider and other harvest goodies. In the winter, it's a chop-your-own Christmas tree farm. There are animals to see, picnic facilities, and children always have fun here. The indescribable mix of nature and holiday themes is a sure hit. But call first if you don't want your visit to coincide with a lot of school groups (this is a popular place with Sacramento's pre-schools and elementary schools).

- Narrated train ride.
- Gift shop, and fresh fruits and vegetables for sale during non-holiday seasons.
- Pick-your-own pumpkins or Christmas trees.

ᕦ Vietnam Veterans' Memorial

At the north side of Capitol Park, between 13 and 14th Streets. I-5 to J Street exit east, or Business 80 to 16th Street north.

Located in a sylvan setting in Capitol Park, this walk-through memorial is both approachable and impressive. Designed in 1985 and paid for entirely by donations, it has an engraved polished granite map of South Vietnam, and several bronze relief and free-standing statues of typical 19-year-old combat veterans. Children find them as fascinating as "real soldiers." The outer surfaces of the walls are faced with twenty-two panels of granite upon which are engraved 5822 names of Californians fallen in battle. In Spring, the blossoming circle of weeping cherry trees against the black granite walls makes it unforgettable for contrast and beauty.

ᕦ Witter Ranch Historic Farm

3480 Witter Way, Sacramento, CA 95834 ᕦ 927-4116. I-5 to West El Camino exit, then El Centro north to San Juan east; Witter Way is on the left. OR: I-80 to Northgate, south to San Juan west, or to the West El Camino exit. Open by appointment (although in the future Mr. Witter hopes to be able to keep the ranch open one day on weekends; call for up-date). Adults, $3; age 6-12, $2; under 6, $1.

This large spread offers children an opportunity to experience first-hand what life was like on a typical farm here from the era between 1915 and 1950. The structures, built in 1920, and the ranch-house, which dates from 1934, are all listed in the National Register of Historic Places and as Points of Historic Interest.

Children's visits here are hands-on experiences. They can prepare food (churn butter, make biscuits the old way, etc.), feed the farm animals, do laundry on a board, make small crafts (like corn-husk dolls) and enjoy the ranch in many other ways.

This is usually a school field-trip; large groups are encouraged, but if you have several families who can go together Ed Witter says they'd be happy to welcome you too. Visits are arranged by appointment, so call first. Before bringing the kids, some of the accompanying adults go first to be "oriented," so they can conduct the tour themselves (although there's always at least one staff member along to assist).

OUTDOOR/FARMERS' MARKETS AND PICK-YOUR-OWN

Ah, the joys of produce fresh from the farm! If you can't grow your own, the next best thing is an open-air market where you can browse, pick, people-watch and generally have a good time while you take care of one of life's necessities.

But open-air shopping is for more than just food. Auctions, flea markets, toys, antiques, furniture, coins, collectibles — in or around Sacramento, you can find just about anything for sale outdoors. That's not surprising, since Sacramento is an out-of-doors kind of place....

❧ Apple Hill
Carson Road, Camino, CA 95709 (east of Placerville) ❧ *(800) 457-6279 (El Dorado County Chamber of Commerce).*

Apple Hill is a phenomenon rather than a place. About an hour's drive from downtown Sacramento, in Camino, just east of Placerville, this is an area filled with apple orchards and wineries — over 50 of them. The farmers here sell their produce and confections, like fresh-pressed cider, pies, fudge, juices and more, to the public during most of the year. Apple season — late summer through fall — is the high point, with special events like Pumpkin Patches and Christmas tree sales. At some of the farms here, you can pick your own produce, and you can always pick your own Christmas tree. See Chapter 6 (Day Trips, Placerville, Apple Hill) for details.

∾ Auction City and Flea Market

8521 Folsom Boulevard, Sacramento, CA 95826 ∾ 383-0880. Highway 50 to Watt Avenue south. Folsom Boulevard right (west) almost a mile. Open 7-5, Sat and Sun. FREE.

Spend a Saturday or Sunday browsing through items of yesterday — and produce of today. Eggs, vegetables, fruit, furniture, clothing, antiques — you name it, someone wants to get rid of it. Open all year.

∾ California Certified Farmers' Markets

8th and W Streets, Sacramento, CA ∾ 363-3663.

Every Sunday, all year round, from 8-noon, you can buy the freshest of produce direct from the farmers. The market takes place in the State parking lot under Business 80 (10th Street exit).

10th and J Streets, Sacramento, CA ∾ 363-3663.

Same fresh produce straight from the farm, available May till December, on Wednesdays and Fridays, 10-2. Indoors.

∾ Davis Farmer's Market

Central Park, bordered by B, C, 4th and 5th Streets.

Located just a few blocks from the UC campus and in a lovely park with play equipment to keep the kids busy while Mom shops. Every Saturday (8-noon) and Wednesday (2-6) you can buy produce straight from the surrounding farms. From May to September, the market moves to 2nd Street on Wednesday nights, 5:30-8:30.

❧ Denio's Farmer's Market and Auction

1551 Vineyard Road, Roseville, CA 95678 ❧ 782-2704. I-80 to Roseville/Riverside exit. Cross the freeway onto Riverside and turn left at the second light onto Cirby Way. Right on Foothills Bd. and right again onto Vineyard to entrance. Open Sat and Sun, 7-5, rain or shine. Smaller market on Tues and Thurs, 7-5.

Jim Denio began this auction selling produce from a small stand in 1947. Now it's become Northern California's largest on-going garage sale! Every weekend, rain or shine, you can wander among the hundreds of vendors of produce, clothing, furniture, jewelry, crafts, household items and more. Don't be shy; there are lots of employees in gold-colored vests throughout, ready to answer your questions or help you find what you're looking for.

❧ 49er's Swap Meet

4450 Marysville Boulevard, Sacramento, CA ❧ 923-9485 (recorded announcement; for more information, call 920-3530). Off I-80 at the Raley Boulevard exit. Open Thurs-Sun, 7-4. $.25 per person walk-in fee; $.25 per vehicle parking, behind the snack bar.

More stuff, for shopping, swapping or just plain browsing. Large snack bar.

❧ Sacramento Natural Foods Co-op

1900 Alhambra Boulevard, Sacramento, CA 95816 ❧ 455-2667. N or P Street exit off Business 80; Stockton Boulevard exit off Highway 50. Open 9am-10pm daily.

The Co-op has the biggest selection of organic produce in the Sacramento Valley, and the largest bulk food selection in Northern California. If your kids accompany you regularly to the ordinary supermarket, this can be an interesting change of pace.

STORYTELLING, LIBRARIES AND BOOKSTORES

Kids live in a world of imagination — and nothing unleashes that imagination like a good book or a well-told story. Each September, Sacramentans get together and prove their commitment to the value of books in their children's lives at an event called "Sacramento Reads!" Here, authors, readers, parents and kids gather to celebrate that world of imagination, and to have a good time together (see Chapter 5, Festivals and Special Events). The Sacramento area abounds with successful writers of all kinds, and with writers' organizations. This is a city dedicated to the power and the fun of the printed word, and here are some of the places where you and your kids can indulge and enjoy.

✎ LIBRARIES

In 1992, the **Sacramento Public Library**, *828 I Street, Sacramento 95814 (440-5926)* moved into this brand new Central facility. The building alone is worth a trip, especially the **Kids' Place** on the Lower Level. Kids and parents can relax here on the cozy custom furniture and take advantage of its many features designed to help guide children toward a successful future. Books, music and story audio cassettes, displays, all levels, novels, non-fiction — children have access to it all, as well as to the library system's entire collection through the new online computer catalog. Also tailored for parents, teachers, day-care providers, etc., the Kids' Place offers books, pamphlets and magazines on infant nutrition, safety, health education, and many other topics related to children.

Once there, be sure to ask for Terry Chekon, the **Coordinator of Children's Programs**; she can help guide you to the program best suited to your needs, and has information about the branch libraries. The Library's offerings for kids vary, and each branch offers different activities — **storytelling, puppet shows, music, arts and crafts, dial-a-story**, etc. Due to current budget concerns, not all programs are offered all the time, so call ahead. You can find out about them at the Central Library or by calling the branch you're interested in.

The branches are listed below, with some of the services offered. Remember that recent budget considerations may have eliminated certain services, and hours differ by branch and may also have been affected by budget cuts. Call ahead to be sure.

Arcade Community Library - 2443 Marconi Avenue • 483-5061

Arden Branch - 891 Watt Avenue • 483-6361

Carmichael Regional - 5605 Marconi Avenue • 483-6055

Colonial Heights Community - 4799 Stockton Bd. • 440-5926

Belle Cooledge Branch - 5600 S. Land Park Dr. • 424-5027

Courtland Branch - 129 Primasing Avenue • (1)775-1113

Del Paso Heights - 920 Grand Avenue • 927-1133

Elk Grove Branch - 8962 Elk Grove Bd. • 685-4798

Fair Oaks/Orangevale Community-11601 Fair Oaks Bd. • 966-5740

Folsom Branch - 638 East Bidwell St., Folsom • (1)983-2780

Galt Branch - 380 Civic Drive, Galt • (209)745-2066

Isleton Branch - 101 C Street, Isleton • (1)777-6638

Martin Luther King Regional-7340 24th St. Bypass • 421-3151

E.K. McClatchy Branch - 2112 22nd St. • 455-8153

McKinley Branch - 601 Alhambra Bd. • 442-0598

North Highlands Branch - 3601 Plymouth Dr. • 331-0675

N.Sac/Hagginwood Branch - 2109 Del Paso Bd. • 927-0652

Orangevale Branch - 8820 Greenback Lane • 989-2182

Rancho Cordova Community-9845 Folsom Bd., R.C • 362-0641

Rio Linda Branch - 902 Oak Lane, Rio Linda • 991-4515

Southgate Community - 6132 66th Avenue • 421-6327

Sylvan Oaks Community - 6700 Auburn Bd., Cit.Hts. • 969-1752

Walnut Grove Branch - 14177 Market, Walnut Grove • (1)776-1412

Special Services:

Administration: 828 I Street • 440-5926

Books-By-Mail • 927-1133

Community Information Center • 442-4995

Dial-A-Story • 441-1234

Dial-A-Book · 442-2442
Friends of the Library · 440-7361
Literacy Service · 966-7323
Mobile Libraries · 440-5036
Non-Profit Resource Center · 264-2131
Readers for the Blind · 966-7323

In West Sacramento, the Yolo County Library, Turner Branch, *1212 Merkley Avenue (371-9274 for information, 371-5612 for hours)* also offers lots of activities for kids and parents, but call ahead to check since they vary according to budget. Some of the recent past offerings include **Pre-school story time, guest puppeteers, Children's Book Week** speakers, a **Cinco de Mayo celebration**, and **Clifford the Big Red Dog** (always a big hit!). They also have **special summer programs** for kids; call for information.

West Sacramento is just across the river from Old Sacramento. Take Business 80 west over the Sacramento River, and take the first exit, Jefferson Boulevard. Turn right on Jefferson Bd. and right again on Merkley Avenue. The Library is on the left, before the street turns. Open Mon and Thurs 1-9; Tues and Wed 10-9; Fri 10-6; Sat 10-5. Call for hours of kids' programs.

✒ BOOKSTORES

A word first about the giants. They don't necessarily offer special children's programs, like some of the smaller bookstores, but they have a wider selection in general, and stock a wide variety of books for young readers. **B. Dalton Bookseller**, at 511 Downtown Plaza (K Street between 5th & 7th; 442-7609) and at 6137 Florin Road (Florin Center; 428-4802) is one of the biggest bookstores in town. They carry everything from A to Z, including a large selection of children's books. If they don't have it, they can order it for you. Some of the other giants include **Brentano's Bookstore**, Arden Fair Mall (920-5277) or Town and Country Village (485-8306), **Scribner's Bookstore**, 1689 Arden Way (923-5178), and, of course, **Tower Books**, at several locations around Sacramento (5950 Florin Road 391-6121; 7830 Macy Plaza Drive, 961-7202; Watt and El Camino Avenues,

481-6600; and 16th Street and Broadway, 444-6688). Tower is Sacramento's supermarket of books — anything you want, you can find it here or they can get it for you. They stock a great number of books for young readers of all ages, including a variety of **foreign language children's books**. Some discounts; inquire.

Newly-opened in the Arden Fair Mall is **Barnes and Noble's Bookstore**, at 1725 Arden Way (565-0644). Here you'll find it all, too, as well as a large children's corner, tables throughout the store, and on-going programs for children, like storytelling and crafts. Bring your coffee in with you; they encourage sitting, sipping and browsing.

Another new bookstore in town is the **Avid Reader**, 1003 L Street (443-7323), across from the Capitol. This is a branch of the original Avid Reader in Davis, which offers a reading area for kids and comes highly recommended by parents. The new A.R. offers seasonal events, like Christmas storytelling, and a large selection of books for kids and parents.

In the Yellow Pages you'll find several pages of listings under Book Dealers - Retail. Many of the smaller ones offer a **Storytelling Hour**, or a **crafts time** or some other children's activity.

Some bookstores in the Sacramento area are just a little bit different in some way and should be mentioned here — like the **Pacific Western Traders Co.**, 305 Wool Street, Folsom (985-3851), a print shop that has an extensive selection of **native American literature**, including children's.

The **Hornet Bookstore**, California State University, 6000 J Street (278-6446) may seem like a surprising place to find children's books. But this University bookstore carries a good selection to augment their **Children's Literature** classes. The first floor contains school supplies and "things"; books are upstairs on the second floor. Paid parking only on campus. Also check other colleges that offer Children's Literature classes for their book offerings.

At **La Raza Bookstore** in the **Galeria Posada**, 629 15th Street (446-5133), you and your children can delve into the world of **Hispanic literature**, for adults and children. This is a bookstore and gallery dedicated to things Hispanic; come in for a real ethnic experience.

Quinby's, at 3509 Fair Oaks Boulevard (Arden Town Center) (488-7071), sells all kinds of children's books, and for parents they offer a **parenting reference** section. Here you can also buy **educational toys, arts-and-crafts materials** and **science kits**. Bring your little ones in on Saturday morning, 11am, for **Storytime** and **Arts and Crafts** (free). Occasional special events, like author's book-signings; call first.

The **Teachers' Exchange** also believes in fun in learning, and it's not at all restricted to teachers, as the name implies. Come browse through their educational materials — books, puzzles, visual aids, workbooks, art supplies, and all sorts of "manipulative" aids that help young minds grasp concepts. According to Miranda Reis, salesperson and resident story-teller, kids walk away from their experience at T.E. "learning something and having a good time!" All three stores offer many programs throughout the year, like **storytelling, readings, arts and crafts**, and **games, workshops** for parents, a **Kids' Birthday Club** and more. Locations: 3421 El Camino Avenue (485-2371), 8089 Madison Avenue, Citrus Heights (965-8921) and 1012 Florin Road (427-5247).

At the **Book Market**, 10917 Olson Drive, Rancho Cordova (858-1735), you can buy lots of books without breaking the bank. This outlet sells a wide variety of books for young and old at a "deep discount"; nothing here costs more than $10, and you can find books for $1 or $2. They get shipments constantly, so you never know what you'll find here, but you'll have fun searching.

TOURS OF THE WORKING WORLD

The tools of the trade can be exciting things, no matter what the trade. Machines that bang, whir, smash, crush, roll, clang, roar — what could be more fascinating to a kid? Finding out how things are made is a source of amazement for kids of all ages, and there are lots of factories, companies or other places of business that are happy to welcome children in the greater Sacramento area. Some have minimum age limits; some have minimum group numbers; some are flexible. Call first.

ᴥ American Institute of Architects

1025 19th Street, Suite 8, Sacramento, CA 95814 ᴥ 444-3658. Meet by arrangement (all tours in the downtown area). FREE.

Sacramento has a rich heritage of architecture, like its wide assortment of Victorian mansions downtown. You can take one of their three guided walking tours, or get their brochures and walk the tour yourself (self-guided). Call for information. More appropriate for older children, who have studied history, architecture, or have an appreciation for the two.

ᴥ Anheuser-Busch Brewery

3101 Busch Drive, Fairfield, CA 94533 ᴥ (707) 429-7595. Located 65 miles west of Sacramento on Interstate 80. Tours available Mon through Fri, 10-2, by reservation only. Weekend tours for groups of 35 or more people. FREE.

Although beer isn't particularly a topic for kids, a brewery this size is a fascinating place to learn about fermentation, horses (in the film about their famous Clydesdales), or assembly-line production (watching the bottle line on the plant floor). You'll learn about the company's history, see a video on the brewing process (for all your budding scientists), and at the end there are samples of beer, soft drinks and snacks. There's also a gift shop.

~ Bel-Air Markets

General Office: 929-6342 (many stores around the Sacramento area). Call to arrange. Tours given Tues, Wed and Thurs, at 10, 1:30 or 3:30. FREE.

School-age children really enjoy this behind-the-scenes tour of how a large, modern supermarket works. They get to see how meats are cut up, how those milk cases get mysteriously filled up all day long from behind, how the air-tight plastic wrap gets sealed on, what to call some of the strange-looking, exotic fruits and veggies, and — the piece de resistance — they wind up at the bakery, where they each get a treat. My second-grade son talked about this tour for weeks!

They require a minimum of 8 children for the tour, so if your own family isn't quite that numerous, you have two options: you and your children can ask to join an already-arranged tour, or you can get together with a few other families and go together. This is a very popular school field-trip, so call well in advance.

~ Cal-Gene, Inc.

1920 Fifth Street, Davis, CA 95616 ~ 753-6313. I-80 to Davis exit (Richards Bd., UC Davis). After underpass, take E Street north to 5th Street east. Tours arranged in advance. FREE.

If you have a serious scientist in your house, you won't want to miss this. Cal-Gene is the leading U.S. plant bio-tech company, and they offer tours by prior arrangement and reservation only. *Their tours are usually aimed at college students majoring in plant technology,* and are not suitable for younger children; call first to be sure it's appropriate for your group.

❧ California State Highway Patrol

3500 Reed Avenue, West Sacramento, CA 95605 ❧ 372-5620. I-80 to Reed Avenue right. Facility is on the right. Tours by arrangement. FREE.

If your little future peace officers are curious how the Highway Patrol trains its officers, this tour will delight them. The facility is more open to large groups (college classes, etc.), but if you have a few people who'd like a tour, call the Staff Office at the above number, and if they have sufficient staff they'll be happy to help you.

❧ California State University, Sacramento

6000 J Street, Sacramento, CA ❧ 278-7362.

CSUS offers tours to anyone interested. You and your children can arrange a personalized guided tour of whatever departments interest you, the library, gym, whatever facilities you'd like to visit. Call in advance, to be sure there are student guides available.

❧ Capital Christian Center

9470 Micron Avenue, Sacramento, CA ❧ 856-5620.

The Center welcomes visitors, and if you call in advance they're happy to arrange a tour of their facility, which includes a large church, school, Bible college, pre-school and more. Best on weekdays; on weekends, obviously, they're busy.

❧ Country Sausage Kitchen

15153 North Jack Tone Road, Lodi, CA ❧ (209) 334-1715. Highway 99 south to Lodi. Route 12 or Kettleman Lane exit east about 6 miles to Jack Tone Road. Tours by reservation. FREE.

Ah, the smells of fresh sausage being made! Come see how they stuff all that meat into those little casings, by hand and by machine. This is a family-run business, and they require that reservations be made at least one week in advance.

⮽ Creative Play Puppets

1881 Walters Court, Suite C, Fairfield, CA 94533 ⮽ (707) 428-1828. I-80 west to Air Base Parkway/Travis AFB exit east. Cross the Railroad bridge and stay right; Walters Court is right after Walters Road. Open 9-4 daily. FREE.

This is the only felt-puppet factory in the US, and they offer children a fascinating 5-station tour that shows them how puppets are created, from first cut to final product. The tour walks them through the process, stopping to talk about each step. Ooohs, ahs and open mouths usually happen when they see the 85 or so puppets on the wall. The factory ships to toy stores, police departments, school supply places, even hospitals (for therapy). An unusual tour that takes about 30 minutes.

⮽ Fire Stations

Fire-fighters in Sacramento, West Sacramento and other outlying suburban areas are happy to show children around their facilities. Look in the telephone directory under the city name. My own little explorers loved climbing on the big trucks, trying helmets and other gear and just wandering around. But remember that these are working crews; don't be disappointed if they have to cancel your tour to go on a call. Just try again, or at another facility; each one is fascinating in its own unique way.

⮽ Folsom Dam & Power Plant

7794 Folsom Dam Road, Folsom, CA 95630 ⮽ 989-7275. Highway 50 east to Folsom Boulevard into Folsom (follow signs). Natoma Street north-east to Folsom Dam Road. Guided tours (about an hour and a half) of the Dam and Powerplant Tues-Sat, 10am and 1pm. Shorter tours available. Reservations are required. FREE.

Folsom Dam, about 20 miles northeast of Sacramento, impounds over a million acre-feet of water in Folsom Lake. Its primary function is flood control — essential in an area that has a history of flooding — but it also stores water for irrigation and electric power generation, and helps preserve the American River fisheries, helps control salt water intrusion from the Delta and provides recreational facilities. (See Chapter 6, Day Trips, Folsom.)

❧ Herman Goelitz Candy Company

2400 N. Watney Way, Fairfield, CA ❧ (707) 428-2838. I-80 west to Abernathy Road. When Abernathy ends, turn left. After about a mile, turn left on Courage Road, and left again on N. Watney Way. Tours weekdays at 9, 10:15 and 11:30; additional tours Tuesday and Thursday, 1:30pm. FREE.

Do your kids love jelly beans? This is the home of the world-famous Jelly Belly, the gourmet jelly bean that put jelly beans in the national limelight. You can see how a jelly bean happens, from the cooking and rolling to the packaging, during this hour-long tour. No high-heeled or open-toed shoes. And they recommend you reserve your tour from 3 to 6 months in advance.

❧ Hershey's Chocolate

120 South Sierra Avenue, Oakdale, CA ❧ (209) 848-8126. Highway 99 south to Manteca (just south of Stockton), then 120 east to Oakdale. The Visitor Center is in the middle of Oakdale, at the intersection of Highways 108 and 120. Open weekdays, 8:30-3. Closed Washington's Birthday, Good Friday, Memorial Day, July 4th, Labor Day, Thanksgiving and the day following, December 24 and 25, December 31 and January 1. Groups should call in advance. FREE.

If you're a chocoholic, the smell alone here will drive you crazy! Imagine — eleven acres entirely devoted to chocolate. You can watch machines melt, grind, shape, sliver, heat, cool, sort and wrap chocolate. It's a veritable labyrinth of conveyor belts, of which the favorite is usually the Kisses... or maybe the huge vats of molten chocolate and peanut butter, for the ever-popular Reese's Peanut Butter Cups!

The Visitor Center, where you stop to sign up for a tour,

is also a candy shop; be prepared for lots of tasting. And save your ticket as you begin the shuttle tour; at the end, it's redeemable for a Hershey's bar.

～ Leatherby's Family Creamery

2333 A Arden Way, Sacramento ～ 920-8382. Arden Way exit off Business 80, take Arden Way east. Located between Fulton and Bell. Open daily, 11am-11pm in winter months; 11am-midnight during summer months. FREE (unless you eat first!).

Everything at Leatherby's is made fresh daily, and you can go behind the scenes for Dave's tour of the freezer and how they make the delicious stuff. Sally Leatherby started the Creamery in 1982, and since then it's been voted the best ice cream in town by several newspaper polls. Bring the kids to see how it's done.

Many people combine a tour with a meal (see Leatherby's, Chapter 7, Family Restaurants).

～ Pizza Hut

5015 Madison Avenue, Sacramento, CA 95841 ～ 323-3700. I-80 to Madison Avenue exit east. Pizza Hut is on the left about a half-mile from the exit. Tours by arrangement; call 2-3 weeks in advance. FREE. $3 to make your own pizza.

Manager Dave Drake gives tours of the kitchen for kids accompanied by adults, any morning before 11am. See where they keep the ingredients and how they make the pizzas. The tour is free, but for $3 per person, kids get to make their own personal pizzas and have a drink with it (accompanying adults only pay if they'll be making pizza too).

～ Port of Sacramento

Harbor Boulevard, West Sacramento, CA 95691 ～ 371-8000. Business 80 to Harbor Bd. west, straight to Port. Call first for tour availability. FREE.

The Port of Sacramento ships wood, wood pulp, rice and other products all over the world. You can take a self-guided tour, free, whenever there's no big ship loading or unloading (in which case it's not safe for the public). Call ahead to be sure; ask for the Main Gate tour information.

Another feature here is that occasionally, Navy ships or other unusual ships are open to the public. Come see the big guns, the relief ships, whatever happens to be in port. Call first. One of the highlights of my son's young life was climbing all over a Navy ship, seeing how the sailors live, where they eat, the guns they carry. Depending on the size and interest of your little dreamers, this can be unforgettable!

After visiting the Port, you can wander through the World Trade Building just down from the Port (2101 Stone Boulevard, West Sac.) and enjoy their display of paintings by local talent, and you have your choice of several parks and playgrounds nearby for picnicking and having fun afterwards (see Parks and Playgrounds, Chapter 1).

∿ Rainbo Earthgrains Bakery

3211 6 Avenue, Sacramento, CA 91817 ∿ 456-3863. Highway 99 south to 12th Avenue exit left. Tours by arrangement. FREE.

There's a 15-person minimum for this popular tour of one of the area's largest commercial bakeries. You get to see how the dough is mixed and raised, put in pans, where and how it's baked, the whole process, right up to slicing and packaging. But the price for popularity is planning ahead; their tours are booked months in advance (it's a popular field-trip, so your chances are better if you can go after school hours). Call and ask for Casey Jones; tour lasts about an hour and a half.

∿ Recycling Center (CSUS)

California State University, Sacramento, 6000 J Street, Sacramento, CA ∿ 278-7301. Located at the southeastern corner of the campus, where Folsom Boulevard goes under Highway 50. Howe Avenue exit off 50, take College Town Drive left (west) into the campus. Left on Jedediah Smith

Drive. Parking available right outside the gate. Tours by appointment; call first. FREE.

Recycling and composting are the foundation of our "garden path" to the future. Everyone is aware now of the importance of tending our planet, and of giving back to the Earth what we take from it. Here, you can arrange a free tour to see how this essential program works.

This Center is a combination Recycling Center / Community Garden / Composting Education Program. They're happy to show you how they do what they do: how they separate materials, where they go, how they're affected by other materials, contaminants, and the steps in the process. In the Community Garden, you can wander through the neat, tidy rows of organically grown food crops raised by community members, and the Center is happy to give you a demonstration of how composting works and how to go about it in your own home. They also give on-site demonstrations, if you'd like them to come to your neighborhood, organization, etc.

Children are the key to a cleaner, healthier planet and future; this tour will help them understand the interdependencies and how best to care for their little part of the planet.

- Picnic table available in the Community Garden area (restroom available).
- Combine with a free tour of the campus (see CSUS, this chapter).

❧ Sacramento <u>Bee</u>

2100 Q Street, Sacramento, CA 95816 ❧ 321-1785. P Street exit from Business 80, to 20 Street. Limited on-street parking; visitor parking at 21 and Q Streets and at 22 and Q. Tours offered daily at 10:00am and at 1:00pm Reservations required. FREE. Children must be at least in fourth grade.

My fourth-grade tour expert classified this tour as "really neat!" In a walk-through tour of about an hour and a half, you get to see the Newsroom and Press area, the "humongous" rolls of newsprint ready to become news-papers, the machinery, old and new, that create this trans-formation, and the presses, seen from an observation deck above. Informative guides explain all and answer kids' questions with enthusiasm.

~ Sacramento City Landfill

921 10 Street, Sacramento, CA 95814 ~ 264-7043.
Accessible from Highway 160. Tours by arrangement.
FREE.

What happens to your garbage after it leaves the curb? You and your kids can find out here. If you can arrange a group of about 30 or more, they're happy to show you around the dumping area, the baler building (where it's turned into bales of solid waste), the area where the bales are stacked, the whole process. It's too big for a walking tour (the facility covers 170 acres), so you must have trans-portation large enough to drive everyone around with the guide. Tours available year-round, although they recommend the cooler months (the barren land-fill area gets extremely hot in the summer).

~ Television Stations

The Sacramento area has several television stations, and most of them offer tours of their facility. Kids enjoy a behind-the-scenes look at one of their favorite pastimes. All of the tours are handicap-accessible, free, and all request that you call at least a few weeks in advance.

KOVR Channel 13, based in West Sacramento, is very small but welcomes group of 10 or more. Since they have only two people on their staff to deal with tours, they require a month's notice. (374-1313)

KVIE Channel 6 — Public Television — offers regular tours, about an hour long, on Wednesdays and Thursdays, between 9am and 4pm (other days sometimes by prior arrangement). Preferred group size is up to 20; minimum is at least two families. Tour the production and technical areas of the station, visit the state-of-the-art building (this is the largest studio in Northern California), see their hi-tech editing and post-production facilities, plus whichever sets are not in use. They recommend you call at least 3 weeks in advance, and please have at least one adult for every 5 kids. Ask for the Tour Mailbox to leave a message indicating when you'd like the tour and how many people; they'll call you back. (929-5843)

KXTV Channel 10 takes you on a tour of their editing and engineering rooms, where they explain the different equipment, and they also show you the newsroom, the assignment desk (where they do the Newsbreaks), the live control room, and their Chromakey studio, where they can make anyone appear is if they were "really" on location. They suggest Tuesdays and Thursdays for a tour, 9am-4pm, although they can arrange another day if necessary. Call at least three weeks in advance. (441-2345)

KTXL Fox 40 offers tours for anyone over the age of 6. Chris Eddy, host of their Fox Kids' Club, does the tours, Mondays through Thursdays, 8:30-5:30. See the news set, Fox Kids' Club set (usually the favorite part of the tour!), Public Affairs set and more. (454-4422).

ᕦ West Sacramento City Tour

West Sacramento Chamber of Commerce, 1414 Merkley Avenue, West Sacramento, CA 95691 ᕦ 371-7042. Business 80 to Jefferson Boulevard exit in West Sacramento (west side of Sacramento River). Right on Jefferson, left on Merkley Avenue. Chamber is on right, free parking in adjoining lot.

The City of West Sacramento, one of the newest cities in California, occasionally offers a City Tour (by bus) that takes you to visit all the major places of business here. Walk through each establishment and see how they do what they do. For example, tour KOVR Channel 13 and see how TV happens. See how MCI manages communications. See how all those salamis and cheeses get from the wholesaler to Tony's customers at Tony's Food Products. Find out where all those Keebler Cookies come from and how they get there.

If your youngsters are studying communities and how they function, this is a fascinating, "real-life" way to get an insider's view. But it isn't offered regularly, so call for information.

TRANSPORTATION

The first adventure in most small lives begins with "Let's go bye-bye!" Whether it's a first trip to Grandma's or an outing to the grocery store, getting there is half the fun for kids. Or rather, sometimes it <u>is</u> the fun! Anything that goes "vroom-vroom", rolls, soars, clip-clops or otherwise gets from here to there can be immensely exciting, and here are some adventures in and around Sacramento to tantalize your young travellers.

∾ California State Railroad Museum
(see Old Sacramento, Chapter 1).

∾ Central Pacific Passenger Station
(see Old Sacramento, Chapter 1).

∾ Light Rail
Adults $1.25, kids 5-12, seniors and disabled, $.50. Exact change required. Bus and Light Rail Schedule Information, 321-2877; TDD Schedule Information for the hearing impaired, 321-2806. (More rail lines projected for 1993-1994.)

Instead of piling into the car again, hop on the Light Rail train/trolley for a trip downtown, or shopping, or just to cruise. Let the kids buy the tickets, and sit back and let Sacramento roll by as you talk and enjoy the scenery. The **K Street Mall / Downtown Plaza** is a popular Light-Rail destination; after a day of shopping, window-shopping or simply having fun (especially during the holidays, when the Mall hosts all kinds of special activities), sit back and relax on the way home. Join in the excitement as your train "races" the cars along the freeway!

∿ McClellan Aviation Museum

825 Palm Avenue, Sacramento, CA; 643-3192. I-80 or Business 80 to Madison Avenue exit. Left on Madison, then right where Madison forks into Roseville Road and Watt Avenue. Follow Watt north to Palm Avenue gate into the base. From the south area: Highway 50 to Watt Avenue exit. Follow Watt north to the Palm Avenue gate. Open Mon-Sat, 9-3, daily except holidays. FREE.

Planes, planes, and more planes! If your young crew is even the slightest bit fascinated by flying, the McClellan Aviation Museum is a real treat. After you've wandered through the self-guiding exhibit illustrating the history of the Air Force, 26 completely restored aircraft beckon. You can wander around them at your own pace, take pictures, read the self-guiding explanations of each plane. Visit the plane that made the landing at the Invasion of Normandy. See the first plane ever used to carry the wounded from battle sites. Take your picture with a Russian MIG. Gawk at the largest propeller airplane engine in the world. See how pilots were trained during WWII.

Although this museum is privately run (it depends on donations), its location on McClellan Air Force Base is part of the appeal, especially for younger children. Access to the public is easy — just stop at the gate for a pass — and once inside, your kids can see what it's like inside a "real" Air Force Base, where people live and work to protect their country. There's a nice picnic area within the museum grounds, and you can buy drinks and souvenirs at the Gift Shop. But they ask that you please clean up after yourselves, since they have no budget for maintenance of that sort. If picnicking isn't for you, there are lots of fast-food places on Watt Avenue near the base.

Handicap accessible; docents available; call in advance. Gift shop.

∾ Sacramento Metropolitan Airport

I-5, about 15 minutes north of downtown.

The miracle of a machine the size of a building rising up into the air is indescribable — and the Sacramento Metropolitan Airport is a pleasant place to come ooh and aah at the sight with your children. The airport is small and simply laid-out, one big semi-circle, so you can easily ride through it on your own. Park in any of the short-term lots and walk through the terminals for a view of America on the move. Watch the planes from one of several observation points outdoors, or go through the security gates and watch from a boarding gate inside.

If you'd rather a more in-depth understanding of the place, contact Shirley Carlson, Operations Manager, for an organized tour (648-0780). Call at least a week in advance.

∾ Towe Ford Museum

2200 Front Street, Sacramento, CA 95818 ∾ 442-6802. Located one mile south of Old Sacramento. Take Broadway west till it goes under I-5, then turn right on Front Street; the Museum is on your left. From Old Sac, take 2nd Street south till it goes under Capitol Mall. When it joins Front Street, turn left. The Museum is about 1/2-mile down, on your right. Open daily, 10-6, except Thanksgiving, Christmas and New Year's Day. Adults $5; Senior Citizens $4.50; High school students 4/2.50; Elementary school students $1; under 6 free. For special group rates, call ahead.

When you walk through these doors, you step back into the golden age of the automobile. This is the most complete antique Ford collection in existence, and maybe the most complete collection of any single make of automobile in the world. Among their permanent exhibition, you can see 8 Fords from before the Model T era, 28 cars (Fords and others) from the Model T years (1908-1927), 35 from the Model A years (1928-1931), 45 cars from before WWII, 50 from after WWI. Studebakers, Edsels, Thunderbirds, retractable hardtops (the forerunner to the convertible), Gubernatorial vehicles (including Jerry Brown's infamous 1974 blue Plymouth), and lots more.

- Extensive automotive research library.
- Free parking.
- Handicap accessible.
- Special Events area, with Alhambra Theatre Courtyard scene and Cecil B. DeMille's "Mighty Wurlitzer" pipe organ.
- Vintage films available daily.
- Rotating exhibits (different car club exhibit each month).

◆ Underground Railroad
(see Old Sacramento, Chapter 1).

PETS AND ANIMALS

Are puppies made for little boys and girls, or is it the other way around? And kittens, and fish, and guinea pigs.... Animals attract children, there's no doubt about it; anyone who's ever tried to walk right past a pet shop with children in tow can attest to that!

Sacramento is a wonderful place for viewing animals — this is still, after all, the "wild west" — and often it's free. Mostly it's simply a question of training yourself and your little scouts to really <u>look</u>. On your drive east on Highway 50 towards Lake Tahoe, Placerville or other points, be sure to keep looking off to the right after you pass El Dorado Hills; the herd of **buffalo** (or are they beefalo?) can usually be seen dozing in the sun or nibbling at the golden prairie grass. At the American River and Nimbus **Fish Hatcheries**, you can sometimes surprise a **wild turkey**, **egret** or other river dweller (besides the fish, of course). And at the **Effie**

Yeaw Center, **river otters**, **foxes**, **turkeys**, **beavers**, and **deer** are common sights, as well as an assortment of other riparian bird- and wild-life.

For a more expensive but unforgettable glimpse of wild animals, **Marine World / Africa USA** is a day trip that your little naturalists will talk about for a long time (see Chapter 6.)

When you go to Folsom, maybe you can arrange a visit to the **emu farm**. And with kids, the **Folsom Zoo** is a must-see stop — an unusual collection of animals that can't be released to the wild for one reason or another. The **Sacramento Zoo**, of course, continues to attract families year-round, just to watch or to take advantage of their many educational, fun programs for kids and adults.

If you want to venture out into the natural surrounding areas, there are several **wildlife preserves** within an easy day's drive of Sacramento. **Gray Lodge** is an outstanding one to the north; out in the Delta you can visit **Grizzly Island** or the **Cosumnes River Wildlife Preserve**. But here in the Sacramento area, you don't need to go to an organized Center to see animals. Right here in the "wilds" of Carmichael, **possums**, **raccoons** and **skunks** are common sights, and in West Sacramento, my little nature-watchers used to count the beautiful white **egrets** and sometimes the **herons** we would see on the way to Linden Park. If you're here during migration time, the Delta is a popular fly-way for many different types of geese. (For a list of Wildlife Preserves in the greater Sacramento area, see Chapter 8, Wildlife Viewing.)

If **feeding the ducks** is a favorite family activity, you can indulge at many of the parks and playgrounds scattered throughout the area, where duck ponds are a common sight. Nothing quite matches the excitement of a toddler's face as these semi-tame creatures just about his own size nibble noisily out of his hand! But a word of warning here: there's something about the abundance of wildlife right in our own backyard that can fool us into thinking those critters are here for our amusement. Be careful: wild animals, no matter how cute or appealing, are <u>wild</u>. Cute little squirrels or foxes can carry rabies. Be sure your children know the rules: don't approach wild animals. The coyotes in the foothills around Sacramento may look like cute little dogs, but their bite is a lot worse than their bark. Don't try to pet those nice, tame-looking cows or horses, either, even the ones in a neighbor's pasture; they spend their lives outdoors here, and can be as wild as the coyotes. If approached with clear ground-rules and a little common sense, your nature-viewing in the Sacramento area will be an exciting, rewarding experience that your children will never forget.

If your taste in animals runs more to the domestic, there are many large pet stores in the Sacramento area that are a treat for youngsters. If you look under Pet Supplies & Pets Retail in the Yellow Pages, you'll find several pages of listings.

One of our family favorites is the **Capitol Aquarium**, 1920 29 Street (452-5556). It's more than just a pet store! My little nature-lovers can spend hours watching the alligators, the huge tanks of fresh-water and salt-water fish, the turtles.... They have a mind-boggling choice if you're actually looking for a pet. But try not to handle the animals unless you're actually serious about a purchase.

If your animal-lovers are crazy about birds, you won't want to miss **The Bird Shop**, 5553 Auburn Bd. (338-0505). Whatever kind of exotic bird you can imagine, it's here — plus all the paraphernalia that goes with it. And they always have birds out loose, to handle and interact with.

And if you're thinking of adopting a pet, take a trip to the **Sacramento SPCA**, 6201 Florin-Perkins Road (383-PETS). Every Saturday at noon they hold a drawing there for a dog or cat who needs a home. But be prepared; it's hard to leave this place empty-handed, especially if you go there with children!

SMALL ART MUSEUMS, GALLERIES AND ART CENTERS

Art galleries offer families an opportunity to experience art in all its shapes and forms, modern as well as traditional, in a small, non-threatening setting. Less imposing or overwhelming than a museum, a gallery is a quiet place to make personal decisions about taste, and just have a good time. And unlike a museum, galleries are free. You can combine a gallery stop with another activity from this guide, or for an illuminating trip through the world of art, hop from gallery to gallery; the comparisons between the different approaches to art can confuse, astound, excite, and often help define your tastes in the visual arts. Here's a list of some of the art galleries in the Sacramento area. Go — look — enjoy!

Joyce Abreu Gallery, 3712 Auburn Boulevard (488-1211)

African American Art Center, 3449 Watt Avenue (485-4516)

American River College Art Gallery, 4700 College Oak Drive (484-8432). Combine with a trip to Foothill Skate Inn Roller Rink on Auburn Bd. (see Chapter 4), or with a concert at the college.

Art Works Galleries, 10239 Fair Oaks Boulevard, Fair Oaks (966-0773)

Artists' Collaborative Gallery, 1007 Second St., Old Sacramento (444-3764) Include in your walking tour of Old Sac.

Artists' Contemporary Gallery, 1200 K St. Mall #9, Hyatt Regency Plaza (446-3694)

Big Art, 1928 L St. (446-2740)

California State University, Sacramento, Library, 6000 J St. Combine with tour of the campus, or of Recycling Center (see Tours of the Working World), or with a concert at the college. (278-5477)

Delphina's, 1027-C 10th St. (441-3330)
Solomon Dubnick Gallery, 2131 Northrop, Suite A (920-4547)
Eagle Dancer Trading Post, 2530 I St. (442-6400)
Else Gallery, Cal. State Univ., Sac. 6000 J St. (278-6156)
Encore One Gallery, 12401 Folsom Bd., Rancho Cordova (351-0777)
Galeria Posada, 704 O St. A focus on Hispanic art. (446-5133)
Gallery W, 9th and W Streets (444-5125)
Gorman Gallery, 7973 Park Avenue, Suite A, Fair Oaks (961-4516)
Michael Himovitz Gallery, 1020 10 St. (448-8723)
Horvath Bass Gallery, 4399 Arden Way (488-1901)
I.D.E.A. Gallery, 3414 4 Avenue (452-0949)
Gregory Kondos Art Gallery, Sacramento City College, 3835 Freeport Bd. (558-2210)
Matrix Gallery, 1725 I St. (441-4818)
Dean Moniz Gallery, 1825 Q St. (448-4039)
Peach Pit Gallery, 1020 22nd St. (443-4025)
Planet Earth Rising, 2931 Sunrise Bd., Suite 125, Rancho Cordova (631-0249)
Pooser Galleries, 3449 Watt Ave. (485-4516)
750 Gallery, 1727 I St. (441-0790)
Sutter Buttes Gallery, 3067 W. Capitol Avenue, West Sacramento. (375-0123)
Viewpoint Gallery, 712 57 St. (451-3063)
Judith Weintraub Gallery, 1723 J St. (442-3360)

SHOPPING AND HOBBIES

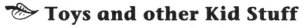 Toys and other Kid Stuff

If you can play with it, climb on it, throw it, catch it, wear it, listen to it or otherwise have fun with it, you can probably find it in one of the many centers of these toy-store giants: **Kay-Bee Toys** (Arden Fair Mall, 2441 Butano Drive, Florin Center, or 6043 Sunrise Mall, Citrus Heights), or **Toys "R" Us** (1919 Arden Fair, 7224 55th Street, or 7800 Greenback Lane, Citrus Heights).

If you'd prefer to browse in a small, less warehouse-like atmosphere, or you're looking for something more person-alized or more unusual, try some of the shops listed below. You won't find as vast an array as you would at "the giants," but you may be surprised at the creative and unusual toys and games you will find.

❧ The Ark

10145 Fair Oaks Boulevard, Fair Oaks, CA ❧ 965-6275.

Hand-crafted wooden toys, art supplies, books and other things kids love, located in the middle of Fair Oaks Village, the old center of Fair Oaks, a lovely place to stroll.

❧ Best Products Co., Inc

1901 Arden Way (next to Arden Mall), Sacramento, CA ❧ 929-6784
6145 San Juan Avenue, Citrus Heights, CA ❧ 969-2200
6990 65 Street, Sacramento, CA ❧ 392-2020

Best is a complete department store, but my children love browsing through their large toy department so much that I had to mention it here. The store on Arden is espe-cially fun with its strange entry — the brick corner of the building slides away from the building when it's open, mak-ing it look as if some giant had taken a bite out of it.

❧ The Country Bear

2894 21 Street, Sacramento, CA ❧ 451-5578

This is an "all Teddy-bear store." Come to be surrounded by the warm feelings only teddy-bears can create. If your little ones (or you) have a bear, want a bear, have ever loved a bear or simply love being around the huggable things, don't miss this!

ᕔ **Fowler's Toys**

2504 J Street, Sacramento, CA ᕔ 444-2933
705 Gold Lake Drive, Folsom, CA

Diane Fowler, owner, takes pride in offering a wide selection of toys that are "entirely powered by your child" — no battery-powered or electronic-powered toys, nothing violent. She believes that every purchase of a toy teaches a child something, so in her shop there's one of every toy out of its box so you and your child can try it and see if it's right for you. Besides toys, they sell books, art supplies, science and nature materials. And every month has an event happening here: Trick or Treating in October, Scottish Days in April...and all summer, storytelling, magic, and other exciting things to experience. Stop by to see their entryway, decorated with tiles designed and created by children.

ᕔ **Hearth Song**

Arden Fair Mall, Sacramento, CA ᕔ 927-9881.

Dolls, dolls, dolls — each one handmade and unique. You won't find these dolls anywhere else. Hand-stitched clothing, hand-painted faces. Halfpenny pocket dolls, music-box dolls, dollhouses and all accessories. A doll-lover's dream!

ᕔ **Imaginarium**

1689 Arden Way (in Arden Mall), Sacramento, CA ᕔ 920-0914.

The focus here is on the imagination — science games, puzzles, wooden toys, computer toys, books, toys that make you think while having fun (or is that, have fun while thinking?).

ᕔ **Kite City**

1201 Front Street (in Old Sac.), Sacramento, CA 95814 ᕔ 443-3478.

What child hasn't dreamed of soaring through the sky? This place has a magical attraction for anyone fascinated with flight. It contains kites of every possible size, shape

and imaginable texture, planes, kits, windsocks, boomer-
angs, frisbees, and "other flying things from around the
world." The imaginations of all those earth-bound tikes (and
their parents) who have ever wished they could fly can take
flight here. A must-stop site on your walking tour of Old
Sac.

∿ Quinby's

*3509 Fair Oaks Boulevard (Arden Town Center),
Sacramento, CA 95864 ∿ 488-7071.*

Quinby's sells all kinds of children's books (including a
parenting reference section), educational toys, arts-and-
crafts materials and science kits. Bring your little ones in on
Saturday morning, 11am, for Storytime and Arts and Crafts
(free). Occasional special events; call first. Quinby's motto
is: have fun and learn!

∿ The Report Card

*6366 Tupelo Drive (I-80 and Antelope Rd.), Citrus Heights,
CA 95621 ∿ 725-5320*

9550-B Micron Avenue, Sacramento (725-5320)

This is an educational resource store, where you'll find
all kinds of helpful "things" to supplement the school cur-
riculum and help kids learn — puzzles, games, gifts for
children and teachers, a quality selection of children's literature, and computer software. They have Story-time on
Saturdays, 11am; listen to stories, and do crafts afterwards
that you can take home. They also offer workshops and
classes on all parenting and teaching topics.

∿ Toys that Teach

*5111 College Oak Drive, Sacramento, CA ∿ 334-4835
12401 Folsom Boulevard, Rancho Cordova, CA ∿
351-9093*

Its name says it all. A wonderful selection of fun things
for kids that help them learn. Plan to spend some time
deciding!

🍃 Factory Outlet Stores

Name-brand quality without paying department store prices — that's the inevitable appeal of factory-outlet stores. From Sacramento, there are two large factory-outlet malls that offer over 200 name-brands to choose from.

🍂 Natoma Station

Folsom Boulevard, Folsom, between Highway 50 and Folsom.

Dramatically poised on the bluff overlooking the road into Folsom, this is a sprawling mall that's home to over 50 name-brand stores. It's a convenient stop on your tour of Folsom (see Chapter 6, Folsom), a trip to the Nimbus Fish Hatchery (see Chapter 2) or a half- or whole-day excursion from Sacramento. Plenty of eateries to make your shopping more pleasant.

🍂 Nut Tree Factory Outlet Store

I-80 at Vacaville 🍂 *(707) 448-6411*

Shop at their 100+ brand-name stores, then stop at the Nut Tree for a half-day fun stop, or just a restaurant stop. There's a little train your youngsters can ride, gift shops, a Pumpkin Patch in October with all sorts of Halloween-related activities, year-round special activities, a family restaurant. Bring your checkbook!

🍃 Food and Supermarkets

Shopping for food is one of life's necessities — and can be an educational, cultural or just plain fun experience. Shopping is easy in Sacramento. Many of the large super-markets are "Superstores," where you can buy just about anything under the same roof — groceries, clothing, drugs, magazines, liquor, fresh-baked goods... some even have a Post Office on location. Taking care of life's necessities just doesn't get much easier!

Like anything else we do often, we can get in a rut

when it comes to buying food. Avoid the food-shopping "blah's" by sampling different markets. Some have live lobsters in tanks; some have samples of food or drinks to taste; some decorate for whatever holiday is coming up in a big way.

Raley's is a chain of "superstores" you'll find throughout the Sacramento area, begun over a generation ago by Tom Raley, a local boy. You can find just about anything here, all under one roof. **Bel-Air Markets**, another superstore chain, was recently purchased by Raley's but retains its own name and style. Bel-Air offers guided tours (see Tours of the Working World). **Safeway** is also liberally scattered throughout Sacramento, and like the other two superstores, offers fresh produce, exotic fruits and vegetables (by season), prescriptions, and everything else you'd expect to find in a supermarket. **Lucky** Supermarkets does the same, but claims to do it cheaper. And for "warehouse supermarket" shopping, try **Sav-Max**; big savings, no frills, you bag your own.

If you're looking for something a little more out of the ordinary, try **Corti Brothers'** Markets. And for your more up-scale, exotic food-shopping, there's now a **Trader Joe's** in Sacramento. Here, you'll find the more exotic, the unusual, the foreign...the more expensive. A trip here can be educational for kids — and for Mom!

The **Sacramento Natural Foods Co-op** at 1900 Alhambra Boulevard has a huge selection of organic produce (see this Chapter, Farmers' Markets and Pick your Own). If your kids accompany you regularly to the ordinary supermarket, this can be an interesting change of pace. They can practice weighing, scooping, bagging and other fun stuff.

And if you're feeling adventurous or feel like a change of pace altogether, try some of the foreign food stores scattered around Sacramento. Along Broadway, west of 16th Street, for example, you'll find a lot of **oriental markets**. Browse through their aisles for a real learning experience. Even if you can't read the ingredients, you never know what find you're liable to take home or what culinary delight you're apt to discover.

🍃 Hobbies

What was your hobby when you were a kid? Don't remember?... or you had so many you can't remember which was your favorite? Kids are inveterate collectors, and love to try new things — just put a kid in a kitchen with a basket full of pourable or measurable ingredients, and watch what happens!

You'll find lots of Hobby shops listed in the Yellow Pages under "Hobby & Model Construction Supplies - Retail." Since the railroad was so important in the development of Sacramento, there seems to be a preponderance of model railroad hobby shops in the area — but you'll also find radio-control shops, graphics, kites, card collecting, plastic models, doll houses, leather working, and just about every other kind of hobby you can imagine. If you are into model trains, don't forget to stop at the **Underground Railroad** in Old Sacramento, 128 J Street (443-7777), and you can also try the **Whistle Stop** at 2828 Marconi Avenue (485-5288).

The **Graphic Hobby House**, 2610 Marconi Avenue (484-1640) has just about anything you can think of as craft or hobby supplies. A trip through their aisles can help spark an idea that can become someone's life-long hobby. **Michael's** can also be a great source of ideas; here, you can find acres of arts and crafts materials. It's fun just to try to imagine what some of them are for! Michael's has three locations: 4241 Marconi Avenue (481-6617), 10913 Olson Drive, Rancho Cordova (631-0340) and 1117 Roseville Square, Roseville (782-2195).

Is sewing a hobby, or a necessity? Or both? Or just plain fun? **Fabricland**, at 3408 Arden Way (972-9000) has everything you need to get you started or keep you going — classes for beginners, kits, material and all the necessary equipment. Call for information on special summer classes. There are other locations.

And at **Tandy Leather**, 7217 Florin Mall Drive (422-5112) or 2864 Fulton Avenue (486-1841), you can learn all about leather-working — cutting, stitching, dyeing, tooling, carving, they teach all the skills here. They also offer summer classes, and kits for beginners or advanced.

And if you haven't found the right temptation here for your little hobbyists, a visit to any of the local flea-markets may prove inspirational. See this chapter under Outdoor Markets, or the Yellow Pages under Flea Markets.

🍃 Hardware Stores

This is where the bits and pieces of our homes and gardens are displayed for us to piece back together — or simply examine with wonder. Grown-ups tend to take it all too seriously; kids find all sorts of treasures in these aisles, and a trip to the hardware store can re-charge their "mystery" batteries!

Ace Hardware is your neighborhood hardward store, chock-full of "neat stuff." You'll find several Ace locations in the telephone directory. My kids love to plunge their hands into the bins of "little things" — nails, bolts, shiny this or that, brass doo-hickeys — and always find something new to touch, examine, weigh, listen to, or otherwise invent new and exciting uses for. Opens a whole new world of imagination.

Call me "Amy," says the sign in front of **Emigh Hardware**, 3555 El Camino Avenue (482-1900). This is a vast assortment of wonderfully enticing "things" just begging to be examined. My son always has to unroll the huge rolls of chains — just a little!

For our explorers, **Home Base** will always be "the beep-beep store." Both locations, 4641 Florin Road (393-9500) and 6001 Madison Avenue (344-9600) are set up warehouse-style; large fork-lifts that move merchandise around beep loudly as they approach. These monster stores contain everything for home improvements, gardening, any do-it-yourself project. Aisle after aisle of puzzling hardware items, parts of houses (doors, toilets, sinks — things that kids find funny when separated from their environment).... Always a fascinating outing.

Save your visit to **Placerville Hardware** for your day

trip to Placerville — but don't miss it when you go. (See Chapter 6, Day Trips, Placerville.)

🍃 School/Office Supplies

Although children quickly get tired of using school supplies for homework, they never tire of looking at new ones! Mine can cruise the aisles of office supply stores for hours, finding all kinds of gizmos and gadgets that make "playing school" or "playing office" more fun. **Office Depot**, at 5400 Date Avenue (338-2582) or 6700 Folsom Boulevard (455-2582), has just about all there is, from paper clips to furniture, and there are other well-equipped stores listed in the Yellow Pages under Office Supplies. Even more intriguing items can be had at School Supply stores like the **Teachers' Exchange** (several locations; see Bookstores, under Shopping, this chapter). A veritable treasure-trove of stickers, papers, notebooks, workbooks, gradebooks, puzzles, and things that make learning fun. See the Yellow Pages under School Supplies.

🍃 Sporting Goods

The Sacramento area is sportsman's paradise, and there are shops all over where you can get supplies for just about any sport you can name. At these establishments, you can learn about whatever activity intrigues your little sport, examine equipment, try it on, buy or rent, and find out where to use it.

One of the biggest is **R.E.I.** (Recreational Equipment, Inc.), at 5961 Sunrise Boulevard, Citrus Heights (965-4343). They sell and rent equipment and clothing, and have recreational information for the entire region (Sacramento Valley to the Sierra Nevada and all points in between). If you want more, they can get it. The **Sierra Club Store**, 1009 J Street (447-9003), is affiliated with the Sierra Club. Your purchase of outdoor equipment or clothing supports the Club in its efforts to protect our environment. They also have quality outdoor gear, outstanding calendars, holiday cards that celebrate the earth's diversity, and information about outdoor sports state-wide.

Some other sporting goods stores you won't want to miss are: **Big 5 Sporting Goods**, 3420 Arden Way (488-5060), the **Army-Navy Department Store**, 4440 Marconi Avenue (487-0100), and if your child can't wait to learn fly-fishing or to try out a new fishing pole, you can find what you need at **Just Fishin'**, 4120 El Camino Avenue (485-3474).

☜ Malls

Shopping malls have become the "downtown" of today's world. With their restaurants, cinemas, walking courses, entertainment centers and whatnot, they attract people for shopping, strolling, dining, "going out" and just having fun together. You don't need to spend a fortune to spend the day at the mall. Here are some of the more familiar sights for shoppers in Sacramento.

Arden Fair Mall (Arden Way, east of Business 80). Aside from being a great place to shop, this mall is fun for kids. Mosaic sculpted animals adorn the lobby, perfect for climbing on and sliding down. The see-through elevator is an adventure, and for entertainment, spend some time in the Mickey Mouse shop watching Walt Disney videos, or in the educational toy stores for hands-on, fun experiences. This mall covers both ends of the spending spectrum, from up-scale Nordstrom's to down-to-earth Taco Bell. At one end of the parking lot is a colossal Toys "R" Us, an Italian restaurant and other fast-food. More shopping across the street, and six cinemas at the freeway-end of the parking lot. A whole-day outing.

The new **Downtown Plaza** opened in October 1993 with the goal of re-vitalizing the downtown area; it combines the best of suburban malls with all the excitement of downtown shopping. Multiple cinemas, lots of places to eat, off-beat shops as well as the usual, the Plaza also offers occasional free entertainment, outdoor fountains and other unexpected pleasures. Located along K Street, between Old Sacramento and the K Street Mall (see below), it can be a walk-through stop or an all-day destination. In the summer, the outdoor Thursday-night Market is a pleasant way to eat, browse, chat and just spend the evening.

Florin Mall (Florin Road and 65th Street, off Highway 99) has big department stores, little shops, small eateries and full-scale restaurants, photographers...and plenty of mosaic benches to climb on. Right near-by, you'll find a large do-it-yourself store, a Toys "R" Us, hobby shops, and lots of other shopping and restaurants.

K Street Mall, on K Street, between Old Sacramento/ Downtown Plaza and Capitol Park, is for shopping downtown during the day. The Mall extends from the Downtown Plaza to the Community Center on 13 Street, and during the business day it's alive with shops, restaurants, and occasional outdoor events. At Christmastime, the Mall, also called the Downtown District, vibrates with music, ice skating, and all sorts of outdoor fun.

Pavilions is a more up-scale place to shop. Not an indoor mall, but a series of one-story buildings with shaded walkways. Amid its labyrinthine walkways and plazas, you can occasionally enjoy a concert or some other cultural event outdoors. Located on the north side of Fair Oaks Boulevard just east of Howe Avenue.

In the suburbs to the east of sprawling Sacramento, **Sunrise Mall** extends east of Sunrise Boulevard and south of Greenback Lane. Here you'll find all the giants and a host of smaller shops and plenty of places to eat. Facing it on the other (west) side of Sunrise boulevard is **Birdcage Walk**, a slightly smaller mall known among budget-watchers for its $1 cinema. Together, the two neighboring malls form a veritable city for shoppers.

This is somewhat smaller than what we've come to consider a mall, in this day of giant shopping "cities," but the **Sutter Square Galleria** is certainly a place to come browse, shop, eat and spend some time. This is the two-part building that brackets Business 80 at K Street. Inside are 35 shops to choose from, restaurants, cafes, and the Visionarium (see Chapter 1).

Town and Country Village, Marconi and Fulton Avenues, is a smaller, older outdoor mall. Small shops, restaurants, no giant department stores. A friendly, western place to shop, very festive at Christmastime.

🐦 Odds and Ends

If you haven't found what you're looking for at one of Sacramento's many malls, or if you prefer a smaller-scale, more personalized shopping experience, try some of these places for something different. (For collectible or second-hand items, try any of the outdoor flea markets and auctions in the Outdoor Markets section of this chapter.)

🐦 Capital Costumes, Inc.

8108 Madison Avenue, Fair Oaks, CA 95628 🐦 *961-2769.*

Need to be a caveman for a school play? Merlin the Magician for Halloween? Whatever the era or costume you need, Capital probably has it — and more, for children and adults. Rental only. From Ancient Egypt through poodle skirts, astronauts, animals.... Fun browsing!

🐦 Chinese Cultural Arts Center

4th, I and J Streets 🐦 *442-7711.*

If your tastes run to the oriental, you can browse through the shops here and then stop in at their restaurant for an authentic Chinese meal. Also open at certain hours at the Center is the Buddhist Church. Examine the art and artifacts for a glimpse of a people who played a large role in the development of Sacramento.

🐦 Crocker Museum Shop

216 O Street 95814 🐦 *264-5423.*

Unusual gifts and souvenirs, not necessarily all related to art but all of the quality you'd expect to find in a fine museum. (See Crocker Art Museum, Chapter 1).

❧ Go To Your Room

5315 Sunrise Boulevard, Fair Oaks, CA ❧ 961-2701.

If you're looking for furniture for your child's room, traditional or unusual, check this out.

❧ Nimbus Winery

Highway 50 and Hazel Avenue, Rancho Cordova, CA ❧ 351-0583. Take Highway 50 east out of Sacramento, and get off at the Hazel Avenue exit. Nimbus is just south of the highway.

This exciting place isn't a winery at all, but a collection of about 22 shops and restaurants. In 1885, Nimbus was reputedly the largest producing winery in the world. But luck changed, vines rotted, gold was dredged under the vines, and when that ran out, Libby cultivated olives there for a while. Now it's consumer gold that's the mainstay of this unusual place to shop.

This isn't off-the-rack shopping. Here you'll find gifts like pure beeswax candles at Mitchell's; gifts that are uniquely Californian at Made in California; things that adorn at Unique Jewelry; and lots of things for the kids at Toys that Teach.

And in between, you can eat at Garbeau's Dinner Theater Restaurant or the Spaghetti Factory (see Chapter 7, Family Restaurants), or simply enjoy the atmosphere of this historical assortment of buildings. Allow lots of time for browsing.

❧ 98¢ Clearance Stores

There are several of these stores around the Sacramento area; look in the white pages under "N" — a wonderland of little "trinkets" that kids love to fondle, examine, wish for, try out, and just plain have fun picking. Lots of seasonal things, decorations, little gifts, party favors, etc.

❧ Thrift/Consignment Stores

Thrift stores can be an adventure for young or old. Treasures can lurk among the humdrum, and "previously owned" can mean simply that someone else loved it before you had a chance to. Prices can be unbeatable, too! Some consignment stores carry new items as well.

~ All About Kids. *75 Natomas Street, Folsom* ~ *985-0606.*

Many new items as well as consignment. Clothing, maternity, toys, brand-new Carters and more. Changing rooms. M-S, 9:30-5:30.

~ Baby Bazaar. *5031 Freeport Bd. (at Fruitridge)* ~ *455-7101.*

Clothing, children's and maternity, name brands. Special 100% cotton section; also carries new items, furniture, cribs and more. M-S, 10-5.

~ Bunny Patch. *3200 Folsom Bd.* ~ *452-8669.*

Clothing from infant to size 10, some furnishings. M-F, 10-6; Sat 12-5.

~ Little Kids. *2302 Florin Road (at 24th)* ~ *393-0427.*

Clothes for newborns through Junior; toys and furniture. T-F,10-4; Sat, 10-4; closed Sun-Mon.

~ Mother Goose. *3218 Riverside Bd.* ~ *447-1733.*

Clothing, size 0 to 14. Special and formal wear (Baptism, Communion, etc.) for boys and girls. Dressing room. 20% of clothing is brand new. T-Sat, 10-5:30.

~ Nice Twice. 209 Vernon St., Roseville ~ *786-9287.*

Women's and children's clothing, toys, books and games. A big place, with dressing rooms. M-Sat, 10-5; Fridays until 6.

~ Northgate Thrift Store. *3000 Northgate Boulevard* ~ *920-4252. (1 mile north of West El Camino)*

~ Fruitridge Thrift Store. *6606 Fruitridge Avenue* ~ *383-3651. (1 block east of 65th Expressway)*

~ Coloma Thrift Store. *10667B Coloma Road* ~ *635-9205.*

All three of the above stores offer quality clothing for the entire family, as well as housewares (new and used), toys, beddings, books, furniture, collectibles and more. All three are open 7 days a week, and on weekdays they're open till 9pm.

Once Again. *2433 Maryal Dr. (between El Camino and Del Paso)* 972-8711.

Children's clothing, formals, lingerie, shoes, furnishings and jewelry. Dressing rooms. M-F, 10-4:30; Sat 10-4.

Once Upon a Child. *3180 Arden Way, Sacramento* 488-8861

Apparel to age 14, books and educational items, toys, footwear, furnishings. M-F, 10-7; Sat 10-6; Sun 12-5.

Once Upon a Time. *318 Arden Way* 488-8861.

Clothing, toys and furniture. F, 10-7; Sat, 10-6; Sun, 12-5.

Recycled Stork. *8807 Greenback Lane, Orangevale* 989-8608.

Clothing new and recycled, sizes Extra small to XXX large; maternity, formal, work and professional clothes. M-Sat, 10-6; Sun, 12-5.

Tiny Tots Trading Post. *9172 Greenback Lane, Orangevale* 989-5965 *and 319 E. Bidwell, Folsom* 983-5319.

Children's clothing, furniture and toys. M-F, 10am-5pm. Sat 12-5pm. Closed Sun.

CHILD PHOTOGRAPHERS

There are moments in every child's life that we cherish and want to save for posterity. Several photographers in the Sacramento area specialize in children, or are simply known for always doing a good job getting their fidgety subjects to cooperate. Here's a partial list; check the Yellow Pages under Photographers for more.

Expressly Portraits, Florin Mall (1-800-34-1HOUR).

House of Photographic Arts, 6743 Fair Oaks Bd., Carmichael (487-1005)

Jensen Photography, 1900 El Camino Avenue (649-2125)

J.C. Penney Portrait Studio, Country Club Plaza (972-8642) or Florin Mall (392-7532)

K-Mart Photographers, 2000 Howe Avenue (922-6721)

Olan Mills Portrait Studio, 2440 Fulton Avenue (493-5491), 9127 Kiefer Boulevard (362-3267) or 6830 Stockton Boulevard (391-0776).

Sears Photography Studio, 1601 Arden Way (924-6133).

The Studio, 3301 Sunrise Bd., Suite B, Rancho Cordova (635-9181)

K. Walker Photography Inc., 9500 Greenback Lane #15, Folsom (989-3190).

HOTEL HOPPING

Travelling can be exciting, even if it's someone else doing it. Big hotels are filled with people from all over, people rushing about, enjoying life, working hard and simply on the move. New ideas can grow from new faces; a change of scenery is sometimes exactly what's called for. So whether your little tourists are suffering from cabin fever, rainy weather blues or just need a change of pace, you'll find distractions, good food and who knows what exciting things to see by visiting some of Sacramento's fine hotels.

If you go to the Capitol and/or Capitol Park, you can combine your visit with a stop at the **Hyatt Regency Hotel**, 1209 L Street (443-1234). Located alongside the park next to Symphony Hall at the Community Center, the Hyatt caters largely to businesses and conferences, and there's always something going on. The people-watching alone is exciting, but you may also happen upon a performing group in the lobby cafe/bar. Some of the regulars are Ragtime music, Jazz groups, even Bell-choirs (usually during the holidays). At Christmastime, you'll want to stop in and see Santa's

Workshop and the extravagant decorations, a frequent photo-stop for families with kids.

Hotels and good eating go hand in hand, and some of the hotels offer kids' specials. At the Hyatt, there's a cafe off the lobby where you can sit outdoors among the greenery. Bugatti's, a northern Italian restaurant also within the Hyatt, offers special kids' menus. For between $2-$5, your kids can enjoy all their favorites — hamburgers, hot dogs, macaroni and cheese, pancakes, waffles, all the staples of kiddom — at a price guaranteed not to break the bank while Mom or Dad enjoy the more sophisticated items they have to offer.

The **Radisson Hotel**, 500 Leisure Lane (922-2020), is the only hotel in Sacramento with a lake in the middle. They offer a Sunday brunch that'll please kids, with the usual assortment of waffles, pancakes, eggs, breads, sweets and not-so-sweets. At about $15.95 per person, $6.95 for under 12, and under 4, free, it's definitely something different, for those days when you just absolutely, positively must do something out of the ordinary! And this one is located next to Highway 16 (the 12th Street approach) as it goes out of the downtown area, so it's easy to schedule a meal here on your way in or out of town.

At the **HoliDome - Holiday Inn**, on Date Avenue at I-80 (338-5800), kids under 12 eat free at J.B.'s Coffee Shop. The Harvard Street Grill at the **Hilton**, 2200 Harvard Street (922-4700), also has kids' specials on their menu, and the **Delta King**, Sacramento's most unusual hotel, offers a Sunday brunch. The Delta King is a floating hotel, a steamboat paddlewheeler permanently moored in Old Sacramento (see Chapter 1, Old Sacramento).

ON THE HORIZON

Sacramento, like life, is always in a state of change. Just when you think you've seen it all, something new and exciting pops up. Some people bemoan it, some welcome it; but one thing's certain: by the time this book reaches your hands, Sacramento will be just a little bit different than it is now. Some of the entries below may already be realities. Some may have disappeared entirely, to be replaced with other, new and exciting possibilities. One thing to remember: When looking for things to do in Sacramento, always keep an eye on the horizon.

～ Excursion Boats

Old Sac currently has two excursion boats available, the Matthew McKinley and the Spirit of Sacramento (on the waterfront at the end of L Street; see Chapter 1, Old Sacramento). In 1994, they're adding another boat to the fleet, but with a difference.

The third boat, the **City of Sacramento**, will be moored permanently just south of the Tower Bridge, where a new parking facility and park will be constructed. This will be an immobile restaurant boat. Call 552-2933 for current information.

～ La Hacienda Tortilla Factory, 8135 Elder
Creek Rd. (381-8600), hopes to have public tours available sometime in 1994, to see how tortillas are made and packaged. Call to see if they're making progress.

❧ Mather Air Force Base. As of the printing of this book, Mather will be no longer; but all that land will be put to some use. Keep in touch with Mather or Sacramento County to see what happens there next.

❧ Sacramento Multi-Cultural Park. Imagine a vast, green park where people from all over the world work and play together in harmony. Side by side, they raise their own types of vegetables and flowers, and exhibit cultural items; together they celebrate their special times of the year. That's what will happen, if all goes well, on the south side of Florin Road, just before it reaches Sunrise Boulevard. The land is already set aside; all that remains is for the various government and community wheels to be set in motion. Keep an eye out for further developments.

❧ Sacramento River Parkway. Just like the American River Parkway (see Chapter 1, Parks), the proposed **Sacramento River Parkway** will extend alongside the Sacramento River, offering green spaces, picnic facilities and all the benefits of riparian parkland. As of this printing, there is no specific date for this to happen, but keep in touch with the Sacramento County Parks & Recreation District (see Chapter 8, Resources) for up-dates.

✎ 3 ✎
Performing Arts for Children

T he lights dim...the hushed murmur fades... Those little bodies that can never sit still, strain for a glimpse of whatever the spectacle has to offer.

What can match the breathless anticipation of those endless few moments before the show starts? Whether it's a puppet show or the Symphony, kids love the drama and the spontaneity of a live performance. A few well-thought-out rules about acceptable behavior at public performances, placed in the appropriate small ears, should ensure their enjoyment of the moment, as well as the enjoyment of those around you. No matter how young, kids like to know what's expected of them.

No one is too young to appreciate the arts. Kids are natural born artists, intimately involved in the arts by instinct — irrepressible actors, singers, dancers — and there's no audience quite as enthusiastic as a young one! So get them ready for their next foray into the world of live entertainment — and their next, and the next.... Sacramento doesn't lack for them.

But don't be satisfied with this list. Shows come and go, and seasonal offerings vary each year. Visiting troupes, special performances, benefits — the world of the performing arts is a constant flux of exciting possibilities; explore them all.

Be sure to check the local publications for more. The Sacramento <u>Bee</u> has a special section every Friday called Ticket, that lists all performing arts events in the greater Sacramento area, and you can find a daily listing in the Scene section, called Today's Events. Also check the <u>Bee</u>'s Community Calendar (Neighbors section), and on Sundays, there's a special pull-out section called Encore that lists all of the area's cultural offerings. There are also publications on the campuses of the many colleges that highlight their performances.

Also check with all the Parks and Recreations districts for performances, especially for children, classes, workshops, etc. There are Children's Drama programs available, children's dance, and lots of other cultural activities for children. See Chapter 8 for Parks and Rec numbers.

And for a final resource for entertainment throughout the Sacramento area, the Bee has a free 24-hour information service called the BeeLine. Call 552-5252, then add (on touch-tone phones) the appropriate category, or extension, number, as follows:

Sacramento area arts - 2787
Local Concerts - 2060
Local Theatre - 2061
Movies by title - 2080
Crocker Art Museum - 4008
Music Circus - 4041
Sacramento Theatre Company - 4026
Happy hunting. Break a leg!

DANCE

There are many dance studios around the Sacramento area; most of them offer regular schedules of performances; some are affiliated with other performances. Some of them are listed here; check the Yellow Pages under Dancing for more.

∿ Broadway Academy of Performing Arts

4010 El Camino Avenue, Sacramento, CA (formerly at 5802 Robertson Avenue, Carmichael, CA 95608) ∿ 493-2775.

At the Broadway, you or your children can learn jazz, tap, ballet, voice, or acting — all the performing arts. Call for information on classes or performances.

∿ Crockett Dance Studio

4050 Manzanita Avenue, Carmichael, CA 95608 ∿ 487-8687.

Barbara Crockett, the owner, was the Founding Director of the Sacramento Ballet. The Crocket Studio offers well-structured classes in classical ballet and other dance types, to all ages. Many Crockett students dance in the annual performance of "The Nutcracker." Each spring, they give performances of all their classes.

❧ Dance Factory

515 Michigan Boulevard, West Sacramento, CA 95691 ❧ 371-5061.

Regular performances, and classes for all ages in ballet, tap, jazz, gymnastics, singing, drama and more. Dancewear shop.

❧ Sue Geller Dance Studio

8110 Madison Avenue, Fair Oaks, CA ❧ 966-8110.

Geller's has students from age 3½ to advanced adult, in tap, ballet or jazz. Performances regularly.

❧ Phares Theatre Ballet / Phares School of Dance

4430 Marconi Avenue, Sacramento, CA 95821 ❧ 484-1188 or 485-7244. For information on Community Center Performances: 264-5181.

Lessons for adults and children in classical ballet and other forms of dance, and performances at the Sacramento Community Center. This spring's selection was Sleeping Beauty, a wonderful ballet for children of all ages.

❧ Sacramento Ballet

2791 24th Street, Suite 16, Sacramento, CA 85818 ❧ 736-2866.

Children under 16 pay half-price at all performances. At least once or twice a year, they do a family-oriented ballet. In December they do the Nutcracker, during a 3-week period. Their season is from fall to spring, with performances on weekends and an occasional Thursday evening. Tickets range from $7.50 to $35.

MUSIC

✎ Bell Choirs

Several churches in the greater Sacramento area offer performances by bell choirs (hand-held bells rung together in concert). They have no set yearly schedules, but a phone call to the church can get you information about the next performance. Some of the churches have youth bell choirs. It's an unusual musical treat, and something your children will remember.

Arcade Baptist Church
3927 Marconi Avenue, Sacramento, CA 95821 ✎ 972-1617
Carmichael Presbyterian Church
5645 Marconi Avenue, Carmichael, CA 95608 ✎ 486-9081
Fremont Presbyterian Church
5770 Carlson Drive, Sacramento, CA 95819 ✎ 452-5437
Northminster Presbyterian Church
3235 Pope Avenue, Sacramento, CA 95821 ✎ 487-5192
St. Mark's United Methodist Church
2391 Saint Marks Way, Sacramento, CA 95864 ✎ 483-7848

✎ Camellia Symphony Orchestra

P.O. Box 19786, Sacramento, CA 95819 ✎ 344-5844. Concerts at the Hiram Johnson Auditorium.

The Camellia's high level of playing obscures the fact that this is a volunteer orchestra. Conductor Nan Washburn has won awards with this group of local talent whose music differs in style from the Sacramento Symphony. Bring the kids for a refreshing venture into the world of fine music.

✎ Davis Musical Theater Company

2121 Second Street, Davis, CA 95616 ✎ 756-3682 (756-DMTC).

This non-profit company presents light musicals, professionally done. Performances on Friday and Saturday evenings and Sunday matinees.

❧ International Jazz Jubilee

Sacramento Traditional Jazz Society, 2787 Del Monte Street, West Sacramento, CA 95691 ❧ 372-5277.

Once a year, in May, the Sacramento area pulses to the beat of jazz in all its forms. Jazz moves in from all over the world — bands come from as far as eastern Europe, Asia, Australia and of course, New Orleans — and you can experience it at outdoor and indoor venues all over town. Not restricted to jazz, it includes singers and musicians from early rag-time through honky-tonk, pre-jazz pops and late jazz. Lots of dancing, toe-tapping and just plain fun!

❧ Oak Park Concert Series

Oak Park refers to the neighborhood; the concerts take place in McClatchy Park, 33 Street and 5th Avenue. In June (dates vary each year; call first), come bask in the cool jazz. In July, move to a Latin beat, and in August, the Big Band era takes over the park. The September concert — there are 4 each year — is usually contemporary music. Call the Sacramento Bee, its sponsor, for information at 321-1800, or at the Bee's 24-hour information number, 552-5252, Category #2060.

❧ Sacramento Music Circus

1419 H Street, Sacramento, CA ❧ 557-1999 (group sales, 446-5880), or Bee Hotline 552-5252, Category #4041.

The Music Circus performs a regular series of Broadway plays each year. During the summer they do 7 shows, at 14th and H Streets, under a tent; in the winter they have 3 shows and 3 again in the spring, at the Community Center. You can purchase individual, group and season tickets.

❧ Sacramento Symphony

Sacramento Philharmonic Orchestra, P.O. Box 162508, Sacramento, CA 95816 ❧ (Box Office Info): 264-5181.

For 80 years, the Sacramento Symphony has been bringing enjoyable fine music to the greater Sacramento community. Through the Symphony, Sacramentans have explored music from centuries past right up till the present moment, with compositions by guest conductors. The Symphony has regularly hosted its series of music in the parks, and has always provided many valuable services for the cultural community. Of special note to parents are the Symphony's Kinder-Concert series, and the concerts in the parks.

✒ Sacramento Youth Band
422-BAND (422-2263)

Students from all over the Sacramento area can play in this non-profit organization. In the summer it's a marching band, in the winter, a concert band, that plays all over California. One annual concert in Sacramento, in the spring at Valley High School.

✒ Sacramento Youth Symphony
8031 Fruitridge Road, Sacramento, CA ✒ 388-5777.

This is a talented group of youngsters from schools all over the Sacramento area. It's wonderful to see and hear young talent brought to such a level of professionalism, and it can be inspirational for your aspiring musicians. The Youth Symphony usually plays three concerts each school year (none during the summer), at the Hiram Johnson Auditorium, at 14th Avenue and 65th Street.

✒ West Sacramento Community Orchestra
P.O. Box 507, West Sacramento, CA 95691 ✒ 483-4961.

A small, volunteer orchestra that performs light classical music at various locations. Kids always welcome. Call for information.

OPERA

There's nothing quite like this extraordinary combination of music and drama to stir the blood — and no one enjoys a good, colorful spectacle more than children! My son still hums tunes he associates with the dashing swordfights of Carmen and the fearsome military pageantry of Don Giovanni. Everyone can find something unforgettable in a well-presented opera. Sacramento offers operas as part of its regular music series, and the Opera House of Woodland is famous not only for its presentations but also for its building, a Historical Landmark.

∾ Sacramento Opera Association

2131 Capitol Avenue, Sacramento, CA ∾ *442-4224.*

Regular performances throughout the year of all the classical and traditional operas. Call for a brochure or up-to-date information.

∾ Woodland Opera House

Main and 2nd Streets, Woodland, CA 95695 ∾ *666-9617.*

Regular performances throughout the year. For information about the historic building, see Chapter 6, Woodland.

PUPPETS

Children can really identify with these "pretend people" as they confront life's ups and downs. Puppets can be a wonderful teaching tool, a source of entertainment, a way for children to learn how to cope with life's vagaries as they identify with these ingenious little creations. Watch their faces as they watch a performance; it's total involvement.

Some book stores around town offer puppet shows as part of their children's program; check the listing in Chapter 2, or the Yellow Pages under Book (Book dealers – retail), and under Puppet. Many libraries offer puppet shows; two such locations are the McKinley Library, 601 Alhambra Bd. (440-5926) and the Colonial Heights Library, 4799 Stockton Bd. (440-5926).

And don't forget to take them to see how and where puppets are made, at Creative Play Puppets in Fairfield (see Chapter 6, Fairfield), the only felt-puppet factory in the United States.

～ Absurd Puppet Shows

8979 Eagleson Court, Sacramento ～ 391-3989.

～ Fairytale Town Puppet Theater

1501 Sutterville Road, Sacramento, CA ～ 264-5233.

～ Fantasymakers' Puppet Playhouse

Gold Country Mall, 884 Lincoln Way, Suite 32B, Auburn, CA ～ 885-8415.

～ Zoopreme Puppet Shows

P.O. Box 24, Rancho Cordova, CA ～ 852-0717.

THEATER

Being experts at "let's pretend," children often get quite caught up in a good drama or comedy. There's good theater, and good children's theater, all over the greater Sacramento area. Some of the entries below feature regular children's

theater; some offer occasional kids' shows. Some involve
the kids, some are only to watch and enjoy. Call first for up-
to-date information. Besides the entries below, you can call
the Bee-line numbers at the beginning of this chapter for
local theater or the Sacramento Theater Company.

~ B Street Theatre

2711 B Street, Sacramento, CA ~ 443-6722.

Timothy Busfield (of Thirtysomething) and his brother
started this intimate little live theater.

~ Broadway Playhouse
(formerly **Carmichael Civic Theatre**)

*4010 El Camino Avenue, Sacramento, CA ~ 483-2775 or
489-6880*

~ Chattauqua Playhouse

*5325 Engle Road, Carmichael, CA 95608 ~ 489-7529
(489-PLAY).*

~ California's Original Theater

922 12th Street, Sacramento, CA ~ 442-2399.

~ Capitol Community Theater

*5802 Robertson Avenue, Carmichael, CA 95608 ~
483-0873.*

~ Davis Musical Theater Company

*2121 Second Street, Davis, CA 95616 ~ 756-3682
(756-DMTC).*

~ Delta King Theatre

1000 Front Street, Sacramento, CA 95814 ~ 558-0803

~ Fair Oaks Youth Repertory Theatre

*Community Clubhouse, 7997 California Avenue, Fair Oaks
Village ~ 966-1036.*

This is an award-winning youth theater group that relies on local talent to produce at least one outstanding musical or play per season.

❧ Garbeau's Dinner Theatre

12401 Folsom Boulevard, Rancho Cordova, CA ❧ *985-6361.*

Is it a restaurant or is it a theater? Yes! Garbeau's is the only children's theater in the Sacramento area that offers a meal, and its performances are usually sold out. During the Christmas season they offer many plays especially for children; the rest of the year, their repertoire is for a general (somewhat old-fashioned, classic-minded) audience, with the assurance that all shows are fit for children — "squeaky clean," no foul language or objectionable material. Price of the performance includes a buffet brunch, beverage and tax. Located in Nimbus Winery, second floor (see Chapter 2, Shopping).

❧ Land Park Theater Shell

William Land Park

Regular schedule of Shakespeare in the Park and other performances. Call Sacramento City Parks and Recreation at 264-5200, or Sacramento City College, the players, at 558-2228.

❧ Sacramento Repertory Theater

4830 7th Avenue, Sacramento, CA ❧ *457-8827.*

❧ Sacramento Theatre Company

1419 H Street, Sacramento, CA ❧ *443-6722.*

❧ The Show Below

22nd and L Streets, Sacramento, CA ❧ *446-2787.*

❧ Stagedoor Comedy Playhouse

2120 Royale Road, Sacramento, CA ❧ *927-0942.*

❧ T Street Theater
4723 T Street, Sacramento, CA ❧ 484-4239.

❧ Theatre El Dorado
El Dorado County Fairgrounds, Placerville Drive, Placerville, CA ❧ 626-5193.

❧ Twenty-Fourth Street Theatre
Sierra 2 Center, 2791 24th Street, Sacramento, CA ❧ 455-6862.

COLLEGES AND UNIVERSITIES

Sacramento area colleges and universities offer a rich selection of cultural experiences all year long. Some are specifically tailored for young people, like some of the seasonal offerings (children's Christmas plays, for example, or young people's concerts), some are outdoors — ideal for kids. Check the newspapers for schedules, prices and changes.

❧ American River College Theater
4700 College Oak Drive, Sacramento, CA 95841 ❧ 484-8433 or 484-8234. I-80 or Business 80 to Auburn Bd. exit. Left on Auburn Bd., then right on Orange Grove. Turn left on College Oak Drive, the theater is on the right at the corner of College Oak and Myrtle Avenues.

All three colleges of the Los Rios Community College District — **American River, Cosumnes River and Sacramento City** — offer opportunities for live entertainment.

American River boasts a fine music and drama department, and its musical and theater offerings are of consistently high quality. Of special note for children are the Orchestra's spring concerts, which take place on the lawn each May.

❧ Cosumnes River College

8401 Center Parkway, Sacramento, CA 95823 ❧ 688-7315.

Smaller than the other two colleges of the Los Rios district, Cosumnes also offers a year-round array of fine music and drama.

❧ California State University, Sacramento (CSUS)

6000 J Street, Sacramento, CA ❧ 278-6604.

CSUS offers a regular schedule of performances in all the performing arts, including world-renowned artists, year-round. Changing exhibits in the visual arts; call for current concerts and exhibits.

❧ Sacramento City College Theater

3835 Freeport Boulevard, Sacramento, CA 95822 ❧ 558-2228.

The Sacramento City College Drama Department often presents children's drama on campus, and each spring they produce several Shakespeare plays in William Land Park. Also many fine musical performances.

❧ University of California at Davis -

Freeborn Hall (music); Main Theatre (Drama)

UC Davis, Davis, CA 95616 ❧ 752-1915.

UCD has outstanding Music and Drama Departments; artists and performers come to Davis from all over the world. Call for information on their year-round schedule, for special events, and for group or season tickets.

REGIONAL PERFORMING ARTS

❧ Columbia Actors' Repertory

Fallon House Theatre, Columbia, CA ❧ (209) 532-4644

❧ Foothill Theatre Company

Nevada Theatre, Nevada City, CA ❧ 265-8587

❧ Magic Circle Theater

P.O. Box 811, Roseville, CA 95661 ❧ 782-1777

Children's plays and adult comedies, plus an occasional musical, throughout the year. They also offer Musical Theatre Workshops for children 6 through 19, and a separate Children's Repertory season.

❧ Old Coloma Theatre

Monument Road, Coloma, CA ❧ 626-5282

❧ Sierra Symphony

Sierra Music Center, 3490 Palmer Drive, 3E, Cameron Park, CA 95682 ❧ 676-3227.

This non-profit, private organization performs 4 concerts each year. Three are at the Foothill United Methodist Church, on Pleasant Valley Road in Rescue, CA, and the fourth, their annual September "Butterfly Concert," takes place at the Placerville Fairgrounds, in conjunction with the Sierra Cultural Art Center Association. It's a family arts festival with lots of hands-on creative activities, workshops and performances. 1993 was the 25th Butterfly Concert.

OTHER PERFORMING ARTS

Each year, the **Ringling Brothers Circus** comes to town, at the Arco Arena. This is a combination of many performing arts — music, dance (human and otherwise), tumbling, trapeze — an event your kids will remember for a long time. *(928-6900)*

Arco also hosts two other shows your small children will love. They can watch Mickey and friends cavort on the ice, at the **Disney on Ice** spectacular, and they can meet their favorite characters from television, at the annual visit of **Sesame Street Live**. Both are popular with families, so get your tickets early.

You can also find some impressive performances happening at any of the **Renaissance Faires** around the Sacramento area (see Chapter 5, Festivals and Special Events). These fairs are chock-full of performers — jugglers, dancers, singers, mimes, musicians — and your children will come home humming, with many happy memories of the timeless, unending possibilities of the performing arts.

4
Sports and Recreation

I f there's one thing that's universal to all children, it's what I call the perpetual motion factor. Kids have to MOVE! Whatever other intellectual pursuits they may explore, they need the balance of regular vigorous physical exercise (as do we all) to maintain physical as well as mental health. The ancients knew it — "mens sana in corpore sana" (a sound mind in a sound body) said some old sage who must have had children. And nothing's changed over the centuries, except the technology. Unfortunately, with more and more children spending their free hours watching television or playing video or computer games, the sound body is often not given equal time.

This chapter offers lots of possibilities for finding just the right kind of activity for their little growing bodies, either individually or as a family. I've included sports that they can watch, for inspiration, but the main focus here is what they can DO.

So if you're not already involved in family or individual sports activities on a regular basis, start now with this list. And if you don't find exactly what tickles your family's fancy here, check with the Parks & Recreation districts (see Resource Telephone Numbers, Chapter 8); they offer all kinds of organized activities, classes, workshops, and other programs. School districts also offer athletics for the community. Sacramento is a great place for outdoor activities, all year round. There's something here for everybody, and I know you'll have fun picking and choosing!

SPECTATOR SPORTS

☙ MAJOR LEAGUE SPORTS

☙ **The Kings** (National Basketball Association). Games are held at Arco Arena, 1 Sports Parkway, Sacramento. Their season goes from November to April, and they play about 41 regular season games. For information call Ticket Information at 928-8499, or the Box Office at 928-6900.

❧ The Gold Miners (Canadian football). As of June 1993, Sacramento has the only team of Canadian football in the U.S. Home games are at Hornet Field on the campus of CSUS (California State University, Sacramento). They play about 10 home games each year, and their season is from July to November. Gold Miners information, 985-4400 (in Rancho Murieta); CSUS information, 278-6481.

❧ COLLEGIATE SPORTS

❧ California State University, Sacramento, *6000 J Street; 278-6481*. CSUS — also referred to as Sac State — has 15 home teams that play a regular season in the following sports: football, softball, basketball, soccer, volley ball, track and field, cross country, gymnastics, golf and tennis. Call the Athletics Department for information.

❧ American River College, *4700 College Oak Drive; 484-8141*, has home games or meets year-round in the following sports: football, baseball, softball, basketball, volleyball, cross-country, track and field, soccer, golf, tennis and swimming. Call the Physical Education/Athletics Department for information.

❧ Cosumnes River College, *8401 Center Parkway; 688-7261*. CRC has home games or meets in baseball, basketball, volleyball, soccer, softball, tennis, cross country and track. Call for a free copy of their schedule.

❧ Sacramento City College, *3835 Freeport Boulevard; 558-2425*. Games seasonally year-round in football, baseball, softball, basketball, volleyball, cross-country, track and field, tennis and wrestling. Call the Athletics Department for information.

🍃 OTHER SPORTS EVENTS

Arco Arena, the only large indoor sports arena in Sacramento, hosts a number of events throughout the year, not all sports-related. **Disney on Ice** usually packs the house with families, as does **Sesame Street Live**. The **Ringling Brothers Circus** comes each year, as do many concerts. Skating fans and families in general usually fill up their annual **Tour of World Figure Skating Champions**, and an annual **Truck and Tractor Pull** usually "pulls" in a big crowd. The **Wrestling Federation** comes to Arco about 4-6 times a year, and you can also see an occasional **ice hockey** game and **pro boxing** match.

In February of '93, Arco hosted the **Wrangler pro rodeo**. Rodeo is the wild west event par excellence, and there are several each year in the Sacramento area. The **Folsom Fourth of July Rodeo** lasts several days, and is reputedly the largest 4th-of-July rodeo in the nation. There are also rodeos in Rio Linda, Roseville and other towns around greater Sacramento; check with Chambers of Commerce (see Chapter 8 for list), the Convention Center, and Arco Arena: Ticket Information at 928-8499, or the Box Office at 928-6900.

For the excitement of **auto and drag racing**, there's the **Sacramento Raceway Park** at 5305 Excelsior Road (southeast Sacramento). They offer drag-racing beginning in February, Motor-Cross each Saturday, Junior Drag Racing and other events. Call 363-2653 for information.

INDIVIDUAL, FAMILY AND TEAM SPORTS

❧ Archery

There's one large archery range in Sacramento, several

other smaller shops with trial lanes, and the local colleges and universities offer classes in the sport. **Frontier Archery Co.**, 9770 Business Park Drive (Highway 50 at Bradshaw), offers indoor lanes that can accommodate up to 30 people. You can rent the equipment or use your own, and their Pro Shop stocks "just about everything." They also offer various Leagues and Youth Programs; call 366-9149 for information. See the Yellow Pages under Archery Equipment for the other shops.

～ Backpacking

Sacramento is a great starting point for backpacking expeditions. The proximity of the Sierra Nevada range and its foothills offers trails ranging from beginner/easy to advanced/strenuous. Any of the local sporting goods store can provide equipment and information, like **R.E.I.**, 5961 Sunrise Boulevard, Citrus Heights, CA (965-4343) or the **Sierra Outfitters**, 2100 Arden Way (922-7500), and for more detailed information contact the State Parks (653-4000).

～ Badminton

Badminton is a perfect family sport, ideal for developing eye-hand coordination and accessible to any age and any budget. The equipment is inexpensive, easily obtainable at most toy stores, and simple to learn. Children of any age can play, simply by adjusting the net level (or not using one). If you don't have your own grassy space to play, it's easy to carry your set to the nearest park, and as you and yours develop more skill, you'll be surprised how physically demanding the game can get!

～ Ballooning

What child, of any age, doesn't dream of floating up in the sky — like a balloon? The Sacramento and Napa Valleys offer many opportunities for balloon flights; in Sacramento, you can find out about it at **MountainAire Balloon Adventures**, 5848 Stonyford Lane, Sacramento (348-8778), or look in the Yellow Pages under Balloons-Manned.

❧ Baseball and T-Ball / Batting Practice

In the Yellow Pages under Baseball Clubs & Parks you'll find a list of Little Leagues and places to hone your skills, including schools and batting ranges/cages. Also contact your local city or county department of Parks and Recreation, your area's religious organization, YMCAs or YWCAs, school districts and other community organizations to find a team for your child to join.

❧ Basketball

Contact your local city or county department of Parks and Recreation, your area's religious organization, YMCAs or YWCAs, school districts and other groups listed in this book or in the Telephone Directory, to find a team for your child to join.

❧ Bicycling

Cycling is a great way for the whole family to get lots of exercise and enjoy the scenery at the same time. It's an activity that requires no special skill, and once you have bikes, can be indulged at any time without any strain on the budget. The Sacramento area abounds with lovely parks for cycling (see Parks, Chapter 1); you can bike around the neighborhood park, or you can go for miles and miles on the Jedediah Smith Bike Trail (American River Parkway). If you can put your bikes in the car, this is the perfect way to see Davis (see Chapter 6, Davis), since the whole town is laid out with bike lanes, and there are several lovely parks within easy cycling range, even for tiny cyclers.

Unlike most other sports, bicycling has the unique advantage of getting you where you're going, so Sacramentans could greatly reduce the damage to their environment if they used their bikes instead of their cars on short errands, to get to work, to school, etc. Be sure to wear helmets, and obey all traffic rules (bikes are considered a vehicle, and are subject to the same rules as all other vehicles).

There are many organized cycling activities throughout the greater Sacramento area; most bike shops can provide information. See the Yellow Pages under Bicycles.

❧ Bowling

This is another sport that the whole family can participate in, regardless of skill level. There are many bowling lanes throughout Sacramento, several of which offer leagues for various age levels. See Bowling in the Yellow Pages.

❧ Boxing

Sacramento's Police Athletic League offers a junior boxing league to the young men in the community, starting at age 9. Your potential junior Olympians train one-on-one with a number of nationally-recognized names in boxing. The gym is open M-F, 4-7pm. (452-9309)

❧ Camping

No other family activity is like camping. Nothing quite compares with the experience of waking up all together under the trees or in the primitive desert, to the sound of birds or a nearby creek or the aroma of a pine forest, knowing that you've met nature on her own terms, been kind to her, and enjoyed all that she has to offer.

For many people who enjoy outdoor activities, California and camping are synonymous. Campgrounds are available through California's extensive and beautifully-maintained State Parks system, through various local Parks & Recreation systems, around PG&E (Pacific Gas & Electric) reservoirs (local PG&E office or (415) 973-5552), on public-use areas maintained by SMUD (Sacramento Municipal Utilities District - 452-7811), and on private campgrounds. For general information on State Parks, call 653-6995; for campground reservations and information, call (800) 444-7275. For general U.S. Forest Service information, call (415) 705-2874 (San Francisco). See the White Pages under Government listings, Parks & Recreation, for local areas.

❧ Cross-Country (Nordic) Skiing

For families who love winter sports, cross-country skiing can be just what you've been looking for. It's less dangerous than downhill skiing (no speed involved, unless you get into downhill cross-country), much cheaper, and easier to stay in groups. Trails take you through pristine, peaceful scenery, and anyone who can walk can enjoy the sport with little or no training.

You can indulge in cross-country skiing just about any-where there's snow, but it's probably best to use maintained trails, especially for beginners. If you don't have your own equipment, most large sporting good stores in the Sacra-mento area can help get you started or rent you what you need. R.E.I. (965-4343) and the Sierra Outfitters (922-7500) have it all, as well as the necessary information to start you on your way. The Sierra Club (444-2180 or 447-9003) is also a good source of information.

The Tahoe region is dotted with ski areas, and most of them offer cross-country trails. The National Forest Service maintains trails in the National Forests; a common destina-tion for Sacramento-area skiers is the El Dorado National Forest (6454-6048). They also maintain a series of Snow-Parks, areas where you can leave your car and go enjoy some fun in the snow — sledding, skiing or just building a snowman.

The world's largest cross-country ski touring center is at Royal Gorge, off I-80 at the Soda Springs exit. They have trails for all levels of difficulty, a separate area for toddlers, overnight cabins, day touring, ski camping and more. Norden and Kirkwood also attract a lot of Nordic skiers. The Sierra offers spectacular scenery in any season, but to glide silently through its winter mantle of pure snow is an experience that cross-country skiers speak of with awe and reverence. No one is too young for such an experience.

∾ Fencing

The **Sacramento Fencing Club** meets from 7-9pm Mon-days and Wednesdays at the Turn Verein Hall, 3349 J Street. Their Olympic Team coach starts new classes every 8 weeks. For beginners, equipment can be rented for up to 2 months. The first night is free. Family rates available. (444-3282)

∾ Fishing

Sacramento is River City — an ideal location for anglers

of any age or skill level. Salmon, trout, sturgeon, shad, catfish...are just a few of the temptations that await you in the Sacramento River, the American, the Cosumnes, the countless streams and sloughs in the area, in the crystalline lakes of the Sierra, in the Delta... even the ocean, only 90 miles away. Check with the California Department of Fish and Game (653-7664) for regulations, limits and season dates. And if fly-fishing is more to your liking, the Foothills and the Sierra are riddled with perfect streams for you. You can arrange personally-guided fly-fishing tours (call Motherlode Angler, Grass Valley, 447-2333), and you can find just about anything you need for fishing at Just Fishin', 4120 El Camino Avenue, 485-3474. See also the Sacramento Sports Fishing Guides, 1531 Wyant Way (487-3392).

❧ Football

Contact your local city or county department of Parks and Recreation, your area's religious organization, YMCAs or YWCAs, school districts and other groups listed in this book or in the Telephone Directory, to find a team for your child to join.

❧ Golf

The choice is enormous! There are at least 15 golf courses in the Sacramento area, all within an easy drive. There's even a computerized golf "course" called Indoor Golf Cafe (in Arden Towne, at Fair Oaks and Watt), where you can "play" various courses (by hitting the ball into a big computerized screen), hit practice balls and even get your golf swing analyzed by computer. For the younger golf set, there are 3 Mini-golf areas (see Golf Courses - Miniature in the Yellow Pages) that have arcades and various family fun attractions beside the mini-golf.

❧ Gymnastics / Tumbling

Gymnastics is one of the best individual sports to help children build coordination, strength, endurance, concentration and self-esteem. There are lots of places in the Sacramento area to indulge in the sport, both for children and adults; I'll list the major ones here. For more, see the Yellow Pages under Gymnastics Instruction.

❧ Byers Gymnastics Centers, *Sacramento (423-3040, 447-4966) Roseville (781-2939).* Byers' has been around a long time. They offer Tot and Kindergym Readiness classes, gymnastics and lifetime fitness classes, Dance (ballet, tap or jazz) and more. Call for a free brochure.

❧ Gymagic, *383-1778.* Classes from age 2 1/2 to adult, from beginners to elite competitors. A National Team Training Center.

❧ Gymboree, *447-7738.* A parent-child play program which offers age-appropriate classes, 3 months to 4 years. Over 40 pieces of specially-built play equipment, enthusiastic instructors, Gymbo the Clown.

❧ Poszar's Gymnastics, *486-9880.* Competitive and recreational class for all levels, all ages, features two 1992 US Olympic Team coaches. Michelle Campi, who took part in the '92 Olympics in Barcelona, trained here.

❧ Sacramento Gymnastics Academy, *Carmichael, CA; 971-1675.* The emphasis here is on fun rather than competition. Richard Burrill, the director, believes sports are to be enjoyed, and that's his approach to gymnastics. His troupe, called the Flying Superkids, is an exhibition team that performs all around town — just for fun! They offer classes for boys and girls 6 days a week. If you're looking to harness that relentless energy of your little tumbler <u>without</u> going in for competition, this may be the place.

❧ Starz Gymnastics, *Orangevale; 989-4230.* Trampoline, tumbling, field trips, fitness and fun, diving, aerosport, cheerleading...and birthday parties. After school daycare; bussing from school to gym.

❧ Technique Gymnastics, *Fair Oaks, CA; 863-5073.* This is the largest facility in northern California, with a 75-foot tumbling trampoline and top-of-the-line equipment. They offer classes for all ages, including KinderGym classes for tiny tots, and team activities, including acrobatics, tumbling, gymnastics, cheerleading and more.

❧ Hiking and Backpacking

Kids love the adventure of exploring the wilderness, and in the greater Sacramento area there's plenty of it to explore! You can meander along some of the milder, level trails within the city or suburbs, or you can head to the hills for more of a challenge. From flat wetlands to rolling hills to steep, rugged mountain terrain, the Sacramento area has it all.

Before you go, though, here are a few safety precautions that will help make it an enjoyable outing for everyone in the family:

- Wear hats. The California sun is famous for a very good reason; the air here is extremely dry, so the sun's rays reach you undeflected by any moisture. The Sacramento Valley really bakes in the summer, and even a mild, flat hike can be unbearable if that strong sun's in your eyes.
- Take water bottles — for everyone. The Sacramento Valley and the foothills are a dry, dusty place, and hiking makes you even thirstier. Kids enjoy the independence and importance of carrying their very own water bottle.
- Take mosquito repellent. Constant swapping and slapping can make even the tiniest hiker miserable.
- Don't move the rocks. Rattlesnakes love to sleep under rocks; never put your hand or foot in a place you can't see.
- Wear solid, sturdy shoes.

Here are some suggestions of places to go for different types of hikes. Whether your goal is a strenuous hike or a leisurely stroll through nature, you'll find it nearby. First, the easy family walks in, or within a short drive of, Sacramento. (For more information, you'll find these entries in the index.)

❧ American River Parkway. The Jedediah Smith Recreational Trail meanders along beautiful riverine landscapes across the whole width of Sacramento. Access at many different points.

∿ Cosumnes River Wildlife Preserve. Gentle wetlands walk, lots of nature viewing. No amenities.

∿ Davis (UC) Arboretum. A thoroughly pleasant meander along the creek, under many different species of trees and other flora. Picnic facilities. On the University of California campus.

∿ Effie Yeaw Nature Center. Gentle nature walks, often lots of nature viewing. Choice of several trails.

∿ Folsom Lake Recreation Areas. Lots of walks, picnicking, lakefront.

∿ Sacramento Science Center. Mild, gentle nature walk, nature viewing, picnic stop.

For longer or more challenging hiking, there are several wildlife refuges within an easy day's drive there and back, and then, of course, there are the foothills and the Sierra.

For hikers with special needs, there's a trail open to explorers in wheelchairs, located about six miles north of Nevada City along Highway 49. It's called the South Yuba Independence Trail, and features waterfalls and spring wildflowers, and totals about two miles for wheelchair users and five miles for hikers. For information, trail conditions or to arrange for disability camping or guided hikes, call 282-3823.

And for all hikers: be sure to check out Bill McMillon's book, "Best Hikes with Children around Sacramento" (see Suggested Reading for Further Exploration).

∿ Hockey

The Sacramento Junior Ice Hockey Association *(797-0454)* meets regularly at Iceland, the region's only ice-skating rink (see Ice Skating).

∿ Horseback Riding

Equestrians, junior or otherwise, can indulge their passion at many locations throughout the Sacramento area.

See the Yellow Pages under Horse Rentals, Horse Stables and Riding Academies. Some colleges also offer courses in riding, and check with Parks & Recreation districts for summer courses.

If your child has special needs, **Project RIDE** (Riding Instruction Designed for Education) is worth looking into. Here, your special child can enhance self-esteem, confidence, and motor skills through riding. Call Carol Meador at 689-2310.

ᔈ Ice Skating

Iceland Skating Arena, *1430 Del Paso Boulevard (925-3121)*, has been here for over 50 years, and it's the only ice-skating rink in the entire greater Sacramento area. You and your family can enjoy public skate sessions, and they also offer lessons (expert instruction from beginning to advanced), hockey (Junior Ice Hockey Association, 797-0454), broomball (925-3529) and a skating equipment shop (648-1887). There are group rates for 20 or more skaters, and you can have private skating parties here or birthday parties (see Chapter 8, Birthday Party Ideas).

ᔈ Martial Arts

Karate, Judo and other forms of martial arts develop discipline and awareness of self, respect for others, concentration, strength, forbearance and the ability to focus and concentrate. Instructors emphasize the defensive nature of the art, and it's always wise to observe a class first before enrolling your child (some places offer a free first lesson). You'll find many listings under Martial Arts in the Yellow Pages, and many Parks & Recreation districts offer martial arts classes during the year and throughout the summer.

Since the programs vary so much, I've listed a few of the bigger centers and what they offer. Call for more up-to-date information.

ATA Family Taekwondo Centers, *481-9693*. Starting from age 3 1/2 to 5 and up, ATA stresses "total physical fitness for self-defense, self-esteem and confidence, to foster respect and discipline." Introductory program: 2 weeks at a reduced rate, including a free uniform. One free lesson, no obligation. Birthday party package (see Chapter 8, Birthday Party Ideas).

International Self Defense, *7518 Fair Oaks Boulevard, Carmichael, 944-0806,* is a member of the International Martial Arts Master Instructors Association. They stress an organized, systematic approach to learning to improve stamina, set and achieve goals, build self-esteem and self-discipline.

Kovar's Karate Center, *7520 Fair Oaks Boulevard, Carmichael, 481-4830,* takes children from age 5 and up — and it's not unusual to see a white head or two among their students. Kovar's main goal is "enhancing youngsters' self-esteem and self-confidence, by developing self-discipline and respect for others." Birthday party package: Kovar's runs it all (see Chapter 8, Birthday Party Ideas).

Rankins Taekwondo & Co., *10621 Folsom Boulevard, Rancho Cordova, 362-4992,* offers instruction for all ages, to develop self-confidence.

∿ Ornithology (Bird-Watching)

The Sacramento area has the privilege of being on a major fly-way for migrating birds, and a major wetlands area for aquatic birds. There are many outstanding opportunities for bird-watching throughout the year and throughout the area. The listings below are only the beginning; contact the Effie Yeaw Nature Center (489-4918) for more information.

Cosumnes River Wildlife Area. Easy walks through the wetlands, no amenities. Abundant birds and other wildlife. (684-2816)

Effie Yeaw Nature Center bird-walks. Family walks with naturalist, 1:30pm Sundays. Learn about birds and local critters. Also has information about bird-watching groups. (489-4918)

Gray Lodge Wildlife Area. Meet in Davis at 9am for a field trip to view spectacular concentrations of geese and other wintering waterfowl. (756-7246)

Yolo Basin Wetlands Area. Scheduled to open to the public in 1994, this wetlands area is just west of West Sacramento. (756-7248)

Yosemite Bird Count. Annually, Dec. 20 in Yosemite National Park. Open to anyone, unlimited numbers. Organizational meeting in Yosemite. $5 fee. ((209) 372-0269).

~ Rafting and Canoeing

The American River is a favorite with rafters of any (or no) experience level. And many other rivers in the Foothill-Sierra region offer exceptional white-water rafting opportunities. Check the Yellow Pages under Rafting, Rafts-Dealers and River Trips for rentals, information, organized trips, instruction, etc. Most raft places can also supply information about kayaking and canoeing.

~ Rock Climbing (Mountaineering)

The **Rocknasium**, *720 Olive Drive, Davis, 757-2902*, offers the opportunity to train indoors for serious rock climbing, or simply have fun climbing the walls. A great place for kids to let off steam while training their bodies and minds (see Chapter 6, Davis). For other places to practice, the **Sierra Club** can help (923 12 Street, Sacramento; 447-9003 (Bookstore) or 557-1100), and you can also get information at **R.E.I.**, 5961 Sunrise Boulevard, Citrus Heights, CA (965-4343), **Sierra Outfitters**, 2100 Arden Way (922-7500) and other larger sporting goods stores.

~ Roller Skating

Skating develops coordination and balance, keeps you fit and it's a sport the whole family can do together with a minimum drain on the pocketbook. There are several rinks listed in the Yellow Pages under Skating Rinks, most of which offer instruction, and many places to get equipment (Skating Equipment). There's also a skate-board park, called the **Daily Grind** (488-4070).

~ Running and Track

A regular regimen of physical exercise is necessary for a

sound body — and what could be easier than just putting on your running shoes and hitting the track, or the park, or the street? There are jogging tracks in many of Sacramento's parks; call Parks and Recreation for your area. Most colleges have a track that's open to the public when there's no meet or other event happening. And many Parks Districts offer Track during their summer sessions.

~ Shooting / Pistol & Rifle Ranges

This is a sport that's alive and well in the Wild West! The City of Sacramento has a Rifle and Pistol Range at 34th Avenue and Bradd Way (277-6007). In West Sacramento, for indoor practice with handguns and rifles up to 22s, try the Firing Pin (372-4867). In Rancho Cordova, you can practice indoors, at the Service Center (369-6789) or outdoors at the Cordova Shooting Center (351-0205). Look in the Yellow Pages under Rifle and Pistol Ranges.

~ Skiing

Sacramento is the gateway to one of the most popular ski resort areas in the world, the Sierra Nevada. A dramatic, rugged mountain chain that runs along the eastern edge of the state, the Sierra offers skiing for novice to expert, in areas scattered from southern to northern California.

The South Lake Tahoe areas are the most accessible from Sacramento. Downhill and cross-country ski equipment can be purchased or rented at most of the sporting goods stores in the Sacramento area, and you can get information about ski centers there, too. For general information, check the Yellow Pages under "Ski Resorts and Arrangements" or "Skiing Equipment;" also try South Lake Tahoe Visitors Authority (544-5050 or (800) AT TAHOE), or the South Lake Tahoe Chamber of Commerce (541-5255). Many sporting-goods stores offer ski-trip packages, as do some of the colleges around Sacramento; also contact Parks & Recreation Districts for possible ski packages.

~ Skydiving

If terra firma is too tame for you, head for the skies —

with a parachute. At most places, you have to be at least 18. See the Yellow Pages under Parachute Jumping Instruction.

✽ Sno-Parks

Sno-Parks provide access to many of the Sierra's best winter recreation areas for cross-country skiing, snowmobiling, sledding, snowball-throwing and any other snow fun you can think of. Permits are available at outdoor specialty stores; the state parks store (1416 Ninth St., Sacramento); various resorts, ranger stations and businesses in the Sierra; and the California State Automobile Association district offices. Season pass by mail at Permit Sales, Sno-Park Program, P.O. Box 942896, Sacramento 94296-0001. Call first for up-to-date prices: 653-8569.

✽ Snowshoeing and Snow Camping

Snowshoeing is a unique way to see some spectacular, unspoiled scenery and get lots of exercise. It requires little preparation other than general physical conditioning, and there's no age limit — young or old. Snow-camping can be the experience of a lifetime — provided you're hardy enough!

Eagle Mountain Nordic has snow-shoe trails; it's about one hour east of Sacramento on I-80, at the Yuba Gap exit (783-4558). Check with other centers for availability. At R.E.I. Sports, Birdcage Walk, Citrus Heights, you can learn about snow camping (965-4343).

✽ Soccer

In recent years, the popularity of soccer has soared all across our country. It's offered at many recreation centers, community centers and churches, and many youth groups also have teams. For general information, see the Yellow Pages under Soccer Clubs, or call one of the sporting goods stores; see the Yellow Pages under Sporting Goods – Dealers. The Soccer Locker (962-0880) offers summer soccer camps, as do some Parks & Recreation Districts and some school districts. You can also get information at the Indoor Soccer Arena at 5560 Palm Avenue (344-4724).

∾ Special Olympics

The Sacramento Special Olympics organization is very active in this area, and they can put you in touch with area coordinators and events. For information, contact their office at 6005 Folsom Boulevard, Sacramento (452-1088).

∾ Swimming and Aquatics

Swimming is the best exercise; no other sport tones all the muscles in the body quite like it. Whether you take your swimming seriously or you just like playing in or near the water, Sacramento is awash with possibilities!

There are dozens of pools in the Sacramento area; see the Yellow Pages under "Swimming Pools - Private" and "Swimming Pools – Public." Many of them offer classes and clubs. During the summer months, most of the Parks & Recreation Districts have swimming and aquatics classes, for babies through adults, as does the YMCA. The community colleges offer youth swim classes during the summer, and CSUS has an Aquatics Center where children can learn water safety and skills (278-6011).

Each year, in the rivers of Sacramento, many people neglect to observe safety rules and become unhappy statistics. Rivers are dangerous, no matter how "citified" they seem or how many people are swimming there. Be sure your children know the rules. Don't let them swim alone. Avoid the middle of the river, where the current is strongest. Be sure they know what to do if they are pulled away by the current. If you go boating, be sure everyone has a snug-fitting life-vest, and see that someone knows where you're going. For everyone's safety, be sure they're all acquainted with these rules, so your family outing to the river ends up a happy one.

∾ Tennis

Like badminton, but bigger — that's how my daughter described this sport that any family can enjoy. All you need is a racket and a few fuzzy balls, and you're ready to head for one of the many public and private tennis clubs or courts around the Sacramento area. See the Yellow Pages under

Tennis Clubs - Private, Tennis Courts – Public, or Tennis Instruction. Many Parks & Recreation Districts also offer summer tennis instruction.

~ Sports Camps

It would be impossible to list all the summer sports camps available in the greater Sacramento area. This is outdoor paradise — if there's a sport you can do outdoors, you can find a camp for it here, for any age or level.

School districts offer summer sports programs; Parks & Recreation Districts have sports training for the summer (see Chapter 8). There are many camps in the Sierra Nevada that offer sports programs, and these are listed in the Sacramento <u>Bee</u>'s summer youth camp listing, which appears as the summer months approach, and in <u>Parents' Monthly</u>, a free newspaper for parents, whose May issue lists all summer educational and sports possibilities throughout the area. Also check with the three community colleges (American River, Cosumnes River and Sacramento City) for their summer sports offerings.

~ Youth Centers and Organizations

Many Community Centers around the greater Sacramento area have sports, educational and social programs for young people. For information and locations of these centers, contact the local Parks & Recreation District (see Chapter 8). Some churches also have youth centers.

Sacramento also has many youth organizations where your child can learn life skills, enjoy social programs, engage in sports and outdoor activities, learn about science, art, and generally have fun growing up. Some of these include:

Camp Fire Boys and Girls, 3560 Business Drive (452-4982)

Boy Scouts of America, 251 Commerce Circle (929-1417)

Girl Scouts, Tierra del Oro Council, 3005 Gold Canal Drive (638-4475 or (800) 322-4475)

Junior Achievement of Sacramento, 2241 Harvard Street (648-1084)

The Salvation Army, 2440 Alhambra Boulevard
(452-2968)
YMCA, 1926 V Street (452-9622)
YWCA, 1122 17th Street (442-4741)

∼ 5 ∼
Festivals and Special Events

The city of Sacramento was born of a special event — the discovery of gold — and since that day, festivals and extra-ordinary happenings have been a way of life here. No matter what the season, there's something special happening <u>somewhere</u> in the Sacramento area. For many of these events, like the Calaveras Jumping Frog Jubilee, a sense of humor is required; Sacramentans don't like to take themselves too seriously. So dig in, and be ready for the unusual.

Most of these events are local; some take place in what's loosely termed the "greater Sacramento area." The Valley, the Delta, Gold Country and the Foothills are all neighbors, and what's a few miles between neighbors? — especially if the goal is to have a good time!

All of the events listed are open to the public; some charge a fee, some are free. But keep in mind that things change; don't be too disappointed if the event you picked isn't happening this year. There's surely another one to take its place, to add to your list of favorites. Check the newspapers for more up-to-the-minute happenings, too, since special events and sponsors come and go (or call the Sacramento Convention and Visitors Bureau at 264-7777; for other areas, see Chapter 8, Convention and Visitors' Bureaus). You'll undoubtedly find things to add to this list — but this should get you started.

❧ JANUARY

❧ **Gold Discovery Days.** Come to the Effie Yeaw Nature Center (see chapter 1) and go gold panning, take part in an old-time sing-along, enjoy puppet shows, films, and make your own pioneer toys and crafts. (489-4918)

❧ **Pig Bowl.** Watch the Sheriff's Department and the Police Department football teams square off to raise money for various benevolent organizations. (399-4918)

❧ **Winterfest** (K Street Mall). A month-long celebration of winter in downtown Sacramento, with outdoor concerts, skating rink, performances and special events. (442-8575)

🍃 FEBRUARY

🍃 **Autorama.** Exposition of custom cars and motorcycles, at Cal-Expo. (487-3994)

🍃 **Banjo-rama**, at the Carmichael Elks Lodge, 5631 Cypress Avenue, Carmichael. (428-3039 or 721-6452)

🍃 **Camellia Show.** Sacramento is the Camellia Capitol of the World, as celebrated by this show and international exposition at the Sacramento Community Center. (442-8166)

🍃 **Carnival Parade**, around the Capitol, the Saturday before Lent. (558-3912)

🍃 **Crocker Red & White Party**, a fund-raiser for the Crocker Museum. Valentine's Day theme. (264-5423)

🍃 **Disney's World on Ice** ice-skating extravaganza, at the Arco Arena. Great for kids. (928-6900)

🍃 **Fasching.** (See Masquerade Ball)

🍃 **Karneval.** (See Masquerade Ball)

🍃 **Mardi Gras Coronation Pageant**, in Old Sacramento. A parade of young men and women formally dressed as Court members (especially cute are the 4- and 5-year-old costumed pages), who prepare to crown their King and Queen of Mardi Gras. (362-4555)

🍃 **Masquerade Ball**, Turn Verein Hall, 3349 J Street. The German Club of Sacramento hosts this gala evening event celebrating the German festival of Fasching, (also called Karneval, or Mardi Gras), to usher in the season of Lent. Bavarian folk dancers in drndls and lederhosen, food, bands, accordion music, singing and celebrating. The first Saturday of February. (442-7360)

🍃 **Music and Sound Expo**, Red Lion Inn, I-80 at Arden Way. Learn all about music and technology, from plain old guitars to four-track, Mac-compatible digital tape recorders, how sound-tracks are made (no, it's not a pit orchestra any more), tips and demos by prominent musicians, and an assortment of vintage instruments. Presented by Skip's Music. (484-7575)

❧ **Rancho Cordova Chamber Crab Feed**, to benefit their high-school scholarship fund. All-you-can-eat crab and shrimp. (638-8700)

❧ **Sacramento Bee Travel Fair**, Cal-Expo. If you've ever wanted to go anywhere, this is a good place to start dreaming! Kids can learn about the world and what it has to offer. (321-1790)

❧ **Sacramento Home and Garden Show**, Cal-Expo. Expositions and information of particular interest to home-owners, do-it-yourself-ers, gardeners. (924-9934)

❧ **Sacramento Sports & Boat Show**, Cal-Expo. Acres of RV's, campers, some boats. (452-6403)

❧ MARCH

❧ **Japanese Spring Food Festival**, 2401 Riverside Boulevard. Its name says it all — come hungry! A real cultural experience. (446-0121)

❧ **Sacramento Boat Show**, Cal-Expo. For 5 days in March, you can see all the latest in boats and boating equipment and accessories. Kids can have fun watching the entertainment, tasting the goodies, and dreaming about their future boats. (482-8190)

❧ **St. Patrick's Day Parade**, downtown Sacramento. The Saturday before St. Patty's, this is a big parade with over 100 entries — the Sheriff's Mounted Patrol, school bands, floats. Rain or shine. (922-3688)

❧ APRIL

❧ **Bockbierfest**, Turn Verein Hall, 3349 J Street. The German Club hosts this celebration of beer. (442-7360)

❧ **Earth Day**, Effie Yeaw Nature Center. The third Saturday of the month; puppet shows, nature walks, crafts and music, all centered on our fragile planet. Free, with a small charge if you participate in the craft session. (489-4918)

❧ **Easter Egg Hunt** - Maidu Park, Roseville (783-8136)

❧ **Easter Egg Hunt** - Polish-American Chapel, Marysville Bd. and South St. (444-8120)

❧ **Highland Scottish Games**, Roseville. Pipes, drums, clans and kilts, highland dancing and sports, food and fun. (557-0764 or 448-6436)

❧ **Jackalope / Easter Egg Hunt** (Saturday before Easter) (443-6223)

❧ **Nordstrom Fashion Show** (264-5423)

❧ **Picnic Day, UC Davis**. This is a great fun day for kids. Lots of food, lots of place to run around, and shows, shows, shows! Dogs, horses, cows, lots of animals doing things, like Police dogs going through their paces. Bring a hat and a water bottle. (752-4880)

❧ **Polish Food Festival**, at the American Legion Hall, Post 392, 21st and K Streets. Pierogi, kielbasa, paczki and all the other favorites. You don't have to be able to pronounce them to enjoy. (444-8120)

❧ **Sacramento Cooks!** A gourmet's delight; something for everyone, at the Scottish Rite Temple, 6151 H Street. (452-5881)

❧ **Sacramento Valley Scottish Games and Gathering**. Last weekend in April (call first to verify date), the Caledonian Club of Sacramento hosts this outdoor event. Pipes and drums, clan tents, athletics, highland dancing, animals, children's activities. At the Placer County Fairgrounds in Roseville. (737-2277)

❧ **Spring Collectors' Faire**. Usually the first Sunday of the month, from 7am-4pm, 300 dealers from throughout the west fill the streets of Old Sacramento with antiques and collectibles. (558-3912)

❧ **Sutter Street Flea Market**, April 18 on Sutter Street, Folsom. (622-7349)

❧ **Teddy Bear Convention.** A whimsical, delightful weekend of cuddly bears and all sorts of "bearaphernalia," including lots of food, music, a parade, face painting, bear clothes, furniture — even a Bear Castle to tour. Unforgettable. Nevada City. (265-5804)

❧ **Wild West Stampede and Rodeo** - Roseville (783-8136)

❧ MAY

❧ **Calaveras Jumping Frog Jubilee and County Fair,** Angels Camp. The town Mark Twain made famous jumps back in time, and celebrates with a fair and all its trappings — and an unforgettable Frog Jump. Rent a frog or bring your own champion. Rodeo, rides, plenty of food and entertainment. See Chapter 6, Gold Country, Angels Camp. (1-(800)-225-3764)

❧ **Cinco de Mayo Celebration,** Southside Park. Celebrate Hispanic culture with food, music, entertainment and camaraderie. (444-8090)

❧ **Crocker Golf Classic,** Rancho Murieta. An alternative fund-raiser for the Crocker Museum; anyone can play, for a fee. (264-5423)

❧ **Elk Grove Western Festival.** Western theme parade, booths, concessions, food, entertainment and a down-home good time. (687-7814)

❧ **Fair Oaks Fiesta,** Fair Oaks Village. The first weekend in May, this is Fair Oaks' big community event. Gather at the Plaza and taste the Chili Cook-out, the Ice Cream Freeze-out, see the car show. Kids enjoy rides and entertainment, take part in a Kids' Walk and other activities. The culminating event, for young and old, is the hilarious Toilet Bowl Challenge! (967-2903)

❧ **International Jazz Jubilee.** This is the BIG event for jazz lovers, ragtime lovers, or any toe-tappers who can't resist moving to the beat! There are performance venues all around the Sacramento area, and groups come to perform here from all over the world. An up-beat experience. (372-5277)

~ **Old Sacramento Triathlon** includes running, swimming and cycling. Second weekend in May. (557-1000)

~ **Orangevale Pow Wow Country Fair** (988-0175)

~ **Pacific Coast Rowing Championship**, in Folsom. (985-7239)

~ **Pacific Rim Street Festival**, Old Sacramento. Celebrates the diversity of the Pacific Asian cultures, with music, dance, food, booths, visual arts and more. (558-3912)

~ **Sacramento County Fair**, at Cal-Expo. Food, music, live entertainment, animal shows, junior exhibits, rodeo, carnival — a real western fair with a flair! (263-2975)

~ **Sutter Street Arts & Crafts Fair**. Folsom's historic Sutter Street fills with arts, crafts, quilts, and collectibles. (622-7349)

~ JUNE

~ **California Railroad Festival**, Old Sacramento. Train lovers and rolling stock come from all over for this main event near the Railroad Museum on the Old Sac waterfront. (445-7387)

~ **Children's Festival**. The streets of Old Sacramento come alive with the sound of children's voices! A celebration about and for children, with lots of music, dancing, food, face painting, crafts and more. (264-5558)

~ **Crawdad Festival**, Isleton. Taste this delicacy of the Delta. (777-5880)

~ **Croatian Extravaganza**, 3730 Auburn Boulevard. (971-0663)

~ **County Bluegrass Picnic**, Freeport (444-7277)

~ **Davis Street Fair**, downtown Davis, first Sunday in June. Craft vendors, food, live entertainment. For families, a petting zoo and Kiddie Carnival. Also a vintage car show. (756-5160)

❧ **Fair Oaks Renaissance Faire**. Kids enjoy lots of games and entertainment at this event filled with costumes, food, music and arts and crafts. (966-1036)

❧ **Family Fun Festival**, El Dorado Hills. The Sierra Cultural Arts Center Association hosts this family celebration the first weekend in June. From noon till about 6pm, wander through the booths and take part in the activities — hands-on art activities, face-painting, food, wine tasting, live music, games, theater vignettes (by the Fantasy Theater). The finale is a concert by the Sierra Symphony. All activities and final concert included in the price of admission. (676-6400)

❧ **Founder's Day**. The Saturday before the first Tuesday in June, West Sacramento, one of California's newest cities, celebrates its founding. Call to verify date first. (371-7042)

❧ **Golden West Track & Field Meet**. The second Saturday in June, at American River College for 1993. This meet brings the top High School seniors, boys and girls, to Sacramento to compete in 33 different events. Come see future Olympians and professionals. (444-8146)

❧ **Laughs in the Park**. The Sacramento Bee and Laughs Unlimited combine to host an afternoon of stand-up comedy, in William Land Park. Local area comedians provide the entertainment. Free; on the fairway of the Land Park Golf Course. (321-1880)

❧ **Nighttime Market**. The K Street mall comes alive every Thursday evening, June through October, from 6-9pm, with outdoor markets (in Cathedral Square), restaurants, live entertainment and more. Stores along the Mall remain open later than usual. Come enjoy a pleasant summer stroll to music, eat under the stars, and experience Sacramento's Downtown District as you haven't seen it in years. (442-8575)

❧ **Oak Park Concert Series**, McClatchy Park, Sacramento. (321-1800)

❧ **Pony Express Ride** re-creates the daring feats of these intrepid young riders, who ride through Folsom this day. (985-2707)

❧ **Portuguese Festa**. Food, dancing, music and more food! The Portuguese played a large role in the settling of Sacramento, and this day celebrates that heritage. (391-3442)

❧ **Sacramento Renaissance Faire**. Costumes, food, music and celebrating in Renaissance style. (966-1036)

❧ **Shakespeare Festival in the Park**, William Land Park. The Sacramento City College drama department does the Bard proud with plays in the park. (558-2228)

❧ JULY

❧ **Championship Rodeo**, Folsom. This is the nation's largest 4th of July Rodeo, with barrel racing, calf-roping, bull and bronco riding, and of course, the antics of rodeo clowns. (985-2698)

❧ **Carmichael Fourth of July Parade** and community fireworks. Del Campo High School, 4925 Dewey Drive, Fair Oaks. (971-5664)

❧ **Eppie's Great Race**. An exciting 3-event race (cycling, paddling and running) along the American River; open to anyone. 1993 was Eppie's 20th anniversary. (366-2940)

❧ **Independence Day Parade and Celebrations** (Sacramento, 264-7777; 558-3912; West Sacramento, 371-7042; Roseville, 783-8136)

❧ **Oak Park Concert Series**. Outdoor music in McClatchy Park. (321-1800)

❧ **Pear Fair**, Courtland, CA. Pears are in important crop in the Delta, and this is the pear-growers' big day. You don't need to love pears to have a great time. (775-1053)

❧ **Placer County Fair**, County Fairgrounds, Roseville, is the real McCoy, featuring livestock exhibits, arts and crafts and carnival rides. (786-2023)

✎ **Rio Linda Rodeo**, at the Horse Arena behind Rio Linda High School. A wild west rodeo sponsored by the Lion's Club. (991-6508 or 991-5929)

✎ **Sacramento Symphony** concerts in the parks. (649-0300)

✎ **Strauss Festival**, Elk Grove. Music by Strauss, decorations by Mother Nature. Bring a picnic dinner, or just listen. (366-2566)

✎ AUGUST

✎ **California Lottery Bicycle Classic**, Old Sacramento. (558-3912)

✎ **California State Fair**. See Chapter 1, Cal-Expo. (924-2000)

✎ **Festa Italiana**. Celebrate the diversity of Italian culture with food, music, and entertainment. (424-8259 or 453-1409)

✎ **History Week**, Folsom. Bring your kids to Junior Historians' Day, cruise the historic exhibits and re-creations. Food, music, entertainment, a week-long antique quilt show. (985-2707)

✎ **International Youth Soccer Festival**. For 3 days at the beginning of the month, soccer players from all leagues battle it out at the Cherry Island Soccer Complex. (264-7718)

✎ **Japanese Cultural Bazaar**. Join with thousands of others at the Sacramento Buddhist Church, 2401 Riverside Boulevard, to explore all the aspects of Japanese culture — lots of food, games, music, activities, people watching and fun. (446-0121)

✎ **Lambtown USA Festival**, Dixon (678-2650)

✎ **Oak Park Concert Series**. Outdoor music in McClatchy Park. (321-1800)

✎ **Sacramento Riverfest and Gold Rush**, Old Sacramento. This is the only community-wide celebration of history in

Sacramento. Historical Societies from all over the region participate with exhibits, events, food, crafts, displays, trade demonstrations, rides. Kids can play historic games, watch the shoot-outs. (264-7057)

~ **Yolo County Fair**, Woodland. See Chapter 6, Woodland. (662-5393)

~ SEPTEMBER

~ **"A Taste of Sacramento."** A fund-raiser for the Downtown District and Easter Seals. For 2 days, Sacramento area restaurants and caterers take to the streets, in and around Plaza Park. There's name entertainment by Sacramento artists, food booths, cooking demos by local chefs. (442-8575)

~ **Autumn Collectors' Faire**. The streets of Old Sacramento fill with antiques and collectibles. (558-3912)

~ **Blues Festival**, Old Sacramento. (482-2215 or 558-3912)

~ **California Indian Days**, Roseville Fairgrounds. A celebration of American Indian culture and arts. Dancing, music, storytelling, basket weaving, food and more. (920-0285)

~ **California State Fair**, Cal-Expo, Exposition Boulevard. See Chapter 1, Cal-Expo. (924-2000)

~ **Greek Food Festival**, Sacramento Convention Center. Celebrate the Hellenic culture with food, dancing, food, music, entertainment — and more food. (443-2033)

~ **Hot Air Balloon Festival**. Watch about 45 hot air balloons take off at the Van Vleck Ranch outside Rancho Murieta, then stay for the fun after the launch — events, concessions, arts and crafts booths, souvenirs. Get there any time after 5:30 for the dawn launch patrol, stay till the afternoon. (441-5282)

~ **Loomis Eggplant Festival**, Loomis, CA. (652-7252)

~ **Mexican Independence Day**, September 20. Southside Park. Food, of course, lots of music and dancing. A family celebration; bring a picnic or cruise the booths. (264-7718)

❧ **Oak Park Concert Series.** (321-1800)

❧ **Peddlers' Faire**, Sutter Street, Folsom. (622-7349)

❧ **Sacramento Multi-Cultural Festival**, at Plaza Park. Celebrate the wonderful cultural diversity of the Sacramento area with food, live music, arts and crafts, dancing and other displays. (444-8120)

❧ **Sacramento Reads**! Businesses, families, writers, kids of all ages join to celebrate the written word. Exhibits, games, educational materials, activities. (552-5252, Category 4023)

❧ **Serbian Festival** (966-5438)

❧ **US National Handcar Races**, Old Sacramento, near the Railroad Museum. Hand-powered train-car competitions. (445-7387 or 558-3912)

❧ OCTOBER

❧ **Black Bart Raft Race** (682-6600)

❧ **"Boats on the Boardwalk"**, Old Sacramento (366-1146 or 566-6435)

❧ **California Vintage Fair** (321-1800)

❧ **Community Day Parade/Heritage Festival.** West Sacramento's community parade along West Capitol Avenue, followed by an outdoor festival of ethnic and American foods, dancing, music, arts, and just plain fun. A multicultural elaboration on what used to be called the Columbus Day Parade. (371-7042)

❧ **Crocker Art Museum Antique Show & Sale**, at the Scottish Rite Temple. Collectibles from all over northern California. (264-5423)

❧ **Crocker Annual Art Auction**, at the Pavilions Shopping Center. Local (northern California) artists auction their work, in all media. (264-5423)

❧ **Harvest Festival** ((707) 778-6300 or 264-5181)

❧ **Maidu Indian Days**, Effie Yeaw Nature Center. Celebrates and honors Indians native to this area. Dancers, acorn grinding and cooking, native foods, crafts demonstrations, storytellers. (489-4918)

ॐ **Oktoberfest**. Turn Verein Hall, 3349 J Street. The German harvest festival. (442-7360)

ॐ **Oktoberfest**, Folsom (622-7349)

ॐ **Old Sacramento Honorary Elections** (558-3912)

ॐ **PGA Raley's Senior Goldrush Golf Tournament**, Rancho Murieta. World-wide golf pro's play for a whole week, for charity. (354-2345)

ॐ **Polish American Heritage Month**. This is usually a Memorial to a Pole who made some contribution to American history or culture, like last year's Commemoration of General Kazimir Pulaski, a famous general of the American Revolution. (444-8120)

ॐ **Pumpkin Patches**. The Sacramento area abounds with them. Call the Chamber of Commerce in your area. (see Chapter 8 for Chamber numbers)

ॐ **Sacramento Blues Festival**. The first weekend in October is the time to sing the blues in River City. (558-3912)

ॐ **Snail Race**, Folsom. Which snail will run away with this year's trophy? Food, exhibits, booths for kids, games, midway, arts and crafts. (355-7285)

ॐ **Zoo Zoom**, Sacramento Zoo. A fund-raiser run for adults and children, in William Land Park. (264-5885)

ॐ NOVEMBER

ॐ **Candlelight Tours at Sutter's Fort**. Step back in time with this unusual tour of one of Sacramento's premiere historic attractions. (445-4209)

ॐ **Christmas Crafts and Music Festival**, Gold Country Fairgrounds, Auburn. Musicians, jugglers, singers, dancers, carolers, elves, weavers, craftsmen, glass sculptors, folk artists, etc. (888-9921)

❧ **Holiday Parade**, downtown Roseville. Right before Thanksgiving, to usher in the holiday season. (783-8136)

❧ **Indian Arts & Crafts Fair** (324-0971)

❧ **Mormon Island Ball**, Folsom. Mormon Island is now under Folsom Lake, but the ball goes on, at the Community Center, 52 Natoma Street. (985-2707)

❧ **Santa Parade**, downtown Sacramento. Go see the jolly old guy usher in the season. (558-3912)

❧ **Winterfest**, K Street Mall. Sacramento's Downtown District rings in the holiday season with outdoor performances, activities, decorations, an outdoor ice-skating rink. Continues till January. (442-8575)

☙ DECEMBER

❧ **Baroque Ball**. Gala dinner and dance at the Crocker Museum. (264-5423)

❧ **Breakfast with Santa**, Downtown Plaza, in front of Weinstock's Department Store. Reservations required. (449-8888, ext. 2261)

❧ **Breakfast with Santa**, Downtown Davis. Call the Davis Downtown Business Association. (756-8763)

❧ **California International Marathon** (983-4622)

❧ **Celtic Music Bash**. An evening of Celtic and Scottish music, dance and merriment. Bagpipes, harps, singing, food and often a sell-out crowd. (448-6436)

❧ **Children's Christmas Faire**, Miner's Foundry, Nevada City (272-8411)

❧ **Children's Christmas Party**. First Saturday in December, at the North Highlands Lion's Hall on Airway Drive. Sponsored by the Polish National Alliance. (444-8120)

❧ **"A Christmas Carol"** at the Sacramento Community Center. (443-6722)

❧ **Christmas Faire**, Silver Dollar Fairgrounds, Chico. 10-

6pm $1-$2, under 6 free. (345-9652)

❧ **Christmas Faire**, Sutter Street, Folsom 8-5pm. (622-7349)

❧ **Christmas in the Village**, Fair Oaks Village. Christmas parade, arts, crafts, booths, kids' games and entertainment. (967-2903)

❧ **Christmas Memories**, Governor's Mansion, 16th and H Streets. Open House 10-4pm, $2-3, under 6 free. (323-3047)

❧ **Christmas Parade**, Main St., Placerville. (626-4990)

❧ **Dickens' Christmas**, Old Town, Elk Grove. (685-2082)

❧ **Dixon Christmas Faire**, Dixon Fairgrounds, 655 S. First St., Dixon. 12/6, 10-5pm. $2, age 10 and under free. (678-5529)

❧ **Holiday Ice Rink**. Ice-skate outdoors amid the bustle of the Downtown District's Winterfest celebration. (442-8575)

❧ **Little Dickens Christmas Festival**, Coloma Community Center, 9:30-5pm; free. (277-6093)

❧ **Messiah Sing-along**. What would Christmas be without Handel's "Messiah?" Sing along with the Symphony and Chorus; call first. (264-5181)

❧ **"The Nutcracker"**, Sacramento Ballet. (264-5181 or 736-2866)

❧ **Old Sacramento Holiday Festival** (558-3912)

❧ **Singing Christmas Tree**, Capital Christian Center. (264-5181)

❧ **Winterfest**, K Street Mall, Downtown District (see November). (442-8575)

❧ **Yuletide Market**, second weekend, at the Freight Depot in Old Sacramento. (264-7057)

🍃 EXTENDED EVENTS

❧ **May-August**
Sacramento Saturday – the Downtown Marketplace (443-6223)

❧ **May-September**
Capitol Park Tours (324-0333)

❧ **July-August**
Music Circus Theater-in-the-Round (557-1999)

❧ **September-December**
Apple Hill Harvest, Placerville (644-7692)

❧ **September-January**
Music Circus Fall Broadway Series (264-5181)

❧ **September-March**
Sacramento Opera Season (442-4224)

❧ **September-May**
Sacramento Symphony Season (264-5181)

❧ **September-May**
Sacramento Theatre Company Season (443-6722)

❧ **October-April**
Sacramento Ballet Season (736-2866 or 264-5181)

❧ **November-May**
Sacramento Kings NBA Basketball Season (928-6900)

❧ **December-January**
Winterfest, Downtown District (442-8575)

🍃 ALL YEAR

Many of Sacramento historic attractions offer **Living History Days** at various times throughout the year, when docents don costumes and live and work there for the day. These are wonderful learning experiences for children, who get to "re-live" life the way it was then. Call the attraction for information.

🍃 EVERY TEN YEARS

Once a decade, in June, train lovers and rolling stock come from all over the world to celebrate **RailFair** with the California State Railroad Museum in Old Sacramento. The last one was 1991. This is the BIGGIE for train enthusiasts. Steam train rides, monster locomotives, entertainment, food and everything you can imagine related to trains and their history. (445-7387)

🍃 REGIONAL FESTIVALS

Contact the California Office of Tourism (322-1396) for information regarding the many festivals that take place throughout the year in northern California.

🍃 1994 YEAR-LONG

Highway 49, the road that winds through the Mother Lode, is celebrating its 75th birthday this year, and will be hosting many events all along the quaint 318-mile track that links the towns and hamlets of gold country. Information is available from the Golden Chain Council of the Mother Lode Inc., in Newcastle, or check with local Chambers or Visitors' Bureaus (see Chap. 8).

🍃 1999 YEAR-LONG

Gold Country celebrates its Sesquicentennial, or 150th anniversary. Special events and celebrations will be happening throughout Gold Country (see Chapter 6) all year long; check with Chambers or Visitors' Bureaus.

❧ 6 ❧
Day Trips

S acramentans consider anything within a few hours' drive "right next door." On a clear day in downtown Sacramento, you can see the Sierra Nevada in one direction (about 90 miles to the east) and the Coast Range in the other (about 60 miles west). You can't really get to know Sacramento without establishing at least a nodding acquaintance with some of the outlying towns and areas that helped shape and define Sacramento. Many of them have a historic center of town, like the ones in the Mother Lode (Gold) country; some offer outstanding outdoor recreational opportunities or wildlife viewing. Whatever your family's focus is for day-trip excitement, this chapter will help you decide where to begin.

The main criterion when travelling with children, of course, is time. Kids don't want to spend the day in the car; they want to get out and DO THINGS. The trips I've outlined here are an easy drive there and back in one day, with time for lots of things to do once you get there.

A word about these entries: If there's a clearly-defined route to take to see the high points, I've followed it here; if the attractions in a particular place are too numerous or too scattered, I've left the choice up to you and simply listed them alphabetically.

And while you're at it, don't forget to see both the forest and the trees; there's a lot of history and a wide selection of recreational facilities right in Sacramento's back yard. Many of the suburbs, like Elk Grove or Fair Oaks, have museums, historical collections, parks and other attractions that you won't want to miss — and you won't have to drive far. Check with the local Chambers of Commerce.

And before you go, check the Bee's Great Outdoors section for more ideas on hiking, camping, skiing and exploring in and around California, and check the Encore section for performances in the area that might coincide with your visit.

So load up the car and get set for a mini-vacation! A

hint, though, for successful exploring, especially during the warmer months (which, in Sacramento, can mean anywhere from March through November!): take along water bottles for everyone. Gold Country is a dusty, dry place, and although these destinations come equipped with all the amenities, including ample feeding and watering places, you'll save lots of time and be able to see and do a lot more if you don't have to keep stopping to find a drinking fountain or store.

Get yourself a good map. And once you get the hang of it, I'm sure you'll dig up your own special places to explore in the Sacramento Valley region. Whatever your family's requirements are for fun, there's lots to be had in them thar hills. Eureka!

Calaveras Big Trees State Park

Highway 16 from Sacramento. Take Route 49 south to Angels Camps, then Route 4 to the Park, just beyond Arnold.

The Big Trees refers to giant Redwoods, or *Sequoia Gigantea*. A tree from this grove caused a scandal in the east; when a slice of one was exhibited at an Exposition in 1853, no one believed a tree that big could be real, and so they declared it a hoax! The stump of the Big Tree they cut down to determine its age was big enough to hold a dance pavilion with 32 dancers and even big enough for two bowling alleys!

The Park is open all year, and offers eight miles of trails and 129 campsites. Cross country skiing is popular here, but the main season is summer, when you can indulge here in fishing, hiking, nature studies, photography and simply wandering through the giant groves in awe of what Nature can do when she puts her mind to it. The last time we wandered through, our path was crossed by a small cinnamon-colored black bear — to the delight of the children and their parents! Early morning and dusk are the best times to see wildlife.

Be sure to stop at the Visitor Center for a better understanding of the trees and their environment through the Park's excellent interpretive exhibits, and for maps and brochures, coloring books and other souvenirs. Trails through the Park vary from flat and short to more challenging in distance and terrain, and there are trails for the handicapped available.

A visit to Calaveras combines well with a stop at one or more of the caves out of Murphys, Vallecito or San Andreas, on Route 4: Mercer Caves (open all summer 9am-5pm, and during the school year on weekends and school holidays 11am-4pm; (209) 728-2101), Moaning Cavern (10am-5pm winter, 9am-6pm summer; (209) 736-2708) or California Caverns (10am-5pm summer, 10am-4pm fall, daily mid-May to October, weekends in winter if not flooded). See Gold Country tour #3, this chapter, for descriptions.

Other Sequoia viewing:
- Placer County Big Tree Grove, the northernmost stand of Redwoods (take the Foresthill exit off I-80, then follow Mosquito Ridge Road about 30 miles out of Foresthill).
- Muir Woods (north of San Francisco, also in this chapter).
- Yosemite National Park.
- Sequoia National Park (off Highway 99 out of Visalia or Fresno).

Columbia State Historic Park
Located in Columbia, off Route 49, north of Sonora. (209) 532-4301.

Columbia was just one of the many towns that sprang up after Marshall's cry of "gold!" echoed around the world. Located in the heart of the Mother Lode, a network of gold-laden quartz that extends along the western edge of the Sierra Nevada, Columbia was still there after other gold-rush towns had sprung up and disappeared. Over the years, it has remained more or less as it appeared when gold-seekers filled its streets.

The entire town is the park, so you can begin your tour anywhere and just wander, or follow the suggested walking-tour route mapped out on the State Parks brochure. Simply imagine you've been transported back in time; there it is, right before you. It doesn't require too much imagination to picture the town the way it looked in 1850. Here are some of the attractions you won't want to miss:

At the Matelot Gulch Miner's Supply store, you can buy a pan and try your hand at gold-panning (for more on gold panning, see the section at the end of Gold Country, this chapter), and the Old Miner's Cabin gives you a good idea of the rough life of a gold miner. Both buildings sit about 10 feet below the original surface here — that's how much earth was washed away by hydraulic mining techniques.

At the Assay Office you can see the equipment used to determine the value of the ore samples brought in with such hope. Next door is the Wells Fargo Office, and in front of the Office you board the Stagecoach for an unforgettable trip around Columbia. This will be the part your kids remember most. Ride inside or on top, for a thrilling, bone-shaking trip back in time. Today's coddled little travellers will wonder how they survived such rides. And maybe, if your luck runs out, your stage will be held up en route....

The whole town is an absorbing walk back into an era of excitement and change. It's comfortably laid out, with rest rooms available from either end of town and barbecue/picnic facilities near the parking area.

Davis

Fifteen miles west of Sacramento on I-80.

The first thing you'll notice when you drive into Davis is the preponderance of bicycles. Cycling is the favored means of transportation in this university town; the flat topography is ideal for it, the bike lanes make it practical, and the climate favors it.

The University of California campus dominates and defines Davis. Its offerings in the performing arts attract people from all over the area (see Chapter 3). Various departments of UCD put Davis on the forefront world-wide; cutting-edge botanical research is carried out here, and outstanding research is done in the fields of primates, raptors (birds of prey) and animal husbandry. UCD is also an international pioneer in energy conservation, being home to the world's largest photovoltaic (solar) power plant.

But there's more to Davis than the University. Davis is a mecca for artists, with its new community-built Art Center, several dozen galleries, a Farmer's Market, and annual Street Faire. Here's a sampling of what you'll find as you wander this compact, vibrant town:

Cal-Gene, 1920 5th Street. This highly specialized facility does genetic research on fruits and vegetables (see Chapter 2, Tours of the Working World). For adults or older children specializing in botanical science or related field. (753-6313)

Central Park is bordered by 4th, B, 5th and C Streets, just a few block from the campus and right in the heart of downtown Davis. There's a nice playground and shade trees, and the **Davis Farmer's Market** meets here Saturdays (8am-noon) and Wednesdays (2-6pm). From May to September, the market moves to 2nd Street on Wednesday nights, 5:30-

8:30pm. This is an exciting farmers' market, with craft and produce vendors, an espresso cart, baked good and the playground to keep the kids entertained as the adults browse.

At the north end of F Street, bordered by F and 14th Streets and Covell Bd, the **Davis Community Park** is center for recreation and culture. **Rainbow City**, a state-of-the-art playground located at the northeast corner of the park, features balance beams, a monster maze, a mirrored tunnel and dinosaur swings. The Park is also home to a library, a community pool, and the **Davis Art Center**, 1919 F Street, which has courses for adults and children, children's theater, martial arts, weaving and more (756-4100). Plan to spend a lot of time here.

Twenty years old this fall ('93), the **Davis Comic Opera Company** (DCOC) offers two performances of light opera each year, in April and November, at the Veteran's Memorial Theater, 14th and B Streets (758-DCOC). Tickets are $12 adults, $10 seniors and children, and performances begin at 8pm. And if lighter musical fare is more to your liking, there's the **Davis Musical Theater Company**, 2121 2nd Street (756-DMTC). Performances Fri. and Sat. 8:15pm; Sun. matinee 2:15pm. Tickets cost $12 adults; $9 students and seniors. Sun prices $10 adults, $8 students and seniors.

Double-Decker Bus. Unitrans of Davis has a fleet of British double-decker busses. Sit on top for a bird's-eye view of the town and campus. (752-2877)

Explorit! *3141 5th Street; I-80 to Mace Bd. exit right. Go over the overpass, then turn left on Alhambra Road. Left on 5th Street, then right onto a small private drive when you see their sign (it looks like someone's home; if you're looking for what looks like a museum, it's easy to miss). Open T-F, 2-4; Sat 10-5; Sun 1-5. $2 (Members and 3-and-under free). Fourth Saturday of each month (changing exhibit) is free admission.*

Formerly the Davis Science Center, Explorit! is a nonprofit, private hands-on museum where kids can explore their physical world. It's arranged by "work stations," where kids do experiments, test physical, mathematical and perceptual laws, read, research and just have a great time! They serve class groups from throughout the greater Sacramento-Davis area, and they welcome families any time.

As you drive up, you'll be surprised at how small the place looks; but don't be fooled — the only limit here is the size of your imagination! There's a permanent exhibit dealing with the world of sand (yes, sand; you'd be amazed!), and other exhibits change every 5 weeks. When I was there, the theme was patterns; kids were doing experiments with repeating patterns and mathematical progression, calculating odds, testing aerodynamics. And they were really getting into it! Other features include:

- A small animal exhibit, and a resource room which serves the double function of a quiet study space and source room. For kids (or adults) who want to study their findings, concentrate on their work, etc.
- Materials and resources that teachers can borrow (slides, hands-on materials, books, "things").
- Public lecture series offered free throughout the year (not just for kids).
- On Saturday afternoons, they offer a speaker on various topics related to science, mathematics and the fascinating world around us.
- Free tabloid-style newspapers on some of their topics.
- Travelling exhibits that go to schools, and a free, once-a-month astronomy club.
- Summer programs for children, craft-oriented, very active-creative.
- Astronomy Club.
- Classes and field trips during school vacations.

They have family memberships, and a lovely picnic area outside the museum, which was originally the Mace family homestead. As of June 1993, there will be an outdoor theater adjacent to the picnic area; call for up-dated information. (756-0191)

Festivals and Special Events. Don't miss UCD's annual Picnic Day in April. And there are other special events throughout the year; call Tours and Events, 752-4880.

The Rocknasium, 720 Olive Drive, is an indoor rock-climbing gym; see Chapter 4, Rock-climbing.

University of California, Davis. There are many wide-open green spaces on the UCD campus where you and your children can wander, picnic, play, run and just have a good time. There are also many good, small restaurants to the east of the campus where you and your children can eat very reasonably. You can pre-arrange a guided tour of the campus (757-3108), or you can combine your picnic with a visit to one of their fine arts galleries (752-8500) or with a tour of one of these facilities:

UCD Arboretum, on the UCD campus along Putah Creek. Not an enclosed arboretum, this wonderful collection of different species of trees, shrubs, medicinal herbs and low-water gardens graces the banks of the creek as it meanders through the campus. Its well-maintained path and lawns are a delightful place to walk, jog, picnic or simply enjoy nature, free. Take the Old Davis Road off I-80, northeast to the campus. (752-2498)

Freeborn Hall is one of several performance centers on campus. Many internationally-renowned artists play at Freeborn. See Chapter 3, Performing Arts.

UCD Raptor Center, 2 miles south of the campus on Old Davis Road. You and your children can explore up to 27 different species of raptors (birds of prey). Read the exhibits, see the eagles, falcons, owls, condors and other raptors that can't be released into the wild; learn from these magnificent birds. You can arrange in advance for a guided tour, or starting sometime in 1994, you can follow the walk-through, self-guiding tour. Open weekdays, 9am-3pm; call to see if the self-guiding tour project is completed. (752-6091)

The Delta

The Sacramento and San Joaquin Rivers have carved a labyrinth of channels and sloughs between Sacramento and the San Francisco Bay. This is explorers' heaven; by car or by bicycle or motorbike, you can meander along the tiniest of sloughs, along edges of myriads of tiny islands, just wandering or going somewhere in particular (like Rio Vista, or Locke, or Walnut Creek, or....)

The other obvious way to explore the Delta is by boat. If you don't have your own, you can take a cruise to San Francisco (any travel agent can help you), or if you're really adventurous you can rent a houseboat ((209) 477-1840) or smaller craft. If you choose to see the Delta by boat, be sure you get good charts before you go. The Delta is literally a labyrinth of tiny sloughs that can confuse even the most experienced navigator.

If you prefer to stick to the beaten track, start your tour by getting on Route 160 south out of Sacramento, and simply follow 160 as it winds along the Sacramento River. You'll pass the little Delta towns of Hood and Courtland, and farther down the road you'll go through **Locke**, which was a Chinese settlement of considerable size during the Delta's development. Stop here and wander along the old street, or continue past Walnut Grove and Isleton, and take Route 12 across the river to Rio Vista.

Founded in 1858, **Rio Vista** is a typical Delta town. Water-oriented activities predominate, of course, but other activities include, according the Chamber, "hunting, camping, relaxing, loafing and the Rio Vista Bass Derby." In February, come for the **Crab Feed**, which attracts people from Alaska to San Diego.

Mid-way between Rio Vista and Fairfield you'll find the

Western Railway Museum, *5848 State Highway 12, Suisun City, CA 94585 ((707) 374-2978). Open Sat and Sun, 11-5; July 4th to Labor Day, open Wed-Sun. Adults $4; 4-15, $2; under 4 free. Includes a ride on the Trolley.* This is a living museum, which means that much of the historic equipment is operated (they still run, and you can ride on some). You'll see a New York "El" car, articulated trains that used to run on the San Francisco Bay Bridge, an electric locomotive that hauled President Taft's special train, a tram from Melbourne (Australia), a "Boat Car" from England's Blackpool Beach, and more. These vintage cars are lovingly tended and restored (many are still in the process) by people who "live" the railroad, and are happy to answer all your questions.

Nearby attractions: At the Railway Museum, you're right next door to the **Grizzly Island Wildlife Area,** and also within easy reach of Fairfield, which has several attractions worth a stop (see **Creative Play Puppet Factory, Anheuser-Busch Brewery** and the **Herman Goelitz Candy Factory,** under Fairfield, this chapter).

TIMING HINTS for a Delta Day Trip:
If you take 160 both ways, as far as Route 12, you can easily visit both Grizzly Island and the Railway Museum in one day. If you don't mind a longer day, you could do both attractions and take the "back roads" one way (ideally in the morning).

OR: For a slightly more adventurous, more leisurely and more scenic route, leave 160 at Ryde (just beyond Walnut Grove) and go west to the Howard Landing Ferry (a delightful crossing). Then drive the Ryer Island road to the Ryer Island Ferry and cross again. Now you're 2 miles north of Rio Vista, and you can get right on 12 to either of the two attractions.

OR: For the real explorer's car tour of the Delta, start in West Sacramento (Jefferson Bd. exit off Business 80). Take Jefferson south till it ends, then — if you have a capable map reader with you — you have a multitude of tiny roads to choose from as you wend your way along islands, cross-ing sloughs left and right, getting lost (the islands often don't have road signs), and really getting the feel for the Delta. This is my family's preferred route — combined with at least one of the ferry crossings. If you get as far down as Brannan Island, you can stop for a picnic at Brannan Island State Recreation Area, and see the Visitors' Center of the Delta Natural History Association.

OR: You can cruise the Delta by boat. One agency that specializes in such tours is Delta & Bay Cruises, 372-3690. They offer a 1- or 2-day excursion for $55, that offers boat both ways, or boat one way and bus the other. Reservations are required.

Donner Memorial State Park

I-80, 2 miles west of Truckee ❧ 587-3841. Museum hours: 10-4 daily.

High up on a pass in the Sierra Nevada, the Donner Party, a group of pioneers from the east, were stopped in this last leg of their long journey west by unusually early snows. Completely snowed in, they were forced to winter here, and suffered cruelly from the cold and lack of food. Eventually, several of the party left to find help, and the rescue party that left Sutter's Fort found very few survivors. One of them, an eight-year-old girl named Patty Reed, made it to Sacramento with her only possession, a doll that you can see now at Sutter's Fort.

The heart-rending story of these intrepid people and the hardships they endured is told and interpreted at this State Park. An excellent museum affords a deep understanding of the rigors of pioneer life and of life in the era of western expansion. Very informative for children studying Califor-nia or American history.

Besides the monument and museum, Donner Lake is a beautiful recreation site, with picnic facilities, walking trails and lots of rocks to climb on.

Fairfield

Off I-80 about 65 miles west of Sacramento, beyond Vacaville but not as far as the turn-off for Napa-Sonoma.

There are several wonderful factory tours here; see Tours of the Working World, Chapter 2, for descriptions of **Creative Play Puppets**, the **Herman Goelitz Candy Company** and the **Anheuser-Busch Brewing Company**.

Also of note is Fairfield's **"All Nations' Festival,"** the third weekend in September. Food, dancing, music and all sorts of cultural activities mark this colorful weekend of sights and sounds from around the world. FREE; Sat 10:30-5; Sun 11-5; 429-2569 or 428-6090.

Folsom

This is a leisurely day trip from Sacramento (about 22 miles east on Route 50) that's chock full of history, nature, and lots of places for everyone in the family to have fun. My itinerary will take you into town first, saving the factory-outlet shopping for the afternoon. You may want to skip the shopping altogether and explore more of Folsom's attractions, or simply pick and choose from all the things described here.

Any way you do it, Folsom is a must. Founded in the mid-1800s by Joseph Folsom, it was originally meant to become a "Chicago of the West," located at the confluence of the north and south forks of the American River. It had ample power (visit the historic Powerhouse), the Dam, and it had gold; what more could a town want, to prosper?

But the Transcontinental Railroad passed it by when its route was finally chosen, and Folsom didn't quite expand as originally intended. Which may be just as well. Standing on the rocks at Negro Bar, looking across the river at the bluffs, I have trouble imagining a metropolis cementing over the banks of the river here. Now a city of about 35,000, Folsom has maintained pride in its history as well as in its future, and it's fun to explore for adults and children alike.

From Sacramento, take Highway 50 east to the Folsom Boulevard exit. Follow signs into town (you'll drive past **Natoma Station**, home of about 50 brand-name factory outlet stores). After a few miles, Folsom Boulevard zigs and zags into town and becomes Leidesdorff, after which you'll turn right onto Wool Street. First stop is the **Chamber of Commerce** (200 Wool Street; 985-2698); the building is a restored old railroad station. Pick up a map and whatever brochures sound interesting, and don't miss the pamphlet put out by the Historical Society outlining the 7-mile historic tour. Before you begin, stop by next door at the **Gold Mining Museum** (985-2698). Volunteer Jim Phillips, a gold miner himself, will give your kids a tour of mining artifacts, buildings and memorabilia they'll never forget. Arrange that in advance; Jim isn't always there.

Now take Wool Street east to Natoma Street, left. Turn left on Stafford Street, then immediately right into the parking lot for the **Folsom Zoo** (10-4:15 daily except holidays; closed Mondays; $2 for 13 and up; $1, age 5-12; under 4 free). This unusual place is called the Misfit Zoo. Its inhabitants are animals that otherwise wouldn't have survived, were wounded, or that nobody wanted — like the cross-eyed tiger, or the albino animals that wouldn't survive in the wild. Small but fascinating, it's just the right size for a short, mid-morning stop.

While you're still parked at the Zoo, the kids can hop on board a **Miniature Steam Train** that takes them on a short ride through the countryside (inquire at the Zoo for hours and prices, which vary seasonally). Also near the Zoo are the **Rodeo Grounds**. The Folsom Chamber says their 4th of July Rodeo is the biggest in the country; see Special Events, below.

From Stafford Street again, turn left and continue up Natoma Street about a half mile to the turn-off (left) to **Folsom Prison**. This is the oldest prison in the state, and sits on 3,000 acres of protected wildlife refuge. Geese, wild turkeys, deer, coyotes and other wildlife are a frequent sight here, and you can admire the beautiful stonework of local granite, all built by the prisoners themselves. There's a **Museum** in what used to be the Warden's house, where you can see all kinds of Prison memorabilia (knives fashioned by prisoners, license plates made there, a cannon, photos and others), and a **Hobby Shop**, where you can buy wooden toys, leather goods, jewelry, and other types of souvenirs and toys made by prisoners.

Continue north on Natoma again as it curves to the left and becomes Folsom Dam Road. Before you get to the Dam, there's a large parking area (20 minutes only) where you and the kids can scramble down the rocks to the edge of Folsom Lake. If your kids enjoy climbing or playing at the water's edge, this stop is lots of fun (the only amenity here is a portable toilet in the parking area).

Follow the road over **Folsom Dam**, a smaller version of Hoover Dam. Originally built for flood control in an area unfortunately prone to flooding, it also provides water and power for the greater Sacramento area, maintains the flow of the lower-lying rivers, preserves the fisheries, controls salt-water intrusion in the Sacramento River, and provides water-related recreation. You can tour the Dam by reservation (989-7275, free). The tour is youngster-oriented, with coloring books and other little souvenirs at the end.

Continue around left on the Folsom-Auburn Road; if

you've brought a picnic lunch, you can cross Greenback Lane here and enter **Negro Bar Recreation Area** (named for the black Americans who found gold here; see the Museum). This delightful area has camping, hiking, a bike trail (that goes all the way back to Sacramento), picnic tables, lots of sylvan walk-ways and wonderful, big rocks that make huge, adventure-filled stepping-stones out into the river. A great spot to burn off some energy and enjoy nature.

Back on Greenback Lane, cross the river and stop at the **Historical Powerhouse Museum** (tours arranged by advance reservation, 988-1707; park open 7am-7pm). This was the first plant in the US to successfully transmit high-voltage electricity over long distances (22 miles to Sacramento) for commercial use, built in 1895 (watch for Centennial celebrations in '95). The tour helps you understand how electricity is produced and harnessed. Near where the tour meets, there's a lovely picnic area. About a dozen tables and a barbecue facility (with out-house) look out over the river, and a trail winds down through the trees to the water. From here you can walk back up to the main historic street of town.

Sutter Street, just up the hill from the Powerhouse, is antique-lover's paradise. Shop after shop beckon you and your wallet, interspersed with gift shops and eateries. Down the street two blocks is the **Folsom Historical Museum** (open Wed-Sun, 11-4; free, accepts donations; 985-2707), where you can learn all about Folsom's history, its culture, gold mining. Lots of artifacts and memorabilia, including some hands-on: a stereoscope (first 3-D pictures), a corn grinder (make your own corn meal and take home a recipe with it), an old scale (weigh yourself against the huge weights). Also available are several historical videos, which last about 10-15 minutes each, and gift shop.

Some interesting places to eat along Sutter Street include Patsy's Soda Parlor, the oldest ice cream parlor in California, which features old-fashioned marble tables and wire chairs, decor to match the original telephone exchange (first one in Folsom), and inexpensive food. Also of note are Hop Sing's Chinese Restaurant, and the Sutter Street Grill, where the food is plain, old-fashioned good. For a more elegant meal, try the Cliff House, on the bluff overlooking the Powerhouse, or the Fish Emporium, off Leidesdorff.

Farther east along Highway 50, you can tour the **Gekkeikan Sake Factory** (1136 Sibley Street, Folsom, CA; 985-3111) to see how Sake is produced. Gekkeikan has been produced in Japan for centuries, and recently they opened this facility near Folsom. Stop by between 10am and 5pm any weekday for a 20-minute self-guiding tour. Free. Take the Prairie City exit off 50 east; turn left on Prairie City Road, go about 2 miles, you'll see the Factory on the left, after the 2nd traffic light.

On your way out of town, don't forget the **Factory Outlets** at Natoma Station, on Folsom Boulevard, and Folsom has several other complete recreation areas near the Lake; you can stop at Park Headquarters on Folsom Dam Road where it joins the Auburn Road for complete, up-to-date information (988-0205). And if you still have time on your way back to Sacramento, get off Highway 50 at Hazel Avenue and stop at **Nimbus Dam Recreation Area** and/or **Nimbus Fish Hatchery** (or make this a destination of its own; see chapter 2, Nimbus Fish Hatchery).

Special Events at Folsom (for more details, get the Calendar of Events at the Chamber; unless otherwise indicated, the number for all events is 985-2707): FEB: Anniversary of Sac. Valley Railroad in Folsom. APRIL: Sutter Street Flea Market (622-7349). MAY: Sutter Street Arts & Crafts Faire (622-7349). JUNE: Re-ride of the Pony Express. End of JUNE: Folsom Rodeo Kick-off Barbecue (985-2698). JULY 4 (several days): Rodeo. AUG. 7-15: History Week. OCT: Great Folsom Snail Race (989-9507). DEC: Sutter Street Christmas Celebration.

Fort Ross State Historic Park

Most direct route: I-80 west to Route 1 north, to Fort Ross. This route takes you through San Francisco. If you want to avoid going through the city, take I-80 west to Route 37 west, then 101 north to 116 (towards Guerneville). This becomes a winding, hilly road that really shows you the countryside; <u>not</u> for those who get carsick.

This is a bit of a ride from Sacramento (2 or 2½ hours, depending on which route you take), but definitely worth it. Few people know that Russians inhabited the shores of California back in its period of settlement. Fort Ross ("Ross"- from "Russ"-ia) was their outpost, and a bit of California history worth exploring. Situated on the oceanside cliffs, it offers spectacular scenery (bring warm clothes; the wind can be biting.)

There's a Visitors' Center, and once inside the wooden Fort you can wander through the look-out towers, visit the old Russian church, climb on the cannons, explore how they lived. Self-guiding tour. One thing I didn't learn from this tour but discovered later at Sutter's Fort (see Chapter 1): John Augustus Sutter, the founder of Sacramento, purchased Fort Ross at one time. It didn't turn out to be the best deal of his career, however, and helped hasten his eventual financial demise.

There's a small snack-bar/restaurant and rest rooms; but I recommend you bring your picnic and eat outdoors. This is the place to sit on the rocks or in the vast fields, listen to the surf crashing way down below the cliffs, and imagine what it must have been like to settle the rugged California coast back then. This was survival at its most elemental, and our past can really come alive here. And for

Californians, who are somewhat isolated from the rest of the world simply due to the immense distances involved, it's definitely educational to see here just how close we are to our foreign neighbors.

Ghost Towns

There are lots of these beauties within a day's drive of Sacramento. Defined as a town that's the ghost of its former self, many ghost towns are located in the middle of nowhere, a tribute to the tenacity of treasure-seekers and the hardy souls who followed them. Gold and silver were responsible for most of the west's ghost towns, gold mostly in California, and silver in Nevada.

The closest ones to Sacramento are in Gold Country. Any one of the Gold Country itineraries in the following section is dotted with ghost towns, some of which were as rich in folklore as they were in precious metals. Here's a partial Gold Country list that'll get you started: Angel's Camp, Chinese Camp, Coloma, Columbia, Fiddletown, Jackson, Mokelumne Hill, Murphys, Rough and Ready, Sonora, and Volcano. All of these are still populated.

If you're looking for a true, middle-of-nowhere, deserted ghost town, try Bodie, in eastern Mono County near Mono Lake. During Bodie's heyday in the 1870s, about $75,000,000 worth of gold was removed from the surrounding hills, and much gold still remains. But the only miners left are ghosts. The many remaining buildings, like the Methodist Church, the jail, the school, or the Firehouse with its old hose cart, are in a state of arrested decay. The climate is fierce, so come prepared for scorching heat in summer and icy, unrelenting winds in winter. A visit in either season gives you a true feel for the isolation and hardships the miners and their entourage endured.

Nevada is also littered with the bare remains of what once were thriving mining towns. Some of the best within reach of Sacramento are Goldfield, Berlin, Rhyolite, Ione, Manhattan and Belmont. Off Highway 80 near the Lovelock area, there are about 30 or 40 ghost towns worth exploring. Get information from the Nevada Commission on Tourism, (800) NEVADA-8 (800-638-2328).

When visiting any of the out-of-the-way ghost towns, be sure to have these items in your car: hats, sunscreen, boots (for hiking), flashlight, first-aid kit, jackets, pencils and paper, compass, binoculars, food and water. And remember: rattlesnakes prefer mornings and evenings. Usually they won't attack without provocation, but they can strike without warning (you don't always hear the rattle first). Be sure your little explorers don't turn over any large rocks, or put their hands in holes or under rocks where they can't see.

Further reading about ghost towns: "Gold, Guns and Ghost Towns," by W. A. Chalfant; "Ghost Towns of the West," by Lambert Florin; "Nevada Ghost Towns and Mining Camps," by Stanley Paher.

Gold Country

This is a broad term that covers a lot of territory. The Mother Lode, a gold-bearing quartz vein, extends for over 100 miles along the western edge of the Sierra Nevada, from northeast to southeast of Sacramento, and was the source of many of the incredible chunks of the precious metal dug from the earth during those tempestuous years called the Gold Rush. This is the American dream at its most elemental: rags to riches instantly, if you could endure the harsh conditions of the mining towns that sprang up overnight or the cruel blows that Nature often delivers here in the Foothills.

To tour the Mother Lode country is to begin to understand the nature of the gold-miner, and the essence of what made Sacramento and all of Gold Country what it is today. You could, of course, live here all your life or visit Sacramento without venturing into this singular world; but then you would have only a partial glimpse of a culture unique to these hills and the valleys around them. The Gold Rush was the Sacramento area's childhood; the gold fever that drove men to madness and the ethnic wars, against Chinese, Japanese, anyone who was "different," were the bullying and scrapping of its youth. Sacramento and its environs are now grown up — or at least on the way. What began as an artificial, transplanted hodgepodge culture based solely on greed has developed into a world of inspiring natural beauty, resilience, environmental awareness and cultural diversity that no one visiting Sacramento should miss.

Before you go, especially if you're going to be touring with children, I recommend you contact the Chambers of Commerce and Visitors' Bureaus of Calaveras and Amador Counties (see Chapter 8). They're very friendly, and delighted to help you plan your tour. Your kids can learn a little of the history before you go, and help choose which points of interest to stop at. It's hard to see it all at once; you'll have to go several times.

Before you go, you might want to take a look at a book called Ghost Towns of the West, by Lambert Florin (Promontory Press). According to Mr. Florin's definition of the term, a town that is now "a shadowy semblance of its former self," many of the Gold Country towns are ghost towns. You can decide as you go which ones fit that description. (See "Ghost Towns," above)

I've outlined here three whirlwind family tours of Gold Country — a little history, some of the frivolous, or "touristy," as well as the essential run-around-and-play-stops. My family has discovered favorites along the way, and yours will too. These have become our repeat destinations. Each year in March we drive to Daffodil Hill near Volcano; Calaveras Big Trees State Park is a frequent summer destination; and they haven't yet tired of exploring the Indian ruins and history of Indian Grinding Rocks. The age and interests of your explorers will eventually define your favorite tour of Gold Country.

So load up your water bottles, hats, and walking shoes, and let's head for the hills!

✺ North Mother Lode – Nevada City / Grass Valley / Auburn

Auburn, Nevada City and Grass Valley together form the heart of the northern part of the Mother Lode. Take I-80 east out of Sacramento to Auburn, the county seat of Placer County. You can stop here either going up to or coming down from Nevada City/Grass Valley; I recommend the way back, since the Auburn State Recreation Area is better explored in the afternoon.

Either way, you might want to wander through Auburn by car, following the **Old Town Auburn** tour outlined on the brochure you pick up at the Chamber of Commerce, at 601 Lincoln Way in Old Town (885-5616 or (800) 433-7575). Auburn was founded by a Frenchman, Claude Chana, who was an adventurer and the first fruit grower in Placer County. Auburn Ravine was one of the richest mining valleys in the world. If you happen to be here on Saturday morning, from May to November, don't miss the Foothill Farmers' Market in the Sierra Elm Shopping Center, Highway 59 and Fulweiler Avenue, from 8am-noon, and take home some real Sierra foothill gold.

From Auburn, take Route 49 north to Grass Valley. First you'll want to stop in at the **Grass Valley/Nevada County Chamber of Commerce**, 248 Mill Street (M-F, 8:30am-5pm, Sat 10am-3pm). This building was the home of Lola Montez, famous chanteuse and actress of Gold Rush days. The

Museum has artifacts of Lola Montez as well as history of the County (273-4667), and you can Pick up a Grass Valley Driving or Strolling Tour brochure.

At the **North Star Mining Museum**, located at the end of Mill Street at Allison Ranch Road, you can learn how the mines operated and what powered the monster machinery. They have the largest Pelton Wheel (used to generate power for mining operations) ever constructed, the largest Cornish pump still operational, and lots more fascinating gadgets. See if your little engineers can guess what it's all for! If they're ready for lunch by now, walk across the bridge and sit by the rushing creek for a secluded picnic in a spot just made for throwing stones in the water.

The **Empire Mine**, 10791 East Empire Street, offers an assortment of guided tours throughout the year, as well as Living History Day 4 times a year, an annual Miner's Picnic, Holiday Open House and more. Empire was the longest operating, deepest and richest California mine. Call ahead for detailed information (273-8522)

Depending on the age of your little tourists, you might want to stop at the **Pacific Library**, at the corner of Church and Chapel Streets. This is a collection of about 10,000 old scientific, reference and history books, some dating from the early 16th century. Also early scientific artifacts and pictures. (June-October, noon-3, Wed-Sat-Sun; 272-8188.) And to pique their sense of history, stop in at the **Holbrooke Hotel**, 212 West Main Street, where the hotel register is on display; they can see the signatures of five U.S. presidents, and — of course! — M ark Twain.

And if history or irony are your cup of tea, take a quick drive out Rough & Ready Highway to the town of **Rough & Ready**, west of Grass Valley (named for "Rough & Ready" Zachary Taylor). In 1850, this tiny town made history by seceding from the Union over a mining tax dispute, creating the Great Republic of Rough & Ready. But when the next Fourth of July rolled around, it dawned on all the residents of this new republic that the 4th was no longer their Independence Day. Gradually, the longings for their traditional 4th celebration won out over ire about the tax, and they "re-joined" the Union — and had a rip-roarin' Fourth of July!

Now back to Route 49, up to **Nevada City**, county seat of Nevada County. Visitors are drawn here seasonally by the breathtaking spring and fall colors, and the downtown center is a designated Historical Preservation District. First, pick up a Walking Tour Guide at the Chamber of Commerce, 132 Main Street (265-2692). This lays out a clear, easy-to-follow route past the major points of interest in town. You won't want to miss **Firehouse #1**, one of the most photographed buildings in Gold Country and now a museum, the 1865 **Nevada Theater**, or the **Miner's Foundry Cultural Center**.

Once you're back in your car, be sure to take the drive about 15 miles out to **Malakoff Diggins State Historic Park**, 23579 North Bloomfield Road (265-2740). Gold was discovered here in 1851, and hydraulic mining began about 1853. By 1884, when operations ended, this was the biggest, richest hydraulic gold mine in the world. The town, or camp, called North Bloomfield in its heyday, fits the description of a ghost town: a shadow of its former self. In the early 1880s, the lively town claimed about 1,200 inhabitants. By 1900, there were only about 730. Today, the townsite is restored to look much as it did then, with a museum and camping facilities, and displays in the park's museum tell the story of hydraulic mining and the life of the miners. The site itself is impressive, with its cliffs, pits, and frequent wildlife visitors. But part of the approach road is dirt and gravel and hard on car and riders; kids love it, but an old car might not!

Before you leave Nevada City, if you have a horse lover among you or simply have the time for a leisurely tour, you can take a ride through town in a carriage drawn by an impressive, pure-blooded French Percheron horse (265-5348).

You can find them during the daytime in front of the Buttonworks or the National Hotel, and in the evening in front of Friar Tuck's Restaurant. Look for the "Carriage for Hire" sign.

And if you have a Teddy Bear lover among your ranks, be sure to plan a trip up to Nevada City in April for the **Teddy Bear Convention**. This irresistible gathering of cuddly critters assembles at the **American Victorian Museum** (also called the **Teddy Bear Castle**) for a weekend of merriment guaranteed to gladden the heart of anyone who has ever hugged a bear. Entertainment like the Flying Bear Circus, a Bearbershop Quartet, a Bear Balladeer, a Big Bear Buffet, Teddy Bear Picnics and more. (265-5804)

🍂 Central Mother Lode – Placerville to Auburn

As you drive out to Placerville on Highway 50, the names you'll pass will remind you of your quest: El Dorado Hills, Mother Lode Road, even Placerville (for placer, a type of gold mined here). Begin your day's tour in **Placerville** (see Placerville, this chapter, listed — deservingly — as a separate, whole-day destination). This should take you easily until lunch-time, depending on how in-depth you choose to go; Placerville or Coloma can each fill up a whole day of family fun. From Placerville, take Highway 49 (the '49ers road) 8 miles north to the **Marshall Gold Discovery State Historic Park** in Coloma (622-3470). This is the place where, in 1848, James Marshall found some small shiny flecks in the dirt at his sawmill and forever changed the course of California history.

The Gold Rush was the one of the greatest mass migrations of all time, although you get no sense of that in the sleepy town of Coloma, which only has about 200 year-round residents. But at Christmastime, the town awakens, and thousands of visitors come here for its annual **Christ-**

mas in Coloma celebration. A visit at any time of year is a living history lesson. The **Gold Discovery Museum** has nuggets, a stagecoach and other Gold Rush artifacts, as well as baskets, beads and bone awls of the local Culluma Indians. Wander around **Sutter's Sawmill**, a faithful replica of the one destroyed in 1855. (Small children have fun playing in the water here.)

The actual site where gold was discovered is a quiet lagoon, a remnant of the original mill tailrace. In the **Catholic Cemetery of Coloma** you can see the graves of over 100 pioneers, many of them buried in large family plots (tombstone rubbings are a fun learning activity for children studying history), and a bronze-coated statue of Marshall stands at his grave overlooking the site of his momentous discovery. And if you care to indulge your sense of the macabre, stop by the **Vineyard House**, on Highway 49 and Coldstream Road. Here, ghosts of insane husbands and prisoners who were hanged in the front yard are said to roam the grounds. Maybe you'll just happen to be the next one to see the shimmering apparitions or to hear the chains rattling!

From Coloma, continue heading north on 49 through the **Auburn State Recreation Area**, a good place to stop for a picnic snack and to run off some energy. Just beyond here is **Auburn**, a historic town you can wander through before getting on I-80 for the express ride back to Sacramento. 49 will take you directly into Old Town Auburn, one of the first gold towns and one of the most productive. Contact the Auburn Area Visitors and Convention Bureau at 885-5616 or (800) 433-7575 for brochures and information.

🐚 South Mother Lode — Amador / Calaveras counties

This is a much longer, much richer circuit of Gold Country, that you and your family will eventually cut into chunks to explore more in-depth. It's my family's favorite part of the Mother Lode. It can be divided into "themes": wine country, an extensive cave network or simply the history of the Gold Rush. As you get more familiar with the area you can divide it up into more manageable destinations. This will get you started:

Take Highway 16 east out of Sacramento (called Folsom Boulevard while in Sacramento; accessible from Howe Avenue, Watt Avenue, Bradshaw Avenue or Sunrise Boulevard). Soon you'll pass Murieta Equine Complex (see Horseback Riding, Chapter 3), and you'll begin climbing into the rolling Foothills. If you're into antiques, you'll want to come back to Gold Country without the kids, and just browse through all the little towns that offer an abundance of antique shops.

The first town of any size that you pass is **Amador City**, where you can stop and visit the old **Printing Museum**. No sooner do you roll into town than you roll right back out; Amador is California's smallest city, both in population and city limits. The whole town nestles along the curve in the road, giving you just a glimpse of the flavor of a typical lower Gold Country town — tiny, usually on windy roads, wooden buildings with covered plank sidewalks, and lots of antiques.

The next town you come to is **Sutter Creek**, a delightful mix of balconied buildings, Victorians and New England style buildings. The lovely **Sutter Creek Inn**, 75 Main Street, is home to an apparition that seems to be the spirit of State Senator Edward Voorhies, and another of the Senator's daughter; and occasionally, strange forces have been known to manifest themselves here, such as the one that picked up a cat from a chair and threw it across the room. You can turn here at Sutter Creek for Daffodil Hill, but I recommend you save that for the afternoon (mid-March is best), when the sun is high and the daffodils glow all over the hillsides.

Plan time for a stop at the **Knight Foundry**, on Eureka Street 200 yards east of Main Street (Highway 49). When mines were opening up all over the Mother Lode, this Foundry supplied the heavy equipment; it's the last water-powered foundry and machine shop in the U.S., in continuous operation since 1873. A self-guiding tour explains it all, or call ahead for a tour ((209) 267-1449 or 267-5543). Just past the town is the **Italian Society Park**, site of the annual Italian festival, and just beyond that, stop at the Vista Point exit where you can read the interpretive display indicating the locations of the tremendously productive **Kennedy and Argonaut Mines**, **St. Sava Church**, a Serbian church built a century ago, and the town of **Mokelumne Hill**.

The next stop is **Jackson**, county seat of Amador County. Stop here at the **County Museum**, two blocks north of Main Street at 225 Church Street ((209) 223-6386). Specializing in Mother Lode memorabilia, this museum highlights the North Star mine stamp mill, the famous and oft-photographed Kennedy Mine Tailing Wheel, and the Mine headframe. The Museum is housed in one of Jackson's oldest homes, built in 1859. Also see Indian artifacts, quilts, a School Room and a model railroad locomotive that starred in movies since 1950. If your group is getting hungry by now, Jackson has a wide range of fast food restaurants to speed you on your way.

About 5 miles beyond Jackson you'll pass the stone ruins of the **Butte Store** on your left, an original general store that served the miners around Jackson. You'll also begin to notice a change in the types of trees at this elevation (1,200-1,400 feet). The light, loosely-shaped pines with long needles are called Digger Pines, named for the Digger Indians. The term doesn't refer to a specific tribe or tribal affiliation; it was a name the miners gave to many of the Indians they saw digging for roots and other foods.

As you crest the hill, you can take the Highway 49 Bypass or the Historic Route 49 into the town of **Mokelumne Hill**. There's little difference in terms of time, and I prefer the historic route. It's only a few miles, and you go past old homes, scenic farms and generally take the scenic route, coming into Moke Hill from the back. As you reach the town, on your left you'll see the tiny, stone building that houses the **Mokelumne Hill History Center**, flanked by other historic buildings, such as the **Odd Fellows Building**, the first three-story building in Gold Country. Park here and walk around the corner; on the left you'll pass the **Hotel Leger**, built by George Leger a century ago. George was a French aristocrat who lived — and died — in Room 7 here, and since his death, his ghost has been seen repeatedly gliding through the halls, sometimes laughing with some giggling and equally invisible ladies in the empty room. You can stop for lunch at Nonno's Italian Restaurant in the Hotel, before continuing on to San Andreas.

The **Historical Society and Visitors' Center** in San Andreas, 30 North Main Street ((209) 754-1058) is worth a stop. Upstairs is the **Museum of Indian Lore** and gold-country artifacts, living quarters from the turn of the century, as well as the beautiful restored **County Courthouse**. Of special note is the set of French dishes, fine porcelain made in France with scenes of Gold Country and short, pithy admonitions or observations about life in *Le Far West*. If you can read the French, they're worth the time. Downstairs and behind the museum you can visit the **County Jail** where the notorious highwayman Black Bart was held, as well as a gold assay office. The pleasant garden of native California plants that surrounds these buildings was once the site for the execution of murderers, the most recent of which was in 1888. The jail was in use until 1964.

Children will enjoy the steep road full of dips that twists its way through **Angels Camp**, the next town along Highway 49. Samuel Clemens, or Mark Twain, spent several months in Calaveras County, and began his climb to fame with his story "The Celebrated Jumping Frog of Calaveras County." In return, the **Jumping Frog Jubilee** has put Angels Camp on the map. Each year, in May, the streets and hotels of Angels Camp swell with the numbers of people who come for this weekend of fun, which transforms the town back into a gold-rush boomtown. The Fairgrounds (called "Frogtown") are at the south end of town ((209) 736-3561).

The town was named for Henry Angel, the first store-keeper here. In 1849, nearly 4,000 miners camped here; when surface and placer gold ran out, hard rock mining began, which has left a honeycomb of tunnels below the surface of the town. In its peak period, between 1880 and 1890, over 200 stamp mills (the machines that crushed the rock to reveal the gold contained within) ran day and night around the area. The legend goes that when the last mill stopped stamping, the town was suddenly so quiet that people couldn't sleep!

Note: at this point you're very close to **Columbia State Historic Park**, in Tuolomne County. But since a thorough visit to Columbia takes the better part of a day, I've listed it separately in this chapter.

Now head out of Angels Camp on Route 4 east. In this corner of Gold Country you have a choice of three out-standing caves to visit. Each one is different: **Moaning Cavern**, out of Vallecito, consists of one enormous cavern room, but you can visit it either the "civilized" way, via the spiral stairway, by rappelling on ropes, or by a combination rappelling and crawling through the tights spots on the "Adventure tour" (age 12 and up). **Mercer Caverns**, out of Murphys, a few miles farther on Route 4, is a labyrinth of rooms, caverns, passageways and other neat spots to explore via a series of stairways that take you down a total of 16 stories. **California Caverns**, at Cave City out of San Andreas, is the most extensive, with undergrounds lakes (frequently closed in winter due to flooding), and offers "wild cave" exploration tours as well as easy tours for the whole family. (See Calaveras Big Tree State Park, this chapter, for cave details.)

Note: You can visit one of these caves on a day-long tour of

Gold Country, but for more than that I suggest you make it a whole day of spelunking, OR combine one or more of the caves with a visit to Calaveras Big Trees State Park OR a visit to Columbia State Historic Park (both in this chapter).

Murphys, on Route 4 about 10 miles out of Angels Camp, is a destination in itself. Park anywhere along Main Street, and wander through the small gift shops, antique shops, restaurants, and make sure to stop in at the **Murphys Hotel.** This historic building, constructed in 1855, is on the National Register of Historic Places and is one of the oldest hotels in continuous use, boasting such names in its register as Mark Twain, Horatio Alger, Henry Ward Beecher, John Jacob Aster and C. E. Bolton, or "Black Bart." If you have small children, wander down the little street behind the hotel to play in the delightful playground, complete with rest rooms, picnic tables and shade trees, next to a splashing creek. The best part is the large rocks to climb on. Quiet and off the beaten track, great for when they're tired of history, shopping or being in the car. Near the rest rooms, don't forget to point out the "pokey", Murphys' old one-room jail. (Murphys' 24-hour Visitor Information: (800) 225-3764.)

From Murphys, besides the caves, you can visit various wineries; see Wine Country, this chapter.

When you reach Jackson on the return trip, turn right (east) on Route 88. In about 13 miles, just past Pine Grove, take a small road to the left to **Chaw'Se Indian Grinding Rocks State Historic Park.** The main attraction of the Park is the limestone out-cropping 173 feet by 82 feet. This rock is covered with petroglyphs (rich carvings and mortar holes (called chaw'ses), which the Miwok Indians used to grind acorns and other nuts, seeds and berries. Near the grinding rock are carefully reconstructed Indian buildings, and the Museum features tours of the structures and interpretive exhibits, some of which are hands-on. The Miwok Indians gather here the fourth weekend of September each year for their **Big Time Days**, a time of ceremonial games, dances, handcrafts and food, all of which is open to the public. Camping also available here. ((209) 296-7488)

Continue along the same road to **Volcano**, a tiny, picturesque gold-rush town. As you pull into town, on the left, below the chain-link fence, is a wonderful place to stop and let the kids play and picnic. **Volcano Memorial Park** offers shaded tables, rest rooms and great, big granite rock formations to climb on. After wandering through Volcano, continue along Rams Horn Grade to Daffodil Hill.

In early spring, for about a four-week period usually during March, **Daffodil Hill** is an unforgettable sight. This private ranch has been owned by the same family since it was purchased in 1887 by Arthur and Elizabeth McLaughlin. In early Gold Rush days, is was a regular stopping place for teamsters hauling timber down from the Sierra for the mines, and for east-bound travelers out of Sacramento heading for the Comstock Lode on the Amador-Nevada Wagon Road (Highway 88). Arthur and his wife Lizzie began planting bulbs (mostly daffodils, but not exclusively) on the Hill in 1887, and have been adding to it ever since. Come up for a breathtaking view of real Mother Lode "gold."

You can take the "bigger" road back to Jackson, the way you came up, or take the smaller, windier Shake Ridge Road (or Sutter Creek Road out of Volcano) back to Sutter Creek for the return trip to Sacramento. Consider when planning your trip that a lot of the back roads of Mother Lode country are twisting, winding mountain roads; if any of your travelling crew tends to get carsick, plan extra time to go slowly and stop often. And beware of icy conditions if you come up in the winter.

Note: Gold Panning is still indulged in throughout Gold Country. The rules are simple and few, and the rewards can be enormous — the fun, I mean; although there still is gold to be found, and people do find it during recreational gold-panning, I wouldn't plan on retiring on it. Here are the rules:

- No special permit is required as long as you use hand-operated equipment only. You may pan in any area where there is public access. Prospecting is legal in state and national forest lands as well as Bureau of Land Management property.
- Equipment: Essential is the pan, made of steel or plastic, whatever size feels comfortable. Also a small pick or old screw driver, shovel, tweezers, magnifying glass, a vial, sturdy shoes, suntan oil, a hat and — depending on age and condition — liniment for a backache!
- Where to pan: downstream from fallen trees, below tree roots, near cracks in the bedrock, grass and moss, sand and gravel beds. Stop in a hardware store up in gold country for pointers, or at Columbia State Historic Park to see how it's done.

Gray Lodge Waterfowl Management Area

P.O. Box 37, Gridley, CA 95948 ❧ 846-3315. About 1.5 hours north of Sacramento. Take Highway 99 north to Live Oak. Turn left (west) on Pennington Road, which zigs and zags, eventually turning north and taking you right into the Area.

Gray Lodge is one of the most spectacular marshes in California, home to countless species of wildlife. It lies on 8,400 acres of wetlands on the Pacific Flyway, criss-crossed by miles of roads and levees, with lots of places to stop and view the area from your car. Many of its ponds are surrounded by hiking trails, and two easy hiking loops offer a very satisfying experience of this peaceful sanctuary.

Each season has its specialties — hundreds of species of birds in the summer, along with deer, muskrats and others; fall brings many different types of geese flying south, along with mallards, swans, hawks, grebes, owls, an occasional eagle. In the winter, you can catch sight of myriads of waterfowl — egrets, herons, teal, pintails, bitterns, all filling the air with their calls. In spring, shorebirds feed on invertebrates in the muddy, receding waterlines — stilts, willets, sandpipers. Resident wildlife are drawn to the cool riparian area — river otters, ducks, coyotes, quail, black-tailed deer. Come walk, hike, or ride through for a view of the amazing abundance of California's flora and fauna.

- Museum with restrooms, public phones, drinking water, literature and maps.
- Interpretive Center with displays, disabled access and fishing access.
- Easy hiking for kids — all level.

Gray Lodge is near **Oroville Wildlife Area** and **Lake Oroville**; you might want to combine two or all three of these destinations into a whole-day outdoor excursion. For information, call the Department of Fish and Game, 653-7664.

For a list of other wildlife areas, see Chapter 8, Wildlife Viewing.

Grizzly Island Wildlife Area

2548 Grizzly Island Road, Suisun, CA 94585 ❧ (707) 425-3828. I-80 west to Highway 12 toward Rio Vista. At the stoplight at Sunset Shopping Center, take the Grizzly Island Road about 10 miles to Grizzly Island Complex Headquarters.

At the heart of a sprawling wetland in the Delta (see

Delta, above), these tule-lined ponds are home to hundreds of wildlife species, including California's native tule elk (and, in the past, grizzlies, before they became extinct in California; hence the name). The elk can be seen all year long, as well as waterfowl, river otters, migratory birds, and many others. Wander the miles of level trails for unparalleled wildlife sighting and an intimate experience of California's marshes.

This destination combines well with a trip down the **Delta** (see Delta, above), to **Rio Vista** or to **Fairfield**. For a list of other wildlife areas, see Chapter 8, Wildlife Viewing.

Marine World / Africa USA

Marine World Parkway, Vallejo, CA 94589 ☙ (707) 644-4000, or (707) 644-ORCA for recorded information. I-80 west about 70 miles from Sacramento to Route 37/Marine World Parkway. Follow signs. Open winter: 9:30-5. Summer: 9:30-6. Spring & Fall: 9:30-5:30. From Memorial Day to Labor Day the park is open daily. The rest of the year it's open Wed-Sun. Closed Thanksgiving Day and Christmas Day.

Marine World is the only combination wildlife park and oceanarium in the United States. All of its animal shows, exhibits and attractions offer fun and entertainment as a means to learning, and visitors come as close as possible to many different kinds of animals. Feed giraffes at eye level, walk among exotic butterflies, be a human perch for tropical birds, ride the elephants, touch the tiger, see and learn about our wild friends. It's often hard to choose among all the shows offered all day long — magic, birds, elephants, water skiing and lots more. The Chevron Aquarium lets you touch all kinds of tidal pool residents, new this year is

"Shark Experience:" submerged in a tropical reef, you and yours get up close and personal with this misunderstood, magnificent predator as well as hundreds of other tropical fish. And for those dinosaur-lovers in the family, don't miss the new exhibit called the World of Dinosaurs.

This is a whole-day excursion, and even then you won't see it all. Be sure to bring hats/visors and sun screen in warm weather. Watch for "wet areas" in the marine shows; the first six rows or so can get soaked (those whales can really splash). Schedule your mealtimes <u>not</u> to coincide with the end of the show next door to the snack bar. And if you plan to ride an elephant, schedule that early in the day.

- Whale of a Time World is a kids's play area that offers outstanding opportunities to climb, bounce, build. But I recommend putting off this stop till later in the day; they may not want to leave here to go see the animals!
- Lots of places to eat inside the park: Lakeside Plaza, with umbrella tables and a variety of food (burgers, hot dogs, fish-and-chips, nachos, spaghetti); Pizza Safari; Clocktower Cafe, a full-service restaurant; assorted kiosks and carts throughout the park. Picnic areas are also available.
- Drinking fountains and telephones are located outside all the restrooms. All restrooms (men's and women's) have baby changing areas.
- Stroller and wheelchair rentals (it's all handicapped accessible). Reserve a stroller or wheelchair in advance by calling (707) 644-4000.
- Information Center and storage lockers.
- First Aid station and Lost Children's Care Center.
- Gift Shop.
- Hand-stamping allows you to leave and re-enter (same day only).

Muir Woods National Monument

I-80 west from Sacramento to Route 1, in San Francisco. Route 1 north takes you right to the park, about 20 miles north of the city. If you want to avoid going through the city, exit I-80 onto 580, then take 101 south to Route 1 north.

Named for naturalist John Muir, who so loved the California wilderness, this is the place to enjoy wandering through the stands of coastal redwoods, Sequoia sempervirens, the tallest trees in the world. Numerous trails wind through the big trees, for long or short hikes. There are rest-rooms or outhouses at the head of all trails, a Visitors' Center, and picnic facilities. If your kids enjoyed the high-speed chase through the trees at the end of "Return of the Jedi," they'll love running around here, where it was filmed.

You can easily combine a few trails here with a half-day at Point Reyes National Seashore, just up Route 1 a few more miles (see Point Reyes National Seashore, below).

And bring warm clothing; it can be very chilly. Whenever you head for the northern California coast, remember Mark Twain's famous observation about the weather here: "The coldest winter I ever spent was a summer in San Francisco."

Placerville

Placerville was originally called Dry Diggins (gold diggings where the creeks dried up during the hot season), but many people called it **Old Hangtown**, after the summary justice meted out here back in gold rush days. Later, the name Placerville sprang from the placer gold found here. This is Gold Country in a nutshell — mines, farms, rugged, impressive scenery, and life with a wry sense of humor, an essential ingredient to surviving the rigors of the gold rush.

On your way east from Sacramento on Highway 50, be sure to point out the small herd of **buffalo** as you climb the rise just beyond El Dorado Hills. They usually roam in the golden pasture south (to the right) of the road. (When you reach Bass Lake Road, you've passed them.)

Your first stop in Placerville should be the Chamber of Commerce (542 Main Street, (800) 457-6279; Bedford St. exit off Highway 50). In this unusual old building, which was a theater during the Gold Rush, you can pick up maps and information about Apple Hill, wine country and all the attractions in the area. In this section I'll list some of the big ones; you'll discover more of your own as you wander around this picturesque town and scenic area.

Two words of caution, though, before you set out: parking is awful in Placerville, simply due to topographical limitations. You'll need your car, of course, to get to many of the out-lying attractions, like Apple Hill; but for walking around Old Hangtown, your best bet is to park in the parking structure on Center Street (3 stories; free). And the earlier you get there, the better!

And remember: Placerville is subject to blistering heat during the summer, and fog or snow/rain during the winter. Try to avoid places like Apple Hill, high up and out in the open, during the warmer parts of a summer day, and if possible, schedule a trip down into the **Gold Bug Mine**, where it's always dark and cool, for a summer afternoon. If you come up to Placerville during the winter, always check the weather conditions first.

Apple Hill (Camino, CA 95709; (800) 457-6279) is a tradition among Sacramentans, a fruit-lover's heaven. No fall season is complete without a trip up here. Dozens of ranches sell their crops directly to the public during most of the year: apples, cherries, pears and even cut-your-own Christmas trees. You can cruise from fruit stand to fruit stand, tasting locally-grown fruit and home-made pies, tarts, juices, sauces, and all possible confections made with fruit (other treats as well, like fudge). At some ranches you can pick your own fruit, and there are many wineries that offer tours.

Apple Hill is a treat for the eyes as well as the palate; the lovely, curving and dipping Loop Road that winds among the orchards is a delight in any season. Late in apple season, drive up for the fall colors; in the spring, the sight of the whole mountain in bloom is breathtaking. Some of the apple farms are also wineries; see Wine Country Tour, this chapter. And there are lots of seasonal festivities, like pumpkin patches, scarecrow contests, etc. Call for information.

To get there: Take 50 east out of Placerville about 6 miles, and turn left at the Camino exit. Take Carson Road left, the "loop road." Refer to the Apple Hill map you got at the Chamber; any one of the roads up here will wind you through the participating farms; just follow the little red barn, the Apple Hill symbol, on the signs. One of the best for children is High Hill Ranch (2901 High Hill Rd., 644-1973). Besides the varied assortment of goodies offered at all the ranches, they have a duck pond where kids can play, a pressing room you can tour (see where the apples are pressed for juice), a restaurant, and a winery (see Wine Country Tour, this chapter).

Continue west along Carson Road to the **Institute of Forest Genetics** (2480 Carson Road, Placerville, CA 95667; 622-1225; look for the small sign on the left of the road). Operated by the USDA Forest Service, this is the oldest facility in the world devoted to forest genetics research and tree breeding. They pioneered the science of forest genetics and the production of pine hybrids, and have become internationally recognized as a center for genetic improvement of the pines of the world. They're happy to show you around (call ahead to reserve a tour; free), or you can just wander through the self-guiding Arboretum. In a world where preservation and protection are so important, this tour is wonderfully instructive and fascinating for kids and parents alike, and can help instill an appreciation of the importance of the resources of our planet. Any kid interested in science will love it. Don't miss it!

As you head back to Placerville, turn right off 50 on Bedford Street, and follow it up the hill to the **Gold Bug Mine** (c/o Parks and Recreation, 549 Main Street, Placerville, CA 95667; 622-0832; open April till June on weekends only; open daily, 9am-5pm, June till November 2). Here, tucked away off this tiny street among the old trees, you can descend into the earth and see how gold was mined here, from the 1850s until World War II. There are picnic tables and rest rooms near the entrance, and a little stream where you're welcome to pan for gold. Slightly further up the hill, you can visit the ore crusher, and there's a group picnic area. But be sure to keep an eye on your little ones; rattle snakes are common here, and poison oak is plentiful. Stick to the marked trails at all times.

Now leave your car in the Center Street structure and wander a few blocks along **Main Street**. You'll pass the Bell Tower, a large structure housing the bell that warned folks when another fire broke out (Placerville, like Sacramento, was plagued by fires). Look up on your left and you'll see the **Hangman's Tree**, where an effigy hangs from the second story in recreation of an actual event in 1849. Shops and eateries abound, and don't forget to stop at **Placerville Hardware** (441 Main Street, 622-1151). This place is a museum of memorabilia, one of only two buildings that withstood a disastrous fire that destroyed the rest of the town. Now 141 years old, it's a family-run, old-fashioned hardware store where you'll find things you never dreamed you'd needed! Kids enjoy browsing and figuring out what some of the items are for — especially if they love a mystery! — and if they're studying history in school, Diane will be happy to help them with the history of the area.

Continue along Main Street and stop in at the **Placerville Historic Museum** (affiliated with the **El Dorado County Museum,** on Placerville Road; 621-5865; open 10am-4pm, Wed-Sat; free, but accepts donations gratefully). Here you can get a feel for Gold Country, if you haven't already.

If the coffee houses and little snack stops along Main Street don't quite do it for your eaters, there are three larger, family restaurants at the west end of Main Street, just past the parking structure. Bob's Big Boy is standard family-diner fare; Walt's Family Restaurant is exactly what its name implies; and the Buttercup Pantry also offers good food for reasonable prices. If that still doesn't do it, fast-food can be found at the other end of Main Street (probably not walking distance).

On your way out of town, you can stop by at the historic **Old Cemetery** on Rector Street (call the Chamber for information on whether the steep, torn-up street is open). The Chamber can provide a guide to the tombstones, which reflect the area's colorful history. A popular pastime with kids is to bring along charcoal and newsprint and do tombstone rubbings — great for their class on California history!

And if this tour has just whetted your appetite for more, the Chamber of Commerce can put you in contact with Marcus Wells. This well-informed young man offers personalized tours throughout El Dorado County (Placerville's the county seat), and is well-steeped in local folklore and little-known facts about the area. (800) 457-6279.

Note: Placerville is about 35 miles east of Sacramento on Highway 50. You'll pass Folsom, its Factory Outlet shopping, and the fish hatcheries on the way (see Folsom, this chapter). About ten miles north of Placerville, between 50 and I-80, is the Marshall Gold Discovery State Historic Park in Coloma, which can be combined with your tour of Placerville, or with your day trip up I-80 to Donner State Historic Park. Or it can be a delightful day trip on its own. See Marshall and Donner, this chapter.

Point Reyes National Seashore

On the coast, 30 miles north of San Francisco on Route 1. (415) 663-1092. I-80 west to Vallejo. Then take Route 37 west to 101 south. From 101 you can take a small road across to Olema, just south of the lighthouse, or you can continue to Route 1 north, which takes you right into the park from the south, along the coast. If you opt for Route 1, you'll pass Muir Woods National Monument (see Muir Woods, above), which you can easily combine with Point Reyes for a whole day excursion.

A rugged, wind-swept scenic coastal park, Point Reyes is famous for its hiking trails, its impressive scenery, and for being one of the best **whale-watching** spots on the California coast. (Whale-watching season is from January through March.) The best place for viewing is at the tip of the peninsula, at the **Point Reyes lighthouse**, which juts out into the ocean about 10 miles farther than its surrounding coast (so the whales come closer here than anywhere else).

This makes a spectacular day-trip any time of year, but bring lots of warm clothing for everybody. The wind is usually incessant, and can be quite cold even in the summer. The winding road along the coast is a scenic treat, and there are lots of places to stop, play, climb, take pictures, collect shells.... If you go for the whale-watching, try to avoid the weekend, and if you can't, try to arrive before 11am. Bring binoculars, and check on conditions before leaving home by calling (415) 669-1534. And if you plan to go to the lighthouse, be ready to carry your toddler: there are 300 steps down to it, which seems like at least twice that on the way up — especially if the kids are tired.

Roseville

Roseville is a small city about 25 miles northeast of Sacramento on I-80. To make this a whole-day trip, combine your visit to Denio's Auction and Outdoor Market (see Chapter 2, Shopping or Farmer's Markets, Denio's Auction) or to the Foothill Farmers' Market (Tower Theater Parking lot, May-November, Tuesdays, 3:30-7pm) with a tour of the town.

Exit I-80 on Douglas Boulevard and go west (left) into the old part of town. About a mile down Douglas you'll see signs for **Royer Park**, a large, well-structured park for children (lots of play equipment, rest rooms, a stream for exploring, and completely wheelchair-accessible). A few more blocks down Douglas, turn right on Oak Street to stop at the **Roseville Arts Center**, or the **Haman House**, 424 Oak Street, Roseville, CA 95678 (783-4117); Main Gallery hours: Sun-Fri, 11am-3pm. Free of charge, the Arts Center offers exhibits of nationally renowned artists. Exhibits change every six weeks. They also offer classes for adults and children, performing arts and special events. A block or so from the Haman House is the **Roseville Theater**, which is home to the Magic Circle Theater, P.O. Box 811, Roseville, CA 95661

(782-1777) (see Chapter 3, Performing Arts for Children), which presents children's plays as well as adult comedies, and an occasional musical. A sample of their children's repertoire includes Sleeping Beauty, Peter Rabbit and Cinderella for 1993.

Turn right on Taylor for a stop at the **Roseville Library** (Taylor and Royer Streets), (774-5221). This lovely facility offers changing exhibits, activities for children, and special events. The larger **Maidu Library** is located at Maidu Park, the largest park in Roseville, on Rocky Ridge Drive. (The Maidu were one of the Indian tribes indigenous to the Sacramento area.) In this park you'll find Roseville's Community Center, with activity rooms for games, classes and special-interest programs.

Continue on Oak Street to Washington Boulevard, left, to the **Placer County Fairgrounds**, home of the Placer County Fair in July. For other special events, call the Chamber at 783-8136.

Sonoma

At the foot of the lovely Sonoma Valley, Sonoma is home to the northernmost in the series of California missions, **Mision San Francisco Solano de Sonoma**. Around the town's central Plaza are clustered a concentration of historic buildings to wander through and absorb some of California's past.

Take I-80 west to Route 12 west (you might want to plan a breakfast stop at the **Nut Tree** in Vacaville). For a while, Routes 12 and 29 are contiguous; when you turn onto 29 North, be sure to look to the right for the huge statue on the hill of the little boy pressing grapes. This marks the beginning of wine country, the first in the chain of famous valleys — Napa, Sonoma and Mendocino — that produce so many of the world's distinctive wines.

After Route 12 turns north toward the town of Sonoma, you'll want to stop at the **Sonoma Traintown Railroad**, about a mile south of the town center. This is the stop that will make Sonoma memorable for small children. Take a 20-minute ride on a quarter-scale railroad pulled by an authentically-scaled locomotive, through the "high Sierra Nevada." The steam train will take you through 10 acres of park landscaped to look like the Sierra, complete with quarter-scale gold-mining towns, camps, waterfalls, bridges — and a stop at a petting zoo where you can feed the animals. While you wait for your departure, you can climb all over a full-scale caboose and climb up the control tower. My 7- and 9-year-old engineers gave this place four stars! Stop here in the morning, on your way into town; the line gets long later in the day. (Open 11-5 winter weekends, daily 11-5 summer; (707) 938-3912).)

Drive north into town, around the right side of the Plaza and around behind the historic buildings to the spacious free parking area, complete with shaded picnic tables. Park here, or for two hours on the street, and begin your walking tour of old Sonoma.

The Mission, across from the parking area, had 27 rooms in 1832, but only 5 remain today. Shortly after the construction was completed, Mexico ordered the secularization of the Missions into parish churches. In its brief 11 years of existence, Sonoma Mission had been one of the most successful of all the missions, but it then began a slow decline. Parts were taken, or sold; parts collapsed. Roof timber was re-used, tiles taken. In 1881, a new church was built, and by 1900, only a few rooms of the Mission remained.

Across the street, you can visit the **Barracks** of the Mexican soldiers. Inside are interpretive exhibits about the Indians, Mission life and the environs, and don't forget to go upstairs for a balcony view of the lovely Plaza below. The Toscano Hotel, next door, is a restored hotel where workers boarded; a tour of the dining room and kitchen out back is an interesting hands-on experience for children. Further down the street stop at **La Casa Grande**, the first home of General Vallejo, Commander of the Mexican Army.

In the Plaza you can read the plaque on the **Bear Flag Monument**, commemorating the tumultuous, month-long period when California was a republic. There are also swings, slides, picnic tables, and shade trees for a pleasant lunch stop, and if you didn't bring your own food, stop by at the Bakery and the Cheese Shop, just down the street from the Barracks, and enjoy your freshly-bought delicacies in the Plaza.

Drive west on Spain Street, along the Plaza and west to **General Vallejo's home**, Lachryma Montis. This Victorian style mansion is furnished throughout with many of Vallejo's personal effects. After a brief stop here, continue west to 12 North. Cross to the other side of the Valley on any of the three east-west streets, Boyes Boulevard, Agua Caliente Road or Madrone Road, and continue north on Arnold Drive to London Ranch Road, the entrance to **Jack London State Historic Park**. The parking area offers shaded picnic tables and rest rooms, and the park is open 10-5 daily.

The famous California-born author Jack London and his wife, Charmian, planned to build their mansion here, in the seclusion of these woods. But fate dealt them a cruel blow; about $85,000 into construction and a short time before they were to move in, the place was destroyed by fire. Only the rock wall foundations remain standing. London survived the fire, but it took a great toll on his health and his outlook. After his death, Charmian built a home on the grounds as a monument to him and his work.

At her home, now the **Visitors' Center and Museum**, you can see London's study, his personal and professional effects, the mementoes they brought back from their world travels; interpretive displays explain his life and work. From here, it's a hike of about .6 of a mile, challenging in hot weather, to the site and ruins of **Wolf House**, with a stop along the way at London's grave. (For those who are unable to hike, a shuttle is available.) It's a delightful, sylvan walk, and an inspiring monument to an amazing man.

If your troupe isn't prone to car-sickness, you can take Trinity Road up and over the mountains that separate the Sonoma and Napa Valleys, and drive back down to the highway along the Napa Valley, for some more lovely wine-country scenery. Or simply retrace your steps back down the Sonoma. Of course, all along both valleys you can pull off just about anywhere to visit wineries. For more on that, see Wine Country, this chapter.

And if you're too busy before you go to do any of the getting-ready accumulation of information, there's a handy resource just for you: Trips on Tape, an audio cassette you just pop into your tape player that lets you listen to the tour as you go. They're called "The Rider's Guide to...", and the destinations currently available are San Francisco, the Napa Valley, Sonoma, and the Monterey Peninsula & Big Sur. Their tours begin in San Francisco, though, so if you're starting from Sacramento you'll join the tour mid-way, when it approaches the destination. Available in Bay Area bookstores, or call (510) 653-2553.

South Lake Tahoe

The Gem of the Sierra, Lake Tahoe, draws tourists from all over the world. A knowledge of Sacramento would be incomplete without at least a brief experience of this place of outstanding beauty. Mark Twain called Tahoe "the fairest sight the whole earth affords," and obviously plenty of people agree with him.

Although it's only about 100 miles to South Lake Tahoe, most of it is a steep climb on a two-lane road which is often crowded, so allow between two to two-and-a-half hours to get there. Before you go, here are some places to contact that can send you brochures and information that will help you choose your destination and activities for the day: Lake Tahoe Visitors Authority, P.O. Box 16299, South Lake Tahoe, CA 96151 (544-5050); South Lake Tahoe Chamber of Commerce, 3066 Lake Tahoe Bd., South Lake Tahoe, CA 96150 (541-5255); Tahoe Douglas Chamber, P.O. Box 7139, Round Hill Shopping Center, Lake Tahoe, NV 89449 ((702) 588-4591). For lodging information, call (800) AT TAHOE.

There are lots of things to do with kids at Tahoe. The obvious summer fun is in the water; swimming, waterskiing, playing on the sand, sailboard rental, cycling, fishing, kayaking.... whichever water sport is your favorite, you can do it here. I'll limit my choices for family fun here to South Lake Tahoe, the only part of Tahoe really within what my family considers a day's drive; although if your crew tolerates riding in the car all day with short stops, a drive around the lake, about 72 miles, is filled with incredible vistas and great places to stop, like Emerald Bay. You can get a self-guiding Shoreline tour from the Visitors Authority.

All kids love boat rides; the glass-bottom **Tahoe Queen**, an authentic sternwheeler, cruises Lake Tahoe year 'round, from Ski Run Marina in South Lake Tahoe to Emerald Bay, past the Scandinavian-style mansion, **Vikingsholm** (541-3364). Other cruise boats leave from other points around the lake. You can all spend several hours visiting the **Ponderosa Ranch**, legendary home of television's Cartwright family from "Bonanza." Here you can explore a re-created Western town, pet the animals, play games of skill, enjoy free pony rides and eat (9:30-5, May-Oct; (702) 831-0691).

The South Lake Tahoe area has a **Museum** with historical exhibits about the Tahoe Basin, and you can all go horseback riding at Zephyr Cove, (702) 588-5664 or at Sunset Ranch, 541-9001. All the local Recreation Departments offer day camps, field trips and other kids' activities throughout the summer season, like swimming, track, dances and others; find out about these before you make the drive up (573-2059).

The Forest Service sponsors many outdoor programs throughout the summer, like nature walks, wildflower walks, boat cruises, ranger talks and other interpretive activities that help you understand and appreciate the natural beauty of the Tahoe Basin. One of their special places that's a favorite with kids is the **Taylor Creek Stream Profile Chamber**, where you can watch rainbow trout, Kokanee salmon and other aquatic life through the windows of an underground viewing chamber. Located along the self-guiding Rainbow Tail at the Lake Tahoe Visitors Center, on Route 89 three miles north of South Lake Tahoe; open 8am-5:30pm (573-2674).

One of the best ways to see Tahoe is from above, looking down; notice the ooh's and ah's at the breathtaking view as you crest the Echo Summit on your drive up. You can get some equally breathtaking views on foot, from the many hiking trails, at all levels of difficulty, that abound throughout the Tahoe Basin. Contact the U.S. Forest Service for information (573-2600).

One way to get a general overview of what's available in the area is to drive around the lake. I wouldn't recommend this in mid-summer, since traffic gets pretty awful on the two-lane road; but the Lake Tahoe Visitors Authority has a brochure that outlines the drive with all the sights and historic stops along the way; you can also get a narrated auto cassette of the tour. The brochure is called "the Most Beautiful Drive in America," and it just might be!

If your little sports are up for it, a hike into the **Desolation Wilderness** will lead you to some unforgettable vistas of the Lake and the area. It'll take the better part of the day. Take lots of water (it isn't safe to drink the water from the streams, and it's thirsty hiking), and if you come up during wildflower season, don't forget your camera. Get information about trails, hiking and camping at the Visitors' Center.

Take a hike to a waterfall, swim in an alpine lake, climb a peak, see a castle, go ballooning, para-sailing, take a ski-lift up to eat in the sky.... The possibilities are endless! On the way back from Tahoe, before you reach Echo Summit, you'll pass a small road off to the right that goes to **Echo Lake**. This is one of my family's favorite stops; we always allow extra time at the end of our day at Tahoe for a stop here. At about 7,000 feet, the lake is icy cold and often frozen over in cold weather; you can hike around it for a spectacular view of Tahoe and the basin; there are horse-back trail rides, a water taxi to the upper lake, and a store to buy refreshments.

A visit to Tahoe is like eating chocolates; you can't just stop at one. Each time, you'll discover more "favorite" things to do, and the more you explore it, the more you'll realize just how much more there is that you haven't done. Happy hunting!

Vacaville

In 1841, Manuel Vaca and Felipe Peña received land grants from the King of Spain on this, the most direct and least hazardous route between the eastern states and San Francisco. The original brick **Peña Adobe** still stands as a historical monument west of the city. Of the original Vaca family, only the name remains — but the "Vaca Valley" soon became known as the center of the fruit industry; by the turn of the century, the Valley produced half of all California's deciduous fruit.

As other California valleys began irrigating, the non-irrigated fruit of Vacaville declined in value; but the city has grown nonetheless into the sprawling city you see today. At the **Vacaville Museum**, 213 Buck Avenue (west of Chandler

St.), Vacaville, exhibits change frequently, and focus on different aspects of local history, such as Native American art, Victorian dining or the life of local botanist and conservationist Willis Jepson. Call first for the current topic. The Museum also offers walking tours of the Buck Avenue and downtown district, as well as special events, workshops and classes throughout the year. (Open Wednesday through Sunday, 1-4:30pm; (707) 447-4513.)

The **Nut Tree** is perhaps Vacaville's most well-known attraction. Located on I-80 and Monte Vista Avenue, (707) 448-6411, it's a refreshment/rest stop for those passing through and a destination in itself. The Nut Tree Restaurant offers traditional meals from breakfast through dinner. Kids can ride the little train around the grounds (boarding in front of the gift shop), or play on the many hobby horses (or hobby giraffe), the funny mirrors, and other children's attractions. A separate children's gift shop has lots to tempt and amuse little shoppers, and the gift shop inside the main building requires hours of browsing. Fruits and nuts in all shapes and forms, breads, cakes, odds and ends, souvenirs, clothing, even an intriguing array of gardening-tool sculpture. (No picnicking at the Nut Tree.)

Just down the road from the Nut Tree is the **Nut Tree Factory Store** complex. Shop here for brand names at less-than-retail prices. Over 80 factory outlet stores attract shoppers from all over the Valley; shuttles leave the Sacramento area. Call for information on hours and shuttles, (707) 448-5764.

West of town, on I-80, lies the Pena Adobe Park. You can visit the historical restored adobe home of one of the founders of the city, and enjoy outdoor recreation in this large, grassy park with barbecue facilities, picnic tables, horseshoe courts, a pond and a native Indian garden.

Wine Country

You don't need to drink wine to enjoy a tour of a wine-making facility. It's a fascinating process to take grapes and turn them into wine, and kids can learn about fermentation and other natural and scientific procedures, about vine cultivation or simply enjoy the lovely scenery and locales.

There are three distinct wine regions in northern California easily accessible from Sacramento: Gold Country north, including the Apple Hill wineries in the Placerville area and those out of Nevada City / Grass Valley; the Napa /Sonoma Valley wineries; and the abundant wineries in Gold Country south of Placerville (Amador and Calaveras Counties).

The most well-known at this point are probably the Napa-Sonoma wineries; here, you'll find some of the most familiar names in the world of wines, and you have your choice of over 125 wineries, many of which offer tours of their facilities. But in recent years, wines from smaller, lesser-known northern California wineries have begun to walk away with the prizes internationally. It's no surprise; the climate here is ideal, the soil rich and fertile; it's probably only a matter of time before Gold Country wines rank right up there with the internationally-known products of Europe. After all, that's probably how the traditions started in Europe hundreds of years ago. Just a question of time....

Wherever you decide to go, contact the Chamber of Commerce of the nearest city or county; they have maps of the wineries and all the contact information you'll need. If you're a member of AAA (locally called the CSAA – California State Automobile Association), they have a wonderful map of the Napa and Sonoma County wineries that includes all tour information. Their office is at 4745 Chippendale Drive

(331-7610). The Chambers of Placerville and of Amador and Calaveras Counties also have similar information about their wine region (see Chapter 8, Chambers).

Woodland / Yolo County

Woodland is the County Seat of Yolo County, which lies to the west of Sacramento. Yolo is rural California, a gentle, fruitful land that varies from the completely flat, endless farmland of the Bypass flood-plains to the rolling hills and rugged canyons of the Capay Valley and beyond.

Woodland itself is small, and there's no particular route to see all of its attractions. One obvious way to begin is on **Main Street**, the heart of the central historic street. You can park on the street for up to two hours and just wander; my first stop would be the **Woodland Opera House State Historic Park**, at 320 2nd Street at Main St. and Dead Cat Alley. This red brick Victorian was constructed in 1895, at the edge of what was then the heart of Chinatown, and offers displays of musical instruments, costumes, props, photos and posters. Tours offered on Tuesday, 10-3:30; call for schedule of performances (666-9617). The Plaza in front of the Opera House is home to the **Woodland Farmer's Market**, Thursday, 3-6pm. Just east of there, on the north side of Main Street, is the Woodland Democrat, one of the county's larger newspapers, which offers tours; call 662-5421.

On the south side of Main Street in the same block is Steve's Pizza, a family restaurant that offers a variety of Italian-style items for reasonable prices. A bonus is the wonderful collection of old photographs on the walls here, which afford a glimpse of old Woodland. You might want to pass back this way for your lunch stop; there's also an assortment of family restaurants towards the west end of Main Street.

While you're walking around Main Street, be sure to notice the Decorating Depot on 2nd and Main. This retail store was designed to resemble the Depot that it was originally, when electric trains used to go down Main Street, turn around, stop at the Depot and leave town again through what's now the front door of the store. And stop for a moment in front of The Music Center, on Main between 1st and 2nd Streets. It's the only business on Main Street that has kept its wooden covered sidewalk storefront; all the stores on old Main Street used to look like this.

College Street offers a magnificent assortment of Victorian homes from the 1870s; the Chamber of Commerce (662-7327) sells a complete guide to these outstanding buildings. Also available at the Chamber is a Woodland Walking Tour, which outlines all the County Buildings, like the modern **Courthouse** and the **Library**, which was originally a Carnegie Library and is now on the National Register of Historic Buildings. On the second Saturday of September, the Chamber conducts a walking tour of Woodland's Downtown District.

The center of Woodland history is the **Yolo County Historical Museum**, also called the Gibson House, 512 Gibson Road (666-1045). This Greek revival mansion was built over 100 years ago by gold miner William Byas Gibson, and houses historical artifacts that date from 1850 through 1940. Its furnished rooms illustrate life during the Victorian era, and there's a dairy barn, root cellar and washroom from the original homestead. It sits in a lovely shaded park, where the Historical Society holds its annual Festival on the third Sunday in May. Open M-T, 8-5, and Sat-Sun, 12-4. Free.

If old trucks make your eyes light up, or you enjoy a glimpse of the past, don't miss the **Hayes Antique Truck Museum**, 2000 E. Main St. This is one of the biggest collections of antique trucks anywhere, all assembled under one unassuming warehouse-type roof at the east end of Main Street, past the freeway. Open Saturdays and Sundays, and by appointment; $3 adults, under 12 $1. (666-1044)

The third week of August, Woodland hosts the **County Fair** at the Fairgrounds on East Street. Admission is free, and you can come cheer at a rodeo, a demolition derby or carnival, see all sorts of farm critters, learn about rural life in the Yolo area through all the educational displays. During the Fair, the **Old School House**, which is located on the Fairgrounds, is open by appointment; call the Historical Society (666-1045) to arrange a tour. In one corner of the Fairgrounds, the Sacramento Valley Historic Railways Society is restoring old railroad equipment. During the fair, kids are welcome to climb all over the massive locomotives or whatever rolling stock is there.

Woodland Biomass Power Ltd., 1786 E. Kentucky Avenue, takes wood-waste products and turns them into methane. Children must be at least 16 to tour their facility. Learn about the different types of wood fuel that power the plant, how it's processed, how emissions are controlled. See the computer that controls it all. Call at least 2-3 weeks in advance; tours by pre-arrangement only. Ask for the Plant Engineer or Plant Manager. (661-6095)

The **Yolo Basin Wildlife Area** will soon be the Sacramento area's newest wildlife viewing center. Still in the process of organization, it plans to open to the public in 1994. You can get a free video-tape titled "Yolo Basin: Echoes of our Future," which tells the story of the creation of the Yolo Basin Wildlife Area, or a free newsletter and schedule, by calling 756-7248.

On or around the weekend of February 28th, depending on the seasonal weather, drive out into the countryside west of Woodland and head for the tiny town of Esparto, poised at the entrance to the Capay Valley, for its **Almond Festival**. It begins with a pancake breakfast and a parade, and all weekend you can bask in the incredibly beautiful almond blossoms and the festivities. This little town was laid out by the railroad that eventually became the Southern Pacific, to ship its abundant fruit out of the valley, and it's a lovely, scenic drive up into the rolling hills and canyons of west Yolo County.

And if enjoying nature is what you have in mind, keep going west out of Woodland, through the small town of Winters and on to the **Lake Berryessa Recreation Area**. Here you can indulge in fishing, camping, boating, picnicking, walking or just playing by the water.

7
Family Restaurants

What Napoleon said about his army is equally true about families: they travel on their stomachs. Every excursion is brightened by a little snack at the right time, or a meal when the travellers are getting grumpy. And being prepared is the best way to ensure that mealtimes are a pleasant break in your day of touring and having fun.

Sacramento has more restaurants per capita than most other cities I've been in — and lots of them welcome children. Many of them are family-run, and know that when you come in to eat with children in tow, you require different treatment than a table of adults. That understanding was my criteria for choosing the items in this list. In this chapter you'll find an alphabetical listing of some of the restaurants around the Sacramento area that understand what kids need, what they like, and — maybe most important — what their parents appreciate when eating out with the kids.

Of course, restaurants come and go, names change, buildings disappear. This is a general guide; call first to be sure. And as you get the hang of what to look for, you're sure to find lots of others that we didn't get to.

And keep in mind that prices are up-to-date as of this printing; they'll certainly change.

Happy hunting — and bon appétit!

❧ Baker's Square Restaurant and Pie Shop

2240 Fair Oaks Boulevard, Fair Oaks 95825 ❧
925-4091
2817 Zinfandel Drive, Rancho Cordova 95670 ❧
638-2418
1235 Harbor Boulevard, West Sacramento 95691 ❧
371-8201
Open M-F, 6am-11pm. Fri-Sat, 7am-12 midnight; Sun, 7am-11pm. (Each restaurant's hours many vary slightly.)

Traditional American food and delicious baked goods to eat here or take away. Lunches — burgers or sandwiches — cost between $5 and $7, and complete dinners range between $7.25 and $11. Children's meals are smaller portions and prices, with high chairs and booster seats available. They don't have any birthday specials, but they will put a candle in your dessert and sing to you.

❧ Black-Eyed Pea Restaurant
7217 Greenback Lane, Citrus Heights 95610 ❧
721-6668

Their "Little Pea-Ple's Menu" includes just about everything a kid could want — grilled cheese, fish sticks, meat loaf, hamburgers — simple meals, portions a kid can handle, and simple desserts. My picky eaters ate heartily. Kids' meals range from $2.49 to $3.39, which includes a drink (soft drink or milk) and fries or other vegetable.

For adults, sandwiches begin at $3.85, appetizers like fried mushrooms and chicken fingers start at $2.95, and complete dinners, including vegetable and potatoes, start at $5.99. The most expensive dinner on the menu, home-style turkey with stuffing and mashed potatoes, was about $6.75. Clearly you won't break the bank here, and the food is home-style delicious. But beware of the acoustics; this isn't the place to come for quiet dinner conversation. Its high ceilings and open floor-plan make all sound bounce and echo such that it's difficult to converse. Can be just the thing for kids!

❧ Bobby McGee's
5623 Sunrise Boulevard, Citrus Heights ❧ *966-1364.*
4-10pm daily.

Prices here are a little higher than at most of the other restaurants on this list, but it's an indulgence your family will enjoy. Servers are dressed in costume here; your children may spot their favorite fantasy character — who may even serve them their dinner. Dinners range from about $12.95 to about $28.95 (for lobster tail combination). There's a special kids' menu, with all the kids' favorites — grilled cheese, cheeseburgers, spaghetti, even fried shrimp, from $2.75 to $3.95. And for your birthday they'll bring you a cake, sing to you, and even take your picture.

ꙮ Bradshaw's and Brookfield's Family Restaurant

9647 Micron Avenue, Sacramento 95827 ꙮ362-3274
4343 Madison Avenue, Sacramento 95842 ꙮ332-0108
11135 Folsom Boulevard, Rancho Cordova ꙮ638-0733
Open 6:30am-11pm, Sun-Thurs. 6:30-midnight, Sat-Sun.
Lunch can be ordered any time after 10am, and dinner, any
time after 11am.

Brookfield's and Bradshaw's restaurants have been run by the same family since 1981. It's good, solid standard family fare, with enough choices for everybody. For a dinner of steak, chicken, prime rib, etc., prices range around $6.95-7.95. Especialidades Grandes is a whole list of Mexican and other specialties (like fish-and-chips), between $5.65-6.25. Desserts — ice cream, delicious deep-dish pies, banana splits — go for about $1.65-3.25. There's lots of seating, so even when there's a line at the door, the wait isn't long, and there are always lots of families here.

- Special children's menu, special prices and a color-it-in menu to keep. Kids can have dinner from $2.39 up; all kids meals include a drink (milk, juice, soft drink or hot chocolate). Dessert is a chocolate chip cookie or a scoop of ice cream for $.25.
- Special senior's menu available.

ꙮ Chevy's

5801 Cypress Avenue, Carmichael 95608 ꙮ483-0782
1369 Garden Highway, Sacramento 95833 ꙮ649-0390
1234 Howe Avenue, Sacramento 95825 ꙮ923-6574
7778 La Mancha Way, Sacramento 95823 ꙮ688-8455
Hours vary at each location; call first.

When they say "Fresh Mex," they mean fresh! If your brood enjoys Mexican food, this place'll please both young and old. The first thing the kids notice is "El Machino," the tortilla-maker (Ed, at the Carmichael restaurant, calls it his "automated baby-sitter"). Mine can stand and watch it work as long as it takes Mom or Dad to finish dinner. On some days there's a balloon artist making balloon creations for the kids.

Special kids' meals, which start at about $2.95, come in a basket and contain lots of small items (like a section of an ear of corn, a piece of melon, chips, etc. to go with the flauta, taco, cheeseburger or more); the pickiest eater will find something to fill up on. All Kiddie Meals come with a Kiddie Cone of ice cream. You can pay between $6.95-$13.95 for an adult dinner, also filling and delicious.

But after the meal comes the real treat: the tour of the kitchen. Kids enjoy seeing all the machines at work making the fresh food, and stepping into the freezer. The best part is the machine that produces that little blobs of masa (corn-meal flour) that will become tortillas. Tours are always available to customers, but be reasonable: if it's Friday night, they may ask you to come back at a slower time so they can devote the time necessary to show you around.

For birthdays, the staff will come sing to you at your table, and you'll leave with a huge Mexican sombrero to remember the day by.

∾ Chuck E. Cheese Pizza

1690 Arden Way, Sacramento ∾ 920-9181
6251 Sunrise Avenue, Citrus Heights ∾ 723-1751
Open each day at 11am; Fri and Sat till 11pm, Sun till 10pm.

A great place to play, although not necessarily to eat. Some kids get too wound up here to sit and eat a whole meal. Mechanized, singing creatures, waving flags, video monitors blaring, and games, games, games! (And noise, noise, noise!) You get tokens with each food purchase, for use in the games and rides (extra tokens can be purchased). Tickets earned by playing can be redeemed for gifts. Pizzas are competitively priced, free refills on drinks. Birthday parties. Not a peaceful place for a meal, but lots of fun.

∾ Coco's Family Restaurant

1830 Arden Way, Sacramento 95815 ∾ 922-6741. Open Sun-Thurs, 6am-11pm; Fri-Sat, 6am-midnight.

Traditional American food for reasonable prices. Coco's

has a Child's Menu that offers small-portion meals between $1.99 - $2.85, and for bigger people, a full dinner can range from $5 - about $10. Nothing fancy, just plain good food.

∾ Eat Your Vegetables

1841 Howe Avenue, Sacramento 95825 ∾ 922-8413. Open M-Sat, 11:30am-9pm. Sun, 12-8pm. Closed 10 days at Christmastime, and on Thanksgiving Day.

Even if your kids break out in hives at the mention of vegetables, they'll probably find something to eat at this unusual vegetarian restaurant. The wide selections of all-you-can-eat cafeteria-style food (home-made, or home-style) have won awards, and account for the steady stream of customers.

You pay for a one- or two-item meal, and that entitles you to the all-you-can-eat salad bar, muffins, pizza bread, fruits, homemade soups (delicious!) and more. For example, a child (6-12) can order a huge baked potato or soup for $2.99, and eat as much as he can to go with it of muffins, pizza bread, ice cream dessert, fruit compote... Adult one-items entrees start at $4.95. Even if you buy several extra entrees, with all the selection of the all-you-can-eat bar, you can really fill up on fresh, home-style fare without making a hole in your budget. And it's so good, you won't notice there's no meat or fish.

Under 5 begins at $.94 per item; special discounts for over 65.

∾ The Fifties Drive-In

7310 Fair Oaks Boulevard, Carmichael 95608 ∾ 482-6357. Open 6am-10pm, Mon-Thurs.; 6am-11pm, Fri-Sat. Closed Sunday.

The first thing kids notice is the cars sticking out of the walls outside — but just wait'll they get inside! If you're old enough to remember family diners from the 50s, you'll be whisked instantly back to your childhood. Kids, of course, just think it's "cool" — half bodies of 50s-model cars, table-tops covered with old comics, Formica counters with twirling stools — even the old songs.

They offer a Blue Plate Special — of course — for dinner ($5.95) and lunch ($3.50 or $4.95), and the usual assortment of diner food, reasonably priced. Special kids' meals cost $3.99 for dinner: burgers, grilled cheese, hot dog or fish fillet, all served w/chips and a drink, and other kids' items begin at $.75; highest-priced kids' meal, spaghetti and meat sauce, is $3.45. Kids can keep their special menu to color (with house Crayons at your table).

But the best part of the kids' meals is the service. Each meal is brought out in little cars, like the ones stuck in the walls, which the kids can keep. And while you're waiting for your meals to be served, you can wander around, read the other table-tops, play in the cars. Take your kids' picture with the replica of the Statue of Liberty. If you call ahead and reserve a car, you or your kids can eat their meal in it — a great way for Mom and Dad to have a peaceful meal "alone"!

This is a neat place to have a birthday party, too. Bring your own cake (order food from the menu), and every child in the party will receive a free balloon and sundae. There's a separate room that seats about 20 children; they suggest you call ahead for large groups.

❧ Fuji Restaurant

2422 13th Street, Sacramento 95818 ❧ 446-4135. Lunch, 10:30am-2pm. Dinner: Mon-Thur, 5-9:30pm; Fri-Sat, 5-9:45pm; Sun, 4:30-9pm. Business 80 to 16th Street exit, left under freeway and right on Broadway.

Fuji serves delicious Japanese food in authentic atmosphere. They have no special children's menu, but I often see lots of children there, and my own little eaters always find something to their liking that comes in small portions.

For $3.15-$7.50 you can get appetizers that can serve as a child's meal, like small chunks of beef or chicken served on a skewer. With rice, it's just enough. For adults, you can gat dinner a la carte from $6.15-$16.50, with sushi from $3.85 up. Their deluxe combination dinners are very filling, and offer an assortment of tempting things like tempura, teriyaki, sashimi, sushi and vegetables, all beautifully arranged and delicious. If you enjoy good Japanese cuisine, don't miss this.

❧ Futami Japanese Restaurant

5609 Freeport Boulevard, Sacramento 95822 ❧ 427-7628. Daily 11:30-9. I-5 or Highway 99 to Fruitridge exit east to Freeport. Just off the south-east corner.

Food here is traditional and authentic Japanese. Sushi, sashimi, teriyaki, tempura, and all combinations thereof, starting about $3.95. Their family combination dinners, beginning at about $8.95, are copious and everyone will find something delicious and satisfying to eat.

❧ Garbeau's Dinner Theater

12401 Folsom Boulevard, Rancho Cordova ❧ 985-6361. Saturday brunch buffet starts at 1pm. Highway 50 east to Hazel Avenue exit. Located in the Nimbus Winery Mall.

A combination restaurant-theater, Garbeau's Saturday brunch buffet performance is usually sold out. The plays are all suitable for children, and the menu includes lots of things kids will eat, like fish sticks, macaroni and cheese, grilled cheese sandwiches, and other culinary delights of kid-dom (plus lots of adult food). For $10 for kids and $12 for adults, you get a copious brunch (beverage and tax included) and an original, hour-long live theater performance. An experience for kids and grown-ups alike.

❧ Good Earth Restaurant

2024 Arden Way, Sacramento ❧ 920-5544. Weekdays, 7am-10pm; weekends, 8am-11pm. Business 80 to Arden Way or Exposition Boulevard exit east; restaurant is just after the Arden-Expo separation. If you're going west on Arden, it's impossible to turn into the restaurant; keep going straight on Exposition and U-turn back.

Good food <u>and</u> good for you? The Good Earth proves that healthful food can be delicious. All of their bread and rolls are ten-grain; even their desserts are healthful — yogurts, fresh fruit shakes (with high protein powder, on request), pumpkin walnut bread and more. Delicious, whole-some soup for $2.25 or $2.95; soup and one of their mag-nificent salads make a copious meal. Full dinners range from $7.25 to $9.95, sandwiches start at $5.45, and for kids 12 and under, there are about 11 smaller-portion meals to choose from, for $1.95 - $3.55 (plus crayons and kids' menus to color). Their fish specials are a good deal, and their shrimp fettuccine with broccoli is this diner's favorite.

❧ Huey's Diner

2100 Arden Way, Sacramento ❧ 929-1950
805 Harbor Boulevard, West Sacramento 95691 ❧
372-1958

There are always lots of kids at Huey's; they enjoy the "old-fashioned" fifties atmosphere, and their parents or grandparents can enjoy the nostalgia. The food is diner food — remember that? Their Little Dinner for kids is $1.99, for a choice of hot dog, hamburger, grilled cheese or junior hot turkey with milk or a soft drink. Breakfast for kids is also $1.99. A Baby Huey sundae for dessert is $.99. For big people, dinners range from $6.99 to about $8.99, with sand-wiches between $4.75-$6.25, and side order ranging from $1.75 for fries to $7.99 for baby back ribs.

❧ International House of Pancakes

3445 El Camino Avenue, Sacramento 95821 ❧ 482-9045
4770 Florin Road, Sacramento 95823 ❧ 392-1125
2216 Sunrise Boulevard, Rancho Cordova 95670 ❧
638-8853
Open 24 hours daily.

If your kids enjoy pancakes, you have to try this. But IHOP isn't only for breakfast — although their breakfast is a good deal, at $2.99 for pancakes, eggs, and bacon or sau-sages. You can get a full family-style dinner, choice of tur-key, pot roast, roast chicken or fried chicken plus side dishes, for $4.99. And between 4 and 10pm, Monday through Thurs-day, 1 child eats free for every adult meal purchased (may vary by restaurant).

❧ Izzy's Pizza Restaurant

3174 Arden Way, Sacramento 95825 ❧ 971-9855
7271 Franklin Boulevard, Sacramento 95823 ❧
393-3601
Open daily 11am-10pm; open Fri and Sat till 11pm.

Izzy's Great Pizza Feed is a great deal: one time through the copious salad bar, and all-you-can-eat pizza and cinnamon rolls from the buffet, for $4.95 per person; children up to 12, $.30 per year of age. Sandwiches range from $2.75 - $5.75, and you can get any combination of their fresh, hot soup, breads, rolls, salad or sandwiches, from $2.45 to $4.75. They have pizza, chicken, lasagna, soups and other wholesome, filling meals for similar low prices. And on Mondays and Tuesdays, kids 8 or under eat free at Izzy's (one for each adult meal purchased).

❧ J. J. North's Buffet

5999 Florin Road, Sacramento 95823 ❧ 392-4060
1030 Howe Avenue, Sacramento 95825 ❧ 922-5577
2342 Sunrise Boulevard, Rancho Cordova 95670 ❧
852-0188

You won't break the bank going the length of this 32-ft.-long buffet. They serve traditional "American-style" fare — roast beef, ham, veggies, potatoes, etc. Tuesday and Saturday are Barbecue days, and Wednesday is Oriental food day. Breakfast and lunch are in the $5-6 range, and dinner costs about $7.

Tuesday is "Family night," complete with a clown who visits tables doing magic tricks and other entertaining things. Sunday offers all-you-can-eat brunch for $5.39. And on all days, kids pay the unbeatable price of $.45 per year of age, up to 12. They also have discounts for seniors. Their prices are changing slightly in March 1993, but it's still unbeatable deal.

❧ Jim Boy's Tacos

4708 Auburn Boulevard ❧ 334-6612
3033 Arden Way ❧ 485-6616

3200 Fulton Avenue ❧ *485-6501*
7401 Fair Oaks Boulevard, Carmichael ❧ *972-8226*
Open Mon-Thurs, 10:30am-9:30pm; Fri, 10:30am-10pm;
Sat-Sun, 11am-9:30 (may vary by location).

More than just tacos, this is a great place to eat out with small children without worrying about social graces. Tacos, which most kids will eat, no matter how picky, cost $.89 ($.69 on Sundays). Probably their best deal is the Fiesta Dinner; you get a beef taco, an enchilada, refried beans, rice and salad, all for $4.85 ($5.39 for a chicken taco with that). High chairs and booster seats available; some Jim Boy's have television, or video games, or something to keep those little bodies busy while Mom and Dad eat!

❧ La Boulangerie

There are about a dozen of these little French-style coffee house/restaurants scattered throughout the greater Sacramento area. Breads, muffins, soups, sandwiches, salads, sweets and drinks. Kids enjoy sitting at their outdoor tables — great for people-watching! Their fresh, crusty French bread hot out of the oven, with chocolate milk, is the treat of choice for my little gourmets. Yours will find something yummy here. A great place for a mid-afternoon snack, or light lunch. Check the White Pages under "La Bou."

❧ Leatherby's Family Creamery

2333 A Arden Way, Sacramento ❧ *920-8382. Open daily.*
11am-11pm in winter months; 11am-midnight during
summer months. Arden Way exit off Business 80, take
Arden Way east. Located between Fulton and Bell.

Dave and Sally Leatherby started the Creamery in 1982, and since then it's been voted the best ice cream in town by several newspaper polls. "Quality is the key to our success," says Dave Leatherby Sr. Everything here is made fresh daily, including the ice cream. For a treat after your taste treat, go behind the scenes for Dave's tour of the freezer and how they make the delicious stuff. Their ice cream is 14% butterfat and 100% scrumptious!

They offer separate kids' menus, with smaller portions

(and prices): sandwiches, soups, salads, and of course, lots of ways to eat their rich, homemade ice cream. For an idea of prices, hamburgers cost about $3.25. But that's not fast food; Dave Sr.'s philosophy is "generous portions" — and their fries are delicious. There's a special meal deal: your choice of a sandwich with soup and a drink, a junior dish and drink, a junior sundae and a drink, or a kid's shake. Prices from $3.25 to $5.29.

They also offer a birthday party special for children under 10 (minimum 5). For $3.25 per child, each one gets a hot dog or sandwich, small drink, a sundae and a party hat. Or for $2.29, each gets a small drink, child's sundae and a party hat. During the summer (ice cream weather), says Dave Sr., it's best to call and reserve for a party; when it's cold out, you can just come in. The restaurant seats about 200, so there's almost always room. And if you like their sauces, you can take some home from their gift shop.

～ Long John Silver's Seafood Shoppe

5245 Auburn Boulevard, Sacramento 95841 ～ 334-1311
1001 Howe Avenue, Sacramento 95825 ～ 929-5889
4219 Marconi Avenue, Sacramento 95821 ～ 485-9135
3298 Northgate Boulevard, Sacramento 95833 ～
649-1836
7228 Stockton Boulevard, Sacramento 95823 ～ 421-4907
Open 11am-9:30pm daily (Fridays, open till 10pm).

Not exactly fast food, not fine dining, something in between. Dinners, which include various combinations of fish, seafood and chicken with fries, salad, and a "hush puppy," range from $3.89 to $4.99. Kids can get a dinner of fish or chicken, fries and a drink for $1.99.

～ Old Spaghetti Factory

1910 J St, Sacramento 95814 ～ 443-2862
12401 Folsom Road, Rancho Cordova ～ 985-0822
Lunch: Mon-Fri, 11:30am-2pm. Dinner: Mon-Thurs, 5-10pm; Fri-Sat, 4:30-10:30pm; Sun 4-10pm. Downtown: I-80 to J Street or 16th Street exit, or I-5 to J Street exit. Rancho Cordova: Highway 50 to Sunrise exit.

Kids, kids, kids — you see lots of 'em here! The "Factory" was originally the train station, and inside there's even a trolley car you can eat in. The decor is turn-of-the-century, and the dark wood is off-set by antiques. But it isn't as expensive as it looks. You can buy dinner for a family of four for about $25-30 and up, without extras like cocktails or desserts.

They have special children's menus for lunch and dinner, with smaller portions, for $2.95-$3.75. Good, traditional Italian and American food. But if you don't enjoy waiting, don't come here on a Friday night; the crowd backs up at the door and you can wait between a half hour and an hour, or more.

～ Sizzler Family Restaurant

5825 Madison Avenue, Sacramento 95841 ～ *344-5824*
2107 Fulton Avenue, Sacramento ～ *481-2282*
8353 Folsom Boulevard, Sacramento ～ *381-3375*
7811 Greenback Lane, Citrus Heights ～ *722-7443*
2204 Sunrise Boulevard, Rancho Cordova ～ *635-2202*

This place packs in the kids. Their Buffet Court (all you can eat salad and dessert bars) has something for everyone, and kids enjoy making their own tacos, salads (including fruits in season) and yummy desserts (cakes, ice cream they pump themselves and all sorts of toppings). Lunch prices start about $1.99 for a kid's meal: burger and potato of your choice. Steak lunch starts at about $4.99. For dinner they have all kinds of chicken, steak and combinations of steak with seafoods, starting at about $6.99, and you can get a kid's meal for about $1.99.

They offer a copious, reasonable Sunday brunch with pancakes, waffles, eggs, toast, just about everything kids dream of for breakfast or brunch, $.399 for kids 10 and under, $.6.99 for adults. And they don't mind if toddlers share from their Mom's or Dad's plate. They'll even sing to you on your birthday, and to top off the meal in the right mood, they bring you lollipops for the kids. I've never been here when there weren't lots of kids, and my own little gourmets gave this place two thumbs up.

❧ Skipper's

Many locations throughout Sacramento and other cities.

Fish, shrimp, or chicken accompanied by fries, potatoes, corn muffins, coleslaw or Jell-O. Even the most finicky eater will find something here. Special kids' plate combinations for 12 and under, served with fries, Jell-O and a Fun Surprise. Priced like fast food, but a nice change of pace from hamburgers.

❧ Strings the Pasta Place

4848 Madison Avenue, Sacramento 95841 ❧ 348-1925
2517 Fair Oaks Boulevard, Sacramento 95825 ❧ 483-9797
7235 Franklin Boulevard, Sacramento 95823 ❧ 395-5711

What kid doesn't like pasta of one sort or another? Their Kids' Menu offers them a choice of pastas with a pick-your-own sauce (on top, or on the side) for $1.95, or a small cheese pizza for $2.95. For adults, prices range from about $5.50 for spaghetti, to about $8.95 for the usual assortment of Italian favorites. Not real Italian style, the way I remember it, but satisfying. Their desserts and ice creams were a little too exotic for my small diners' palates, but the balloons made up for it.

❦ 8 ❦
Resources

I f you haven't found what you're looking for in the previous chapters, this one will help you find it, or find out how or where to find it.

Convention and Visitors' Bureaus

This listing includes greater Sacramento as well as places listed under Chapter 6, Day Trips.

AMADOR COUNTY Chamber of Commerce
P.O. Box 596, Jackson, CA 95642 ☎ (209) 223-0350
AUBURN Chamber of Commerce
601 Lincoln Way, Auburn, CA 95603 ☎ 885-5616
CALAVERAS COUNTY Chamber of Commerce
P.O. Box 115, San Andreas, CA 95149 ☎ 1-(800) 225-3764
CONCORD Chamber of Commerce
2151 A, Salvio St., Concord, CA 94520 ☎ (510) 685-1181
DAVIS AREA Chamber of Commerce
228 B St., Davis, CA 95616 ☎ 756-5160
FOLSOM Chamber of Commerce
200 Wool St., Folsom, CA 95630 ☎ 985-2698
GALT AREA Chamber of Commerce
P.O. Box 442, Galt, CA 95632 ☎ (209) 745-2529
GRASS VALLEY Chamber of Commerce
248 Mill St., Grass Valley, CA 95945 ☎ 273-4667
LODI DISTRICT Chamber of Commerce
P.O. Box 386, Lodi, CA 95241 ☎ (209) 334-4773
NAPA COUNTY Chamber of Commerce
P.O. Box 636, Napa, CA 94559 ☎ (707) 226-7455
NEVADA CITY Chamber of Commerce
132 Main St., Nevada City, CA 95959 ☎ 265-2692
PLACERVILLE Chamber of Commerce
542 Main St., Placerville, CA 95667 ☎ (800) 457-6279
RIO VISTA Chamber of Commerce
60 Main St., Rio Vista, CA 94571 ☎ (707) 374-2700
ROSEVILLE Chamber of Commerce
650 Douglas Bd., Roseville, CA 95671 ☎ 783-8136
SACRAMENTO Convention and Visitors' Bureau
1421 K Street, Sacramento, CA 95814 ☎ 264-7777

SACRAMENTO DOWNTOWN DISTRICT (Special Events)
717 K Street, Sacramento, CA 95814 ~ 442-8575
SACRAMENTO STATE Chamber of Commerce
1201 K Street, Sacramento, CA 95814 ~ 444-6670
SOUTH LAKE TAHOE Chamber of Commerce
3066 South Lake Tahoe Bd., South Lake Tahoe, CA 96150 ~
    541-5255
STOCKTON Chamber of Commerce
445 W. Weber St. #250, Stockton, CA 95203 ~ (209) 466-7066
VACAVILLE Chamber of Commerce
400 E. Monte Vista Av., Vacaville, CA 95688 ~ (707) 448-6424
WEST SACRAMENTO Chamber of Commerce
1414 Merkley Bd., West Sacramento, CA 95691 ~ 371-7042
WOODLAND Chamber of Commerce
520 Main St., Woodland, CA 95695 ~ 662-7327
YUBA-SUTTER Chamber of Commerce
P.O. Box 1429, Marysville, CA 95901 ~ 743-6501

Top 20 Places to Go in Sacramento

Cal-Expo (Fair, Expositions and Waterworld)
California State Indian Museum
California State Railroad Museum
Community Center
Crocker Museum
Effie Yeaw Nature Center and Hoffman Park
Fairytale Town and William Land Park
Governor's Mansion
McClellan Aviation Museum
The Mine Shaft
Nimbus Fish Hatchery / American River Fish Hatchery
Old Sacramento
Port of Sacramento
Sacramento Museum of History, Science and Technology
(formerly the Sacramento History Museum and the Sacramento Science Center)

Sacramento Public Library (Central Branch)
Sacramento Zoo
Scandia Family Fun Center
State Capitol and Park
Sutter's Fort
Visionarium

Free Activities/Outings for Families

American River Fish Hatchery
American River College free outdoor concerts (spring)
Art Galleries
Bookstores
Cathedral of the Blessed Sacrament
Children's Festival
Concerts in the Parks
Downtown Plaza
Effie Yeaw Nature Center
Farmer's Markets
Heritage Day Parade
Hotel Hopping
K-Street Mall
Kite-Flying Day
Nimbus Fish Hatchery
Nurseries
Old Sacramento
Parks
Pet Shops
Playgrounds
Port of Sacramento
Public Libraries
Sacramento <u>Bee</u> (tour)
Sacramento Metropolitan Airport
Sacramento Science Center Nature Walk

Sacramento Symphony Summer Outdoor Concerts
Santa's Parade
Shakespeare in William Land Park
Shopping Malls
State Capitol Tour
Toy Stores
William Land Park
Winterfest (K-Street Mall at Christmastime)

Birthday Party Ideas

ATA Taekwondo Centers, 2621 Alta Arden Way (for a list of other centers, see Chapter 4, Martial Arts, or call). Bring the gang — and the energy! Birthday party package includes Taekwondo demonstrations, workouts for all kids, games and more. You supply the goodies (cake, etc.), they supply the fun. Reasonable. (481-9693)

Byers Gymnastics Center. For 1½ hours, two coaches run your Olympic-theme party. Organized non-competitive games, then an ice cream cake, fruit juice and all the necessary paper goods. The coaches do it all; you can relax and enjoy (or have your own party while you watch them do all the work!). $85 for up to 10 children ($5 each additional child, to 15). The birthday kid gets an "Olympic medal," and everyone gets a balloon. (447-4966)

Trish Chancey, P.O. Box 5035, Fair Oaks, CA 95628. Trish specializes in children's music, and can liven up any party (not only birthdays) with traditional and original sing-alongs that kids love to join in. For about $85, you get an hour of live music plus some magic tricks, balloon animals and a pre-party personalized card for the birthday kid. For a few dollars more, she'll bring along a cassette of her birthday favorites and autograph it.

Chuck E. Cheese Pizza. If you can stand the noise, the kids'll have a great time in this kids' wonderland of a restaurant! For $5.69 per child (minimum 6), you get 1 large pizza with 2 toppings and a pitcher of soft drinks for each 6 children. The birthday kid gets a personal pizza, 10 game tokens and a T-shirt. A hostess will help serve at your 1½-hour long party. Call at least a month in advance. (Arden Way, Sac. 920-9181; Sunrise Bd., Citrus Heights, 723-1751. See Chapter 7.)

Fairytale Town. West Land Park Drive (in Land Park), across from the Zoo. How many kids do you know who get to celebrate in Sherwood Forest, sitting in Robin Hood's very own chair? Or inside King Arthur's Castle? Call to reserve your party in this very special setting kids can relate to. (See Fairytale Town, Chapter 1.) (264-7061)

Fifties Drive-In. Celebrate amid 50s cars, comic-book table tops and 50s music. Bring your own cake, order from the menu (food is reasonable) and all kids get a free balloon and sundae. Separate room accommodates about 20 small people, about 10-14 adults (no age limit for birthdays). Call ahead for large groups. (See Fifties Drive-In, Chapter 7; 482-6357)

Fun for All at 6412 Tupelo Dr., Unit G in Citrus Heights offers three theme parties for kids — All American (hot dogs and chips), Mexican Fiesta (taco and chips) and Traditional (pizza and popcorn) — as well as a standard party that includes snacks, soft drinks or juice, party balloons and 20 game tokens. After one hour of play in the gym and the game area, kids gather for a 45-minute celebration in a pre-decorated room, assisted by a staff member. $6.95 per child, 10 guest minimum. Other options available. (762-2111)

Funderland (in William Land Park) Sutterville Road and 17th Avenue. For 10 children, about $40-50 gets them each 2 hours of unlimited rides in this kid-sized amusement park. This also entitles the group to use the special birthday area (covered gazebos) for their celebration. Available from about Feb. 1 till Oct. 30. At this printing, the management is in the process of changing their prices, so call first. (see Funderland, Chapter 1; 456-0115)

Gymagic, 8360 Rovana Circle, Suite 3. Birthday parties

are available on Saturday evenings or Sundays. $60 for up to 10 kids ($5 each additional kid) gets two hours of organized gymnastic age-appropriate activities (age 3 and up), a card from the staff, decorations and gift time. No refreshments inside, but there's a picnic area outside. Reserve 3 to 4 weeks in advance, with a $25 deposit. (383-1778)

The Hay Barn, 8320 Hazel Avenue, Orangevale. For an unusual birthday party, take the kids on a hay ride; packages available. (988-3765)

Iceland Skating Rink, 1430 Del Paso Boulevard, Sacramento. Kids can ice-skate to their hearts' content, then gather in the separate "coffee shop" (just a separate room with table booths and counter seats) for cake or whatever goodies you want to bring with you. Depending on which session you attend and the age of the kids, prices vary from $3 each to $4.50, with a special rate if there are more than 20 skaters. Sunday and Monday evenings and after-school sessions cost $3 each, with skate rental included in that reduced price (at other times rental is $1). (See Chapter 4; 925-3529)

Kids-n-Us Characters. Choose from over 40 characters to come animate your child's party — Ninja turtles, clowns, Santa, Batman, etc. — with games, magic, face-painting and more. (922-KIDS)

Kovar's Karate Center, 7520 Fair Oaks Boulevard, Carmichael, CA 95608. Bring your child and friends to the Center on the Saturday before or after their birthday, and they'll teach them a beginner's karate class, and play organized games for about an hour. Parents bring whatever refreshments they want. $65. At the end of the party, you'll all get guest passes entitling you to a couple of sample classes. (481-4830)

Leatherby's Family Creamery, 2333 Arden Way. With a minimum of 5 children, you have two options: for $3.25, each child gets a hot dog or sandwich, small drink, sundae and party hat; for $2.29, each child gets a child's sundae, small drink and party hat. They have lots of seating, but in the summer months (ice-cream season) Dave recommends you call first. (See Leatherby's, Chapter 7.) (920-8382)

Little People's Parties. For busy working parents who want to have the birthday at home, this can be the answer. Pam Yocum, who runs the service, is extremely organized and will come to your home before the party, decorate, and then run the whole thing. Her prices range from $95 to $250, depending on the party you choose. All of her packages assume a guest list of 8 children, and a 2-hour party; additional guests, $3. You provide the punch and ice cream; she can provide everything else.

Magic Birthday Shows. Have a magician come entertain at your child's party, with live animal productions, and "amazing magic." (393-3683)

Bobby McGee's, 5623 Sunrise Boulevard, Citrus Heights. This fine restaurant has a birthday package: not exactly a party, but for $7.95 the birthday person gets a cake, a song (the servers all come sing at your table) and a souvenir photograph. (966-1364)

Roller Skating Rinks can be an exciting place to celebrate, and birthday party packages vary at each rink. For example, **Sunrise Rollerland**, 6001 Sunrise Vista Drive, Citrus Heights, has a $50 package: your kids and friends can skate all they want, and party for 1/2 hour in the King Arthur Room; the rink provides ice cream, Pepsi and cake. Or for $40, they can skate and then party at the snack bar. Both plans get you a host or hostess to help with the party, and the necessary paper goods. (Rollerland info 961-3333; reservations 961-3339). For other rinks, see the Yellow Pages under Roller Skating.

Sacramento Children's Museum, 1322 O Street. For $60 (up to 10 children; $2.50 each additional child), the Museum supplies the cake, punch, place settings, and an hour-long party in their separate party-room. They direct a craft session, their mascot Dewey the Dragon comes to visit and help with presents and serves the cake. Then the kids are free to wander through and enjoy the Museum (see Chapter 1). Dewey even gives the birthday-kid a present! (See Chapter 1; 447-8017)

Scandia Family Fun Center, 5070 Hillsdale Boulevard. Here's a place to let 'em loose! Bring your own cake, and

and for $5.00 per person, the little revelers are entitled to play miniature golf, they get tokens for the center Arcade, and you get plastic silverware and napkins for your party. You have your choice of an indoor party room or the outdoor gazebo, and the mood is as festive as can be. Also available: bumper boats, Little Indy races, batting cages (hardball and softball), and a snack bar. (See Chapter 2; 331-5757 or 331-0115)

Visionarium Children's Museum, 2701 K Street, in the Galleria Shopping Center. Beginning at $4 per child, you can have the use of their special party room for an hour. Before or after that hour (your choice, arranged in advance), the kids can enjoy the museum for as long as they want. (See Chapter 1; 443-7476)

And more...
Bowling
Capitol Tour
Children's Theater
Downtown District (November-January)
Effie Yeaw Nature Center
Fish Hatcheries
Gold Miners games
Gymnastic Centers
Kings games
Martial Arts Centers
Metropolitan Airport
Playgrounds
Parks
Sacramento Old City Cemetery (tombstone rubbings tour)
Swimming
Tours of the Working World

Rainy Weather Ideas

Animal Shelter (SPCA)
Art Galleries

Bookstores
Bowling
California Railroad Museum
California State Indian Museum
Capitol Tour
Citizen-Soldier Museum
Concerts
Crocker Museum
Governor's Mansion
Gymnastics Centers
Hardware Stores
History Museums (outlying cities)
Hobby Stores
Hotel Hopping
Ice Skating
McClellan Aviation Museum
Pet Stores
Public Libraries – Storytelling, Children's activities
Roller Skating
Sacramento <u>Bee</u> tour
Sacramento Children's Museum
Sacramento Museum of History, Science and Technology *(formerly the Sacramento History Museum and the Sacramento Science Center)*
Shopping Malls
Stanford Mansion
State Archives
Tours of the Working World
Toy Stores
Visionarium

Wildlife Viewing

American River Parkway (from downtown to Folsom; various points of entry)

Colusa National Wildlife Refuge (near Colusa)
Cosumnes River Wildlife Preserve (Sac. County, near Galt)
Delevan National Wildlife Refuge (near Colusa)
Effie Yeaw Nature Center (Carmichael)
Gray Lodge Waterfowl Management Area (Butte County,
   near Gridley)
Grizzly Island Wildlife Area ((Solano County)
Nimbus/American River Fish Hatchery (Fair Oaks)
Oroville Wildlife Area (near Oroville)
Sacramento National Wildlife Area (Glenn-Colusa Counties)
Sutter National Wildlife Refuge (in Sutter By-pass,
   Sutter Co.)
Yolo Basin Wetlands Area (planned for 1994, Yolo County)

Summer Classes, Workshops, Programs and Camps for Children

The Sacramento area offers something for everyone when it comes to summer activities. On a local level, call the Parks & Recreation district (see Resource Numbers, beginning of this chapter) to receive their announcement of summer programs. Local schools and religious centers also offer summer classes and workshops, as do many community centers. For a free Camp Directory, call (800) 362-2236. Also check the YMCA / YWCA, and other youth groups. You or your children can learn to swim, to do crafts, to act, sing, play music, dance — just about anything you can think of — somewhere around Sacramento. Here are some ideas to help you get started looking.

California State University, Sacramento (CSUS) Aquatic Center, 6000 J Street, Sacramento, offers a summer camp for children where they can learn sailing, canoeing, kayaking, motorboat safety, etc. Beginner, intermediate and advanced. Overnight camp, too. (985-7239)

Camp Sacramento, located at 6,500 feet elevation (17 miles from Lake Tahoe and 2 hours from Sacramento), offers families an unbeatable outdoor experience. June through August is family camp time: families can attend camp for a full week or go to a 4-day "mini-family camp" from Wednesday to Saturday. Parents can enjoy their own outdoor activities in the Sierra without worrying about their kids, who are having their own kind of supervised fun. Its 64 rustic cabins are also available to backpackers, campers and there's a special camp for senior citizens. Prices are expected to change, so call for information. (264-5195)

Dance Academies all over the Sacramento area offer special summer courses for children of all ages and adults, in ballet, tap, modern dance and others. See the Yellow Pages under Dancing Instruction.

Explorit!, the Davis Science Center, 3141 5th Street, Davis, offers summer classes and programs that are craft-oriented activities, very "active-creative," says the Director, and geared for a K-6 level. Classes take place in Davis, at the Center, and there are also some classes and workshops offered in Woodland and in West Sacramento. Price ranges from $3-50, depending on the activity. (756-0191)

FabricLand, 3408 Arden Way (972-9000) or 10639 Folsom Boulevard, Rancho Cordova (368-7394), can acquaint your child with the creative art of sewing. Their beginning and intermediate sewing classes repeat every 6 weeks, at $40 a month for 4 classes. Also quilting classes and other crafts. They may be expanding their offerings, so call first. FREE.

FutureKids, Lyon Village Shopping Center, 2580 Fair Oaks Boulevard, Suite 22, offers summer camps for computer literacy, any age. Also Holiday camps throughout the academic year. Their focus is on academics (no video games): reading, writing, math, logical thinking process, decision making processes. Summer: about 2 hours, about a month long. Summer session: about $100 3, 2-hr classes. 40-min classes, 4 for $100. Also check schools for outreach programs, and Parks and Rec.(488-9695)

Many of the numerous **Gymnastics** centers in the Sacramento area offer special summer sessions for children and adults. See Chapter 4, Gymnastics.

Horseback Riding. For youngsters 6 and over who love horses, this can be a summer camp they'll never forget! They can learn to care for their horse, and to ride with confidence. Many riding academies in the Sacramento area offer summer courses; see the Yellow Pages under Horse Stables or Riding Academies.

Los Rios Community College District
American River College
4700 College Oak Drive, Sacramento 95841 ✎
484-8433 or 484-8234
Sacramento City College
3835 Freeport Boulevard, Sacramento 95822 ✎ 558-2228
Cosumnes River College
8401 Center Parkway, Sacramento 95823 ✎ 688-7315

All three of the colleges in this district offer community classes during the summer. Swimming is always a popular one with children of all ages. Offerings vary each year, so call for information during the spring semester.

Math Masters Learning Centers. Help your student prepare for next year's math classes. (488-MATH or 725-MATH)

Michael's, 4241 Marconi Avenue, offers all sorts of children's and adults craft classes during the summer (see Chapter 2, Shopping). Between age 4 and 10, the child must be all right unsupervised. Call, or come in for a schedule. Other locations. (481-6617)

Micro-Kids offers computer camps and classes all year long (including summers) at various school sites throughout the greater Sacramento area. Their focus is pre-school education, children at risk, teacher workshops and thematic instruction. They also do software-consultation (if you have problems with your child's software at home). They've been around the Sacramento area for 11 years, and they're all credentialed teachers. Call 444-5233, or your local school.

Real Genius, Nimbus Winery, Highway 50 at Hazel (985-8580) can help your kid get excited about learning, in math, reading, language skills, science, computers, music and more.

Tandy Leather, 2864 Fulton Avenue (486-1841) or 7217 Florin Mall Drive (422-5112) can teach your children basic leather crafts. Learn basic leather carving, stamping, dyeing, lacing and assembling, for about $25 for 6 weeks of classes, one evening a week. Summer classes depend on requests. They also sell lots of starter kits for do-it-yourself projects, and they're always available to answer questions.

For Kids with Special Needs

Childhood Language Disorders Clinic
Scottish Rite Temple
5161 H Street, Sacramento ☞ (452-5881 or 731-4357)
The Temple offers this free Clinic to help kids with aphasia or dyslexia.
Dyslexia Consultants of Northern California
5740 Windmill Way, Carmichael 95608 ☞ 471-9870
This school provides support groups for parents of dyslexic children, scotopic screening, learning strategies that can help your child succeed in school. For adults, too.
Lindamood-Bell Learning Processes
486-8183 or (800) 233-1819
Lindamood-Bell specializes in treating Dyslexia and Attention Deficit Disorder.
Melvin-Smith Learning Center
4436 Engle Road, Sacramento ☞ (483-6415)
A diagnostic and tutorial center for children with learning disabilities. For clients from age 3 to adult, to help remediate dyslexia, attention disorders, head trauma, and many other learning disorders.
Project RIDE
8850 Southside Avenue, Elk Grove ☞ (689-2310)
The purpose of Project RIDE is to enhance the self-esteem

and physical coordination of children with special needs, through therapeutic horse-back riding. Part of a highly successful nation-wide program, Project RIDE (Riding Instruction Designed for Education) operates year-round in Elk Grove (south of Sacramento). Carol Meador began the program in 1979 with only 32 riders, and now they have more than 160 regular clients. Call Meador for information.

Publications

～ Sacramento Newspapers

The Business Journal, 1401 21 Street (447-7661), is a weekly review of business activities in the greater Sacramento area. It has a monthly special pull-out section that show-cases different industries in the area, and generally keeps a finger on the business pulse of Sacramento.

Parents' Monthly, 8611 Folsom Bd., Suite A (451-4905), is "Sacramento's good parenting publication." Chock-full of informative articles on parenting, books, education/schools, child development, travel, family activities and more it's published monthly and available free in doctor's offices, business offices, at newsstands, in restaurants, and wherever free publications are stocked, throughout the greater Sacramento area.

The Sacramento Bee, McClatchy Publications, 2100 Q Street (321-1000, or 321-1785 for tour info.; see Chapter 2, Tours of the Working World), is Sacramento's major daily newspaper. It offers several features for children — a special comics page with puzzles, jokes, etc. on Sundays, and on Fridays there's a section by and for teens called Sidetracks. Children's books are reviewed regularly, and Dr. William Russell, noted child psychologist, has a regular column. Weekly and daily calendars of events include children's listings, and a separate section on Fridays called Ticket that lists all entertainment and performing arts for the weekend. On Sundays, the special Encore section offers the week's entertainment calendar, and there's a special number, called BeeLine, that gets you up-to-the-minute information on all events in the Sacramento area; call for a list of their BeeLine category numbers.

ᴧ Newspapers from Other Cities

These newspapers from other Northern California cities are regularly available in Sacramento.

Davis Enterprise, 315 G Street, Davis 95616 (442-1718).
San Jose Mercury News, 925 L Street, Sacramento 95814 (441-4601).
San Francisco Chronicle, (800) 792-0725.
San Francisco Examiner, (800) 792-0725.
Woodland Democrat, (662-5421).

ᴧ Community Newspapers

Smaller newspapers from communities, towns or cities in the greater Sacramento area.

Carmichael Times, 4807 El Camino Avenue, Carmichael 95608 (483-0946).
Catholic Herald, 5890 Newman Court, Sacramento, CA 95819 (452-3344).
Chico Enterprise-Record, 420 P Street, Chico 95814 (444-6747).
Elk Grove Citizen, 8936 Elk Grove Boulevard, Elk Grove 95624 (685-3945).
Folsom Telegraph, 825 Sutter Street, Folsom 95630 (985-2581).
Murieta Times, 11171 Sun Center Drive, Rancho Cordova 95670 (852-6680).
Natomas Journal, 520 Garden Highway, Natomas 95833 (921-9151).
News-Ledger, 816 West Acre Road, West Sacramento 95691 (371-8030).
Nichi-Bei Times, (Japanese-American) 441-1040.

Orangevale News, (351-0112).
Rio Linda News, 6757 5th Road, Rio Linda 95673 (991-3000).
West Sacramento Press, 834-D Jefferson Bd., West Sacramento 95691 (371-2397).

❧ Neighborhood Newspapers

Distributed free in restaurants, libraries, etc.

Sacramento News & Review, 2210 21 Street, Sacramento 95818 (737-1437).

❧ Magazines

Comstock's Magazine, 1770 Tribute Road (924-9815) is Sacramento's executive monthly business magazine. Its glossy, no-nonsense format takes an in-depth look at business in the Capital region.

Outdoor Family, P.O. Box 191893, Sacramento 95819 (451-9466) is a glossy magazine devoted to outdoor fun with kids.

Sacramento Magazine, 4471 D Street (452-6200), is a glossy, attractive publication that offers a broad-based view of Sacramento, from business to cooking to travel to home and garden. It provides an economic forecast for the Sacramento region, business surveys, and editorials — and a good idea of what's going on in Sacramento.

Sacramento Parent, P.O. Box 9311, Auburn 95604 (888-0573), is a free, tabloid-size monthly magazine that covers all parenting issues. Free.

Step Parenting Today, 8360 Bluebell Court, Citrus Heights, CA 95610 (721-8386), is a new monthly magazine dedicated to the special issues of step-parents. Free.

Colleges and Universities

Sacramento, California's capital, offers many opportunities for continuing education, including universities, colleges, and many business and vocational schools. Listed below are the major institutes of higher education in Sacramento. For further information or more listings, see the Yellow Pages under Schools – Academic, or Schools – Business and Vocational.

American River College, 4700 College Oak Drive (484-8433 or 484-8234) is part of the Los Rios Community College District. It offers a 2-year AA degree in arts or sciences, leading to transfer to a 4-year college, or preparation for a skilled, non-academic career like nursing, fire technology, etc. Also offers a broad range of community courses, such as music, art, swimming, physical education, writing, and many more. The state-of-the-art Learning Resource Center offers individualized, computer-assisted instruction in many areas.

California State University, Sacramento (CSUS), 6000 J Street (985-7239) is part of the State University system. It offers 4-year degrees, BA and MA, in arts and sciences, and is a common transfer point for students graduating from Sacramento's Community Colleges.

Chapman University, 4020 El Camino Avenue (485-7832) and Bldg. 8, McClellan AFB (929-1388) is a 4-year, private college that functions as a satellite of its main campus in Orange County, CA. The Sacramento campus is geared for professional students who work during the day, with evening classes only.

Cosumnes River College, 8401 Center Parkway (688-7315), also part of the Los Rios District, offers 2-year degrees in arts and sciences, leading to transfer to a 4-year institution or to a vocational degree.

Lincoln Law School, 3140 J Street (446-1275) offers preparation for a career in law.

McGeorge School of Law, 3200 5th Avenue (739-7105), prepares students for a legal career. It is an extension of the **University of the Pacific**, in Stockton.

Sacramento City College, 3835 Freeport Boulevard (558-2228), is also a member of the Los Rio Community College District. Like ARC and CRC, it offers a 2-year degree in arts or sciences, for transfer to a 4-year college or for a vocational career.

Rudolf Steiner College, 9200 Fair Oaks Boulevard, Fair Oaks (961-8727) is a private training center for people who want to teach in a Waldorf school. There are approximately 600 Waldorf schools world-wide, based on the philosophy of Rudolf Steiner.

And although it isn't in Sacramento, the **University of California at Davis** is right next door, and a common transfer destination for students who graduate from Sacramento's Community Colleges. It offers full 4-year degrees, BA, MA and Ph.D., and has earned world renown for research in various areas of veterinary medicine, primate development and plant technology. There is a UCD Medical Facility in downtown Sacramento, and artists from all over the world come to UCD's Freeborn Hall to perform. UCD has shaped the town of Davis, and even if you're not considering attending, it's worth a trip (see Chapter 6) to this "city of learning."

SPECIAL ASSISTANCE
TELEPHONE NUMBERS

Ambulance, Fire, Police	911
Abducted-Abused-Exploited Children	(800) 248-8020
Al-Anon/Alateen for Families	483-4806
Alcoholism and Drug Programs (Sac. County)	366-2736
Alcohol Abuse Hotline	(800) 234-0420
American Cancer Society	446-7933
	or (800) 227-2345
American Diabetes Association	920-8575
American Lung Association	444-5864
American Red Cross	368-3131
Animal Control (information & service)	366-2632
	(emergencies) 366-2000
Boys Town National Hotline	(800) 448-3000
California Missing Chidren Hotline	(800) 222-3463

California Youth Crisis Line	(800) 843-5200
California State Automobile Ass'n. (AAA)	
Emergency Road Service - 24 hrs. (members):	Elk Grove 441-3740
	Roseville 961-5480
	Sacramento 331-9981
California State Boating and Waterways Dept.	445-2615
Catholic Diocese of Sacramento	444-8108
Catholic Social Service Counseling	368-3260
Child Action, Inc. (free workshops for parents)	453-0713
Child Protection Center	
(U.C.Davis Med. Center)	734-8396
Community Information Center	442-4995
Community Centers:	
Belle Cooledge, 5699 S.Land Park	264-5610
Clunie, 601 Alhambra Bd.	264-7719
Coloma, 4623 T St.	277-6060
Evelyn Moore, 1402 Dickson St.	433-6380
George Sim, 6207 Logan St.	277-6161
Hagginwood, 3271 Marysville Bd.	566-6440
Lambda, 1931 L St.	442-0185
Oak Park, 3425 Martin Luther King Bd.	277-6151
Robertson, 3525 Norwood Ave.	566-6419
Sac. Senior Cit. Cntr, 915 27 St.	264-5462
Shepard Center, 3330 McKinley Bd.	443-9413
Woodlake, 500 Arden Way	566-6403
Cystic Fibrosis Foundation – N.Cal.	(415) 677-0155
Deaf Blind Services	641-5855
Deaf Communications TDD (U.C.Davis)	752-2222
Diogenes Youth Services	363-0063
Family Service Agency	368-3080
Family Support Program	366-2374
FEAT (Families for Early Autism Children-	
Support Group)	334-9210
Heart Fund - American Heart Association	446-6505
Hemophilia Council of California	448-7444
Homework Helpers	483-0303
Homework Hotline	973-1313
Humane Society SPCA	383-7387
Jewish Family Services	921-1921
La Leche League	338-5896
Make a Wish Foundation	448-9474
March of Dimes – N. Cal.	922-1913
Medical Assistance	
University of California, Davis, Medical Center	
2315 Stockton Bd., Sacramento	734-2011
(Emergency)	734-3797

Kaiser-Permanente Medical Center
  2025 Morse Avenue, Sacramento(Pediatrics)   973-5080
  (Emergency)   973-6600
National Runaway Switchboard   (800) 621-4000
Neighborhood Alternative Center
  (counseling for minors)   366-2662
Nursing Mothers Counsel   682-5070
Parent Effectiveness Training   678-2301
Parent Support Program   366-2374
Parents without Partners   487-5154
Parks & Recreation Districts:
  City of Sacramento   264-5200
  County of Sacramento   366-2061
Outside Sacramento:
  Arcade Creek   482-8377
  Arden Manor   487-7851
  Arden Park   483-6069
  Auburn, CA   (1) 885-8461
  Carmichael   485-5322
  Rancho Cordova   362-1841
  Davis   (1) 757-5626
  Elk Grove   685-3917
  Fair Oaks   966-1036
  Fulton-El Camino   927-3802
  Mission Oaks   488-2810
  North Highlands   332-7440
  Orangevale   988-4373
  Placerville, CA   (1) 642-5232
  Roseville, CA   (1) 781-0242 Ext. 229
  Southgate   428-1171
  Sunrise   725-1585
People Reaching Out (alcohol and drug
  counseling)   971-3300
Pharmacies:
  Kaiser-Permanente Pharmacy –
    2025 Morse Ave.   973-5362
  Kaiser-Permanente Pharmacy –
    3240 Arden Way   973-7652
  UCD Medical Center Pharmacy –
    2315 Stockton Bd.   734-2476
Poison Control Center   734-3692
     or (800) 342-9293
Sacramento Children's Home   452-3981
Sacramento Children's Medical Clinic Inc.   422-2229
Sacramento County Probation Dept. parent
  support group   386-7700

Sacramento Plasma Center	44-2830
Sacramento Police Athletic League	452-4069
Sacramento Regional Transit District (bus & rail info)	321-2877
St. Jude Children's Research Hospital	(800) 877-5833
United Way	368-3000
YMCA	452-5451
YWCA	442-4741
Youth Crisis Hotline	(800) 448-4663

Recommended Reading

for further exploration...

Best Hikes with Children, by Bill McMillon and Kevin McMillon. The Mountaineers Publishers, 1993. 65 hikes and walks within 60 miles of Sacramento, starting within 20 miles of downtown.

California Gold Country, by Paul Jones and Dan Flora. 1973. Places and events of special interest in the Mother Lode Country of northern California.

California with Kids. Frommer's Family Travel Guide. Prentice Hall Travel, 1993. This guide covers all of California, including hotels and attractions.

Discover Historic California, by George and Jan Roberts. GemGuides Book Co., 1988. A guide to historic places you can visit all over California.

1000 California Place Names, by Erwin G. Gudde. University of California Press, 1959. Fascinating reading for historians, linguists, anyone interested in how and why places get their names, and what they mean.

Places to Go with Children in Northern California, by Elizabeth Pomada. Chronicle Books, 1993. Attractions throughout the northern state.

INDEX